On February 18, 1910, French pilot Louis Paulhan flew his French-manufactured wood and fabric Farman biplane from a field on the outskirts of Houston, resulting in the first recorded aircraft flight in Texas.

Aviation in Texas

by
Roger Bilstein
and
Jay Miller

★

Published by Texas Monthly Press, Inc. and The University of Texas Institute of Texan Cultures at San Antonio and made possible through the generosity of Southwest Airlines.

Texas Monthly Press, Inc.
P.O. Box 1569
Austin, Texas 78767

A B C D E F G

Library of Congress Cataloging in Publication Data

Bilstein, Roger E.
  Aviation in Texas.

  Bibliography: p.
  Includes index.
  1. Aeronautics—Texas—History. 2. Aircraft industry—Texas—History.
I. Miller, Jay, 1948– II. Title.
TL522.T4B54 1985   387.7'09764   85-8089
ISBN 0-932012-95-7

The prototype for the Windecker "Eagle" sits at the company's Midland-Odessa Regional Air Terminal facility shortly before Windecker's economic collapse. The all-composite "Eagle" was an innovative design typical of its brilliant designer, Dr. Leo Windecker.

Contents

Katherine Stinson, one of the most famous woman fliers of the pre war era, was sworn in as a mailplane pilot for a special 30-mile flight between Seguin and San Antonio on May 24, 1915. Katherine's mother, on the left, looks on along with several unidentified relatives during the ceremony executed by a local postmaster.

Acknowledgments

There would be no pictorial history of aviation in Texas without the kind assistance of many contributors. We would like to take a moment to mention those whose efforts on our behalf have helped make this book possible: John Hotard of American Airlines; Marty Reisch of Bell Helicopter Textron; Linda, Paul, and Alex Bilstein; Tony Bingelis; Peter Bowers; Rudy Bowling; Lee Bracken; Erwin Bulban; Leo Childs; Dave Chocci; Jane Coats; Mike Kingston of the *Dallas Morning News*; Vincent Dolson; Gary Emory; John Kumpf and John Sutton of E-Systems; Jerry D. Ferrel; Emily Finn; "Lefty" Gardner; Bill Williams and Joe Thornton of General Dynamics Corporation; George Haddaway; Gary, Bruce, Jr., Don, Mark, and Enid Hallock; William Horne; Dr. Thomas Kreneck of the Houston Public Library; Dr. John Davis of the Institute of Texan Cultures; Barbara Joy; George Bradley of the Kelly AFB Office of History; Janie Kitchens; Sgt. Randy Krites; Gloria Livingston of the Lackland AFB History and Traditions Museum; Gayle Lawson; Robin Loving; Kirk McManus; Larry and Tehila Miller; Susan and Anna and Miriam Miller; JOC Wayne Mishler; David Morgan; Linda Ezell and Dominic Pisano of the National Air and Space Museum; Lloyd Nolen; Ann Whyte of Pan American World Airways; Alvin and Mildred Parker; Mrs. Dorothy Patterson; Bobby and Pearl Ragsdale; Ken Ragsdale; Lt. Com. Richard Recordon of VF-201; Jim Roth; Patti Benoit of the *San Antonio News-Express*; Leon Sanders; Robb Satterfield; John Schroeder; Lewis and Janet Shaw; Leland Snow; Southwest Airlines; Ernie Stepp; James Street; Dora Strother; Com. Carl Swan of VF-202; Texas Aeronautics Commission; Brig. Gen. Belisario Flores and Dorothy Esba of the Texas Air National Guard; Col. Herbert Purtle of the Texas Army National Guard; Ed Rice and Dr. Larry Sall of the University of Texas at Dallas; Paul Bowers and Jim Croslin of Vought Corporation; L. L. Walker, Jr.; Barbara Wasson; and Jim and Kay Wogstad.

L. L. Walker, Sr., climbs out of a homebuilt monoplane he made from plans based on the design of the French Bleriot. He flew this aircraft during the autumn of 1910. Though most Bleriots were powered by a small air-cooled rotary engine, Walker modified his aircraft to accommodate a water-cooled inline type of more modern design.

Preface

When the Institute of Texan Cultures, located in San Antonio, was planning a major exhibit on the history of flight as it related to Texas, it also intended to publish a book related to the project. By coincidence, Texas Monthly Press in Austin was considering a book on the same subject. An agreement was reached to cooperate, and this volume is the result.

This photographic history of aviation and space flight relating to Texas should not be considered as a definitive study. As the authors discovered in the process of putting the book together, the varied aviation and aerospace stories concerning Texas are just about as infinite as the tall tales and yarns that have always been a hallmark of the state.

Our book should be seen as representative of the people and events that have contributed a rich heritage of aviation and space progress. In addition, we have also tried to show the influence of aviation and space flight on the citizens of Texas and to remark on trends that have had national, as well as international, implications. Hopefully, additional writers will continue to add to our awareness of aerospace personalities and events relating to Texas.

As the credits suggest, the authors owe much to the individuals and organizations listed above. The authors also owe much to their respective spouses and families, who remained supportive through the retelling and rewriting of many "hangar stories" and who navigated through stacks of photos spread across living room floors. Our thanks also to those who read and commented on all or part of the manuscript. The errors that remain belong to us.

Jacob Brodbeck, a German emigrant and tinkerer, allegedly designed and built a flying machine, which he referred to as an "airship," near Fredericksburg in 1865. Some observers later claimed that spring-powered propellers were used to get the craft airborne.

1. Men, Myths, and Machines

Early Civil Aviation and Its Legacy

On August 7, 1865, Jacob Brodbeck crawled into a machine of his own design and manufacture and proceeded to make the first flight in an airplane. At least, that is the story accepted by many Texans, especially around San Antonio and Fredericksburg—both locations having been mentioned as the site of the event. It is possible that Brodbeck got into the air, although the vagueness about the actual location of the event is consistent with the fuzziness surrounding many details of the flight itself.

Jacob Friedrich Brodbeck was born in Germany on October 13, 1821. He became a teacher in his hometown, but he had been fascinated by mechanics since the age of eighteen, and worked at designing a self-winding clock. In 1846, Jacob and a brother, George, planned to emigrate to Texas, even though their parents decided to remain in Europe after hearing stories about wild Indians in the states. The brothers settled in Fredericksburg, where Jacob resumed his teaching career in the famous eight-sided Vereins Kirche. Jacob married a local girl, and the Brodbeck family eventually included twelve children.

At some point, apparently during the Civil War years, Brodbeck began tinkering with model gliders, some of which were driven by propellers powered by clock springs. In this fascination with flight, he typified the activities of dozens of American and European experimenters in the nineteenth century. Brodbeck's models evidently gained considerable local fame and highlighted a number of regional fairs in Texas between 1863 and 1865. Eventually, he decided to build a full-sized aircraft.

The most complete extant description of Brodbeck's aeronautical design appeared in the *Galveston Tri-Weekly News* for August 7, 1865:

> We find in the San Antonio News, a call made by Mr. F. Brodbeck of that place, upon the people of the United States to aid by Stock Subscription in construction of an Air-Ship, constructed on new principles. As Texas inventions are novelties in the world of art and science, we hasten to lay the case before our readers and the world at large:

> For more than twenty years I have labored to construct a machine which should enable man to use, like a bird, the atmospheric region as the medium of his travels. First, trying empirical experiments, without a guiding idea I soon satisfied myself that the means heretofore used were hopeless. I left this barren field and took up the way which had been so sucessfully [sic] followed into the mechanical laws, governing these wonderful structures, and observed the various peculiarities of the air, and so in the year 1863, I was at last able to construct a machine, which, requiring comparatively little power, imitates the flight of birds, inasmuch as it makes use of the same peculiarities of the air, and moves with the same celerity in every direction, with the wind and against it, not resembling however in form a bird, but being constructed like a ship, which has caused me to call it "AIR-SHIP."

> A small model constructed in that year proved by successful experiments the correctness of my principles; later experiments, with some improvements in the model, resulted still more favorably.

> The blockade, and the state of the country during the war, prevented me from progressing in my invention and from opening a new era in intercommunication by a larger ship, arranged for practical purposes, but now I hold it to be my duty, after those impediments do no longer exist, to follow without hesitation the path shown me by Providence and the spirit of progress.

> The construction of a large Air-Ship requires more means than I possess, but this surely should not be an insupportable difficulty. Should I not be justified to call upon the aid of my fellow-men who will be all, directly or indirectly, benefitted by the result of my

invention!

I have therefore concluded to collect subscriptions, in order to build, under the protection of a U.S. caveat, a large air-ship, and then to take out a patent. These subscriptions I shall not ask as donations, but as shares, to be refunded together with a part of the proceeds of the sale of the patent right, or the sale of air-ships, as the case may be. I have put the price of one share at five dollars. Every shareholder will receive a certificate, securing to him a proportionate interest in the proceeds of the enterprise.

I will give a few ideas indicating generally the character of the air-ship and what it will be able to accomplish.

The AIR-SHIP consists of three main parts.
1. The lower suspended portion, formed like a ship with very short prow to cut the air; it serves to hold the aeronaut, as also the power producing engine with all the steering apparatus. This portion is shut up all around to prevent the rapid motion from affecting the breathing of the man within. In this, as low as possible, lies the centre of gravity of the whole structure, so as to steady the motion. At the back end of the ship there is a propeller screw which will make it possible to navigate the water, in case that by any accident the aeronaut should have to descend, while he is above the water. In this case the ship can be detached from the flying apparatus.
2. The upper portion, or flying apparatus, which makes use of the resistance of the air, consists of a system of wings, partly moveable, partly immovable, presenting the appearance of horizontal sails, but having functions entirely different from the sails of vessels.
3. The portion producing the forward motion consists either of two screws, which can be revolved with equal or unequal motion, so as to serve the purpose of lateral steering, or of wings of a peculiar construction. The preference to be given to one or the other depends on the *force* of the motive power. Another apparatus *controls* the ascending motion.

The material is so selected as to *combine* the greatest strength with the least *weight.*

When the air-ship is in motion, the aeronaut has in each hand a crank, one to guide the ascending and descending motion, the other the lateral steerage. Immediately before him is the compass, while a barometer with a scale made for the purpose shows him the approximate height. Another apparatus, similar to the ball regulator of a steam engine, shows him the velocity, as well as the distance passed over.

It is self-evident that the speed of the air-ship depends upon the motive power and on the direction and force of the winds; according to my experiment and calculations it will be from 30 to 100 miles per hour.

Brodbeck's notations for barometers and other equipment to measure speed and altitude are noteworthy. Few aspiring fliers of the era seem to have bothered with such potentially useful devices, and the German mathematics teacher's instinctive fascination with useful flight data sets him apart. In other respects, the story of Brodbeck's alleged flight is not so convincing.

Although no drawings or blueprints of Brodbeck's "air-ship" have survived, it is possible to make several assumptions from this intriguing description. Brodbeck says that his machine, although constructed like a ship, "imitates the flight of birds"; that the wings are "partly moveable"; that forward motion, while relying in part on two screws (propellers), also occurs as a result of the action of "wings of a peculiar construction." He also refers to a flying apparatus using the "resistance of the air," and to the presence of a "system of wings...presenting the appearance of horizontal sails." All of this suggests a contraption similar to the ornithopter—a dead-end concept that captivated many aeronautical tinkerers of the era. The news article mentions a "power producing engine," which subsequent written accounts have treated as meaning a clock-spring device. Even though Brodbeck stresses his goal of using lightweight materials, the boatlike structure to contain the "engine," the steering gear, and the occupant must have been fairly heavy, especially since it seems to have been fully enclosed in order to permit the aeronaut to keep breathing at the fierce speeds its inventor envisioned.

Newspaper accounts published years later appear to be the major source for Brodbeck's flight, placing it on August 7, 1865, the date of the Galveston news item. These accounts say that Brodbeck's airplane flew, although, as one journalist noted many years later, the airship's backers reported to be present never mentioned the event in their diaries. The plane crashed, it was said, because the inventor failed to perfect a system to rewind the spring at the same time it was unwinding, making it impossible to maintain continuous flight. Brodbeck's failure seems to have discouraged other potential investors, even though he toured other parts of the United States in the late 1800s. The plans were either lost or stolen, and no patent was ever filed. Brodbeck returned to a farm in Gillespie County, where he died on January 8, 1909.

Did Brodbeck really fly? There are a number of nagging questions that are not easy to dispel. Numerous accounts following the event stress the fact that Brodbeck flew as high as the tree tops. How high were the trees? Did he fly over them? This seems unlikely, making it more probably that observers made a quick estimate by relating Brodbeck's altitude to trees located some distance from them. This raises the question of perspective, especially in the case of people who had never seen a plane before and who must have made hasty judgments in a state of considerable excitement. Here perspective is especially relevant, since a plane seeming to rise to tree-top height was being viewed against trees at some distance. Comparatively speaking, a distant tree line is very low in relation to an object much closer to the viewer, especially if the object is off the ground by only a short distance. Assuming that Brodbeck's plane rose at all, it need not have risen very high to seem impressive to unskilled viewers.

Could the plane have risen in any case? That is an even more relevant question. A metal spring in 1865 would have been exceptionally efficient in order to lift a man, an aircraft with considerable wingspan, and a system of gears and transmission belts to turn two propellers and movable wings. Finally, there remains a question about the source of power itself. Later writers seized on Brodbeck's experiments with spring-driven models and may have assumed that a similar spring arrangement was used with the full-sized airship. Perhaps not. One of Brodbeck's sons, Hilmar, wrote a column for the *Fredericksburg Wochenblatt* during the 1920s. In one story, Hilmar says that his father "spent all his energy... inventing an airplane which could be driven by human force through the air like a ship on the ocean." In view of Brodbeck's own description of the airship as imitating the flight of birds and having movable wings, it seems most likely that his airplane was designed for muscle power and for clock springs. The stories of Brodbeck's airship are appealing but not very convincing.

But if Brodbeck was not the first to fly, there are other claimants from Texas. Consider, for example, the story of William Downing Custead, born in Delaware on April 14, 1867. He was a cousin of "Buffalo Bill" Cody and later evinced some of the showmanship that made Cody a public figure. Unlike Cody, Custead failed to achieve fame, living out his final years as a recluse on a beach in Hawaii.

In 1891, Custead moved his family to Texas and settled in the community of Elm Mott, near Waco. Two rail lines ran through the area, known for cotton farming, and Custead became a dispatcher for the MK&T railroad, better known as the "Katy." As a member of the Brotherhood of Telegraphers, Custead was probably involved with one of the more spectacular events of the era, when promoters arranged a head-on collision of two old but heavy locomotives in 1896. One of the principal organizers was a railroad passenger agent appropriately named W. G. Crush. At a time when any event out of the ordinary relieved the tedium of frontier life, the locomotive crash drew a crowd of some thirty thousand; two of them were killed and many were injured by flying debris. It was in this atmosphere of intense, naive interest in curious events that Custead devised his own airship.

When news of Custead's aerial device was published in 1899, newspapers in the area had already printed stories of mysterious flying vehicles. Custead apparently experimented with small models, possibly ornithopters driven by a rubber band. He proceeded to a full-sized ornithopter design powered by a steam engine, but changed to a gasoline engine developed by Gustave

Whitehead, who was working on his own flying machine in Connecticut and who became one of Custead's collaborators in later years. Descriptions of Custead's machine are comparatively detailed, based on contemporary stories in the *Fairfield Recorder* (February 17, 1899) and the *Waco Times Herald* (April 2, 1899), which published drawings of the contraption. One of the men who helped build the airship, J. L. Bergstrom, of Waco, gave a long interview to a reporter on the *Waco Tribune Herald* (October 30, 1949).

The Custead Airship Company, capitalized at $100,000, was incorporated on April 12, 1900. The ship Custead originally built incorporated bamboo, chicken wire, and oilcloth. Bergstrom became involved when Custead gave up on the bamboo frame, which kept coming apart. Bergstrom's bicycle shop ordered 500 feet of tubular steel, which Bergstrom then fashioned into a framework to Custead's specifications. Although early drawings show the airship with eight wings, Bergstrom's interview in 1949 mentions only two, each thirty feet in length, which flapped up and down. Geared to the engine, the wings were required to flutter at 160 strokes per minute, with the wing tips making a six-foot stroke. Air resistance on the upward stoke had bedeviled every designer of ornithopters over the centuries. Custead's approach was ingeniously simple.

To the tubular frame of the wings, Custead attached the chicken wire. Next, he attached strips of oilcloth, running them lengthwise under the wing and fastening the forward edge of the strip to the wing framework. On the upstroke, the strips opened to allow the air to pass through them; on the downstroke, the strips were forced upward against the chicken wire. Thus, Custead presumed, his airship would be lifted and propelled forward. Bergstrom saw the airship lift off the ground in tethered tests; he did not see the plane in free flight, although it was reported that Custead flew from Elm Mott to Tokio and back—about five miles.

In 1974, a transplanted Briton, Nick Pocock, published a thorough little study of the Custead episode. Pocock was an engineer who flew with the Royal Air Force Volunteer Reserve and then became a professional aerobatic pilot of note in Europe, the United States, and Central America. Eventually settling in Texas, Pocock was able to interview many individuals who claimed to have seen Custead fly at one time or another, or who at least had seen the airship. The "eyewitness" accounts, many of them made when the individuals were youngsters of five to twelve years of age, are contradictory and inconclusive. Pocock, an engineer and professional pilot, finally concluded that the Custead machine could not have flown. The extremely rapid motion of the wings would have caused intolerable stress on them as well as on the gear mechanisms. The alleged flight from Elm Mott to Tokio and back was probably a story that started as a local joke, playing on the resemblance of the name to Tokyo, Japan. But local pride dies hard, and the Custead legend is as persistent as the Brodbeck legend.

Like Brodbeck, Custead pursued his aerial dreams

for a few years after his reported flights in Texas. About 1901, Custead returned to the East Coast, to Connecticut, where he joined forces with Gustave Whitehead, the man who had supplied the engine for Custead's early design. Whitehead had also designed his own airplane, and there have been continuing stories that he beat the Wright brothers into the air in August, 1901. As a designer and builder, Whitehead may have been somewhat more advanced than either Brodbeck or Custead, but his claim to aeronautical fame, like that of so many tinkerers of the era, was inconclusive. Custead apparently moved to New York and subsequently applied for three different patents between 1904 and 1905. All three were described as "variable speed mechanisms," although it is not clear that they related to aircraft.

Custead's family remained in Texas, and he never saw them again. They heard from him only occasionally as he drifted from New York, to Panama, to California, to New Orleans. He eventually arrived in Hawaii, where he lived as a recluse, a man who rarely wore clothing and survived on his garden plot and a few chickens. He continued to read the newspapers; when several unread issues piled up near the door of his shack in March, 1933, a neighbor who went to investigate found him dead. The news item reporting the incident began with a reference to "the hermit of Nanakuli."

It is likely that the ballooning craze of the late nineteenth century spurred scores of inventors to plan assorted sizes and designs for elaborate balloons and complicated aerial vehicles called airships and to organize companies for their construction and commercial operation. Considered from the perspective of twentieth-century airline transports, the elaborate plans of airship promoters seem quaint and naive. However, at a time when successful powered airplanes were still a chimera, the proven lifting capacity of balloons made airships of some sort appear to be feasible candidates as commercial aerial vehicles of the future. Airship inventors put together elaborate prospectuses and fancy stock certificates that were bought not only by speculators, but also by thoughtful citizens who perhaps saw airships as a parallel to railroads—which, after all, had been scoffed at by earlier skeptics. The Ezekiel Air Ship Manufacturing Company represented Texas' contribution to the airship phenomenon.

For years, the Reverend Burrell Cannon devoted his time to his family, his Baptist ministry, and his sawmill. Around the turn of the century, Cannon added a new goal to his life—human flight. He drew his inspiration from the biblical descriptions of chariots in the sky as related by the Old Testament prophet Ezekiel. In another biblical conceit, Cannon and his eleven supporters represented the twelve apostles behind the Ezekiel Air Ship Manufacturing Company, formed in the summer of 1901. The company sold shares for $25 each and eventually raised enough for the construction of an airship, which was prepared for its maiden voyage in 1902. The Ezekiel Air Ship took its power from a small kerosene engine, apparently rigged to power a series of large wheels. These in turn moved fanlike wings, which were to drive the airship through the sky and steer it at the same time. Some accounts claim that the craft did indeed leave the ground, covering perhaps 100 feet; nevertheless, the project fizzled. The Reverend Mr. Cannon himself is said to have remarked that "God never willed that this airship should fly"—a likely epitaph for the Ezekiel Air Ship.

Thus it was that the first people in Texas to become airborne were balloonists. In the mid-nineteenth century, ballooning became a national craze. Ascents enlivened countless sporting events and fairs, and the sight of humans in the sky was so intriguing that a balloon flight, all by itself, often became a major public event. This seems to have been the case with the first recorded balloon ascent in Texas, which took place in Dallas on April 16, 1861. The balloonist was an individual known as Professor Wallace (academic accolades—sometimes warranted, sometimes not—were often bestowed on people reputed to have out-of-the-ordinary scientific skills or unusual educational backgrounds). Professor Wallace made his flight and appears to have validated his honorific title to the satisfaction of the spectators in Dallas that day.

There were other ventures into the skies over Dallas during the early part of the century. In May, 1908, a craft described as an airship (it is not clear whether it was a balloon or dirigible) called the *Aerial Queen* ventured aloft for a series of exhibition flights in the vicinity of Oak Cliff. One year later, an adventurous man named Frank Goodall piloted a dirigible around a local landmark known as the Praetorian Building. Although balloons and dirigibles continued to appear over Texas during the next decades, they were usually participants in staged events, such as fairs and balloon races, or were engaged in military training.

The romantic appeal of ballooning took the fancy of many young Americans, including William Ivy, of Houston. Ivy was born on July 31, 1866. At an early age, he seems to have decided on a career as a circus acrobat. He secured a reputation in Texas by walking a high wire stretched over a lake at San Pedro Springs, a feat that apparently got him a job with the Thayer-Noyes Circus. During a stint in Indiana, Ivy made a flight aboard a homemade hot air balloon and quickly added ballooning and parachuting to his circus credentials. In the meantime, he continued his high-wire act, despite occasional mishaps. At Wichita Falls, in 1882, a tipsy cowboy spurred his horse through the circus workers handling the guy wires during Ivy's tightrope act; Ivy crashed to the ground and suffered a broken ankle and several cracked ribs. Ivy's young bones soon mended, and he went back to work, catching the eye of Captain Tom Baldwin, one of the more successful impresarios of the airship exhibition circuit.

In 1890–1891, Ivy joined Baldwin's troupe on a Far Eastern tour. After opening in Tokyo, the Baldwin entourage worked its way down the coast of China, then made numerous flights in Southeast Asia, including Java, French Indo-China, Burma, and India. Following this exotic experience, Baldwin settled down in an amusement park in Quincy, Illinois, where Ivy ran the saloon, made spectacular leaps into a safety net, and conducted aerial weddings in balloons floating over the countryside. By this time, he had become so much a part of the Baldwin troupe that he called himself Ivy Baldwin, a name he kept for the rest of his picturesque career.

In 1893, Ivy traveled to Mexico to do some ascents with a tethered passenger balloon. Then he was off to Denver, where he headed the showbill at the famous western amusement park Elitch's Gardens. In Denver, Ivy met army personnel eager to start a balloon unit in the Signal Corps. In 1894, he signed up as a sergeant and took command of the army's lone balloon, stationed at Fort Logan, Colorado. Over the next four years, Ivy trained army recruits in ballooning techniques, experimented with ground-to-air telephone communications, and made aerial photos. He and his wife also put together a new balloon made of domestic dress silk. In the Spanish-American War of 1898, this home-built vehicle went into combat as the first army war balloon since the Civil War. Arriving in Cuba, the balloon was christened the *Santiago*. Several years old and adversely affected by tropical humidity, it leaked hydrogen everywhere. Ivy's commanding officer grumped that, if they had tried to fly it in peacetime, it would have been grounded.

With Ivy aboard, the wheezing *Santiago* nevertheless performed significant reconnaissance in several engagements, including action at El Caney and at approaches to San Juan Hill. But the balloon missions became highly controversial. Spanish riflemen peppered the observation basket and the balloon envelope with so much fire that it was eventually brought down. The balloon then became the target for both small-arms fire and artillery. A wartime reporter, novelist Stephen Crane, described the scene. "The front had burst out with a roar like brushfire," he wrote. "The balloon was dying, dying a gigantic and public death before the eyes of two armies. It quivered, sank, faded into the trees amid the flurry of battle that was suddenly and tremendously like a storm."

Although the army continued to work with various balloons, Sgt. Ivy Baldwin was discouraged; he resigned in 1900 and returned to the peaceful atmosphere of Elitch's Gardens in Denver. Eventually, he gravitated to California, where he rejoined Tom Baldwin and discovered a new aerial adventure in the frail, powered airplanes of the early twentieth century.

One of the first airplanes to appear in Texas was evidently introduced as an exhibit for the annual state fair. In September, 1909, the eccentric millionaire Ned Green brought a Wright brothers biplane to Dallas as an attraction at Fair Park. But it was only there to be seen, not flown. The following February, one of the first air meets was organized in Dallas, featuring a well-known early "birdman" named Otto Brodie, who dazzled crowds in his highly maneuverable Curtiss biplane. Brodie, like other fliers of the era, would not risk his fragile biplane in gusty weather, so spectators received

"wind checks" if it was too turbulent to risk taking off. This early activity stimulated local adventurers in Dallas to take to the air. A site known as Caruth Field, located in the river bottoms (of the Trinity) near downtown, became an active flying field. Local aviators in Dallas included Harry L. Peyton (ca. March, 1912) and Morris Titterington (ca. 1914).

But Dallas was probably not the location of Texas' first plane flight, since delays kept Brodie grounded until late February. It seems that Houston was the site of the first flight in the state. The person who has the most likely claim as the first airplane pilot was a Frenchman—the famous aviator Louis Paulhan. He was drawn to Houston by a highly lucrative contract in the amount of $20,000, contributed by the *Houston Post* and the Western Land Company, a developer active in the area of South Houston. Paulhan held license no. 10 from the Aero Club of France and had completed a series of notable flights in Europe as well as in the United States. In January, 1910, he participated in a major aviation meet in Los Angeles, and he arrived in Houston in mid-February, along with his Farman biplane, which had been crated up for shipment by rail.

Because of the Western Land Company's interests, Paulhan's exhibition flights naturally took place in South Houston. The site was near the intersection of present-day Spencer Highway and Old Galveston Road (Highway 3). In 1910, the location was an industrial area, and tenants included the Texas Fireworks Factory and the South Houston Iron Works, whose principal product was a line of stoves. The location was accessible by road, as well as by local rail line and the Galveston–Houston interurban railway, which ran about one mile to the west, parallel to Old Galveston Road. Curious onlookers could easily travel to see the daring Frenchman and his flying machine. Paulhan probably made at least two and possibly more flights on February 18. Among the intent observers that day were three men with more than passing interest, since they were in the process of building an airplane in a garage located in downtown Houston.

The three keen observers were local Houstonians: L. F. Smith, Guy Hahn, and L. L. Walker. At the time of Paulhan's appearance, Smith worked in the fireworks factory and had a reputation as a mechanical whiz. In later years, he served the city of South Houston as councilman, mayor, and president of the school board. Hahn appears to have lived a comfortable life as the son of a wealthy landowner and probably supplied the money for a later aircraft project in partnership with Smith. The third man, L. L. Walker, was popularly known as "Shorty," in recognition of his five-foot-three-inch frame. Walker was the first to become deeply involved with aeronautics and was responsible for the plane then under construction in the downtown Houston garage.

Walker was born on October 2, 1888, and grew up in east Texas. After finishing high school, he decided to attend Oklahoma A&M (now Oklahoma State) in Stillwater. After a couple of years, he evidently decided that life was more exciting outside the college campus

11

and signed on as an apprentice machinist with one of the organizations building the Panama Canal. By 1908, he had returned to Houston, working as a machinist in various shops. He became a foreman with a company known as the Auto and Motorboat Works, located on the corner of Capitol and Milam. Like many young men and women of the era, he became fascinated with the concept of airplanes and flying. Several pioneer manufacturers offered either plans or kits for popular aircraft of the period. It is not clear whether young Walker obtained a kit or used detailed plans, but the plane he built was a Bleriot Model XI, similar to the machine in which Louis Bleriot had flown the English Channel in 1909. Walker had help on the project from a fifteen-year-old shopboy, Mike Guseman, who worked with Walker for the next fifty years. As the plane took shape on the top floor of the garage, the news of Paulhan's flying exhibition must have seemed particularly exciting, since neither Walker nor his helper had observed a plane in flight. The Farman they saw was a biplane, making its appearance much different from that of the Bleriot monoplane. Still, the Bleriot's cross-channel flight gave it a considerable reputation.

Walker left little in the way of records, and local newspapers were not informed of his project. The best account of his early activity was written by his son, L. L. Walker, Jr., based on conversations with his father and with several of his father's contemporaries. As his son emphasizes, Walker was not seeking fame or fortune, but was engaged in a project for personal satisfaction.

The prestige of the Bleriot name notwithstanding, the design made for a tricky and inadequate aircraft, and, by the time my father's aircraft was complete, it was obsolete by comparison with the most advanced designs of the day. Then too, limited finances forced him to compromise in many ways, including the choice of engine.

A French-built engine, the best of the day by far, would have cost too much, so he purchased an American-built engine of more weight and less power. Inherent design flaws, together with the low-powered engine, were factors which would sharply limit the capabilities of the finished product. Perhaps it is just as well that he did not realize this at the time.

Some time in the latter part of 1910—perhaps late summer or early autumn—construction was complete. The wings were removed and fuselage was towed on its own wheels from downtown to South Houston, where it was reassembled. There then remained only one slight detail; the owner had yet to learn how to fly. There was no one to teach him, and, even if there had been an instructor, the aircraft had only one seat. Whatever he had to learn, he had to learn alone.

Remarkably enough, no records of any kind were kept, and so there is nothing to document what I am about to tell you. But, from many conversations with my father and with Mr. Smith, I have concluded that he would have first made sustained flight in October or November of 1910. This and subsequent flights were made from the same field in South Houston where Paulhan had flown earlier in the year. He may have been the first Houstonian to fly; I think he was, and several writers on the history of Houston have so suggested. I can tell you, however, that I never once heard him make that claim. For him, the accomplishment of building and flying his own aircraft was enough.

Walker's interest in flying led him into a lifelong association with aviation. In 1915, he received pilot's license no. 759, issued by the Aero Club of America. During World War I, Walker became an instructor with the Curtiss School of Aeronautics and worked in the area of Lake Charles, where he also learned to pilot biplane Curtiss flying boats. In the postwar era, he continued as an active pilot and eventually set up an engine repair and maintenance business, converting used aircraft engines for boat racing. Walker also serviced engines for pilots into the 1930s. About 1940, his shop was awarded government certification as a propeller repair station. Although the senior Walker died in 1960, his son ran the business until 1980, making it the oldest continuously certificated station in Texas.

Walker's flight in the autumn of 1910 turned out to be one of several aviation events of the season. Before the end of that year, the Moisant International Aviators, Inc., played Houston during a tour of the Southwest. John B. Moisant, a promoter from Chicago, had learned to fly only a few months before appearing in Houston. His aerial troupe included both American and French aviators, among them Rene Simon, who piloted a Bleriot to make the first flight over Houston proper. During the years before World War I, the plane built by Smith and Hahn was completed and was probably flown by a professional birdman, Fred DeKor, who also owned a Curtiss pusher. From Houston, DeKor traveled around the southwestern United States giving flying shows.

The touring troupes of international aviators probably motivated many aspiring aviators to build planes and to become pilots. It is also likely that many failed. Those who succeeded probably combined a sound mechanical knowledge with a sense of adventure. At least one, Jan Pliska, had a smattering of aeronautical lore as well. In 1897, at the age of eighteen, Pliska made the voyage from Austria-Hungary to Galveston, and eventually settled in Flatonia, near La Grange. Pliska's interest in aeronautics began much earlier, before his migration to America. As a conscript in the Austro-Hungarian army, he had been assigned to units working with balloons. Eventually, Pliska set up a successful blacksmith shop, but his fascination with balloons and gliders persisted.

Pliska obviously kept up with aeronautical events in the United States; during the winter of 1911–1912, he put the finishing touches on a biplane, built from plans sold through aeronautical magazines of the day. He acquired a powerplant from the Roberts Motor Company, manufacturers of a four-cylinder, 50 hp engine. By the spring of 1912, Pliska and a friend, Gray Coggin, loaded the plane into a horse-drawn wagon and hauled it out to a dry lake bed about six miles northwest of Midland. Pliska had the presence of mind to make several brief trial hops before getting high into the air for his first flight. This cautious self-training made him a successful pilot, and he evidently made several flights in the Midland-Odessa area.

Despite his early success, Pliska prudently decided to rest on his laurels before fate overtook him in the air. Sometime during 1912, he hung the plane from the rafters in the rear of his blacksmith shop, where it stayed for fifty years. The shop was finally torn down in 1962. Pliska's descendants deeded the historic aircraft to the City of Midland, and it eventually found a permanent home in a special wing of the Midland-Odessa airport terminal building.

Flying fever prompted other Texans to build and fly aircraft. In Temple, George W. Williams constructed a Bleriot and probably flew it early in 1911. He received support and encouragement from his brother, E. K. Williams, who published the *Temple Daily Telegram* from 1907 to 1929. In January, 1911, the newspaper sponsored a flying show in Temple, which included Rene Simon, J. K. Hamilton, and Roland Garros, who were traveling east by train after an air meet in Los Angeles. George Williams is said to have continued flying in the area, and he became a leading figure in Texas aeronautics in the 1920s.

Inevitably, crowds tired of merely seeing a plane take off and circle a racetrack; promoters had to find something more dramatic to lure spectators and generate headlines. Coincidentally, as the range and reliability of early planes began to improve, more fliers began to consider long-distance jaunts. An aerial tour across the continent became a powerful lure, especially in 1911, when news magnate William Randolph Hearst offered $50,000 for the first coast-to-coast flight. As prospective entrants considered potential routes across the United States, logic brought them through Texas and the Southwest, where the weather was bright and sunny and the terrain was flatter. For years, the barrier of the Rocky Mountains prompted other record-seeking fliers and early airlines to take the southwestern route for the same reasons.

The logistical support for this trip proved to be considerable, and only one individual bid for the prize: an ex–motorcycle racer named Calbraith P. Rodgers. When Rodgers took off from New York City, on September 17, 1911, he had a total of 60 hours' flying experience. His plane was christened the *Vin Fizz*, in honor of a soft drink purveyed by his sponsors. In support of the Wright biplane that Rodgers piloted, the sponsors provided a three-car train carrying $4,000 in spare parts, several mechanics, his mother, and his wife. The Hearst offer stipulated that the winner must complete the transcontinental flight in thirty days. For the cigar-

chomping Cal Rodgers and his crew, it was a formidable challenge.

Rodgers made it to Pasadena, California, after 82 hours and 4 minutes in the air, but there were a total of sixty-nine stops along the way—many of them planned, most of them not. Winds were wrong, the weather was sour, and there were nineteen crashes of varying severity. By the time he reached Pasadena, on November 5, the whole process had taken forty-nine days. Although Cal Rodgers failed to win the Hearst prize, he captured enthusiastic attention along the entire route. Texas was no exception, especially since twenty-three stops occurred within the state, giving Texans plenty of opportunity to see the daring airman (chewing the cigar that had become his trademark) and to take a big share of the headlines that followed America's first coast-to-coast flight. Regrettably, the career of Cal Rodgers paralleled the careers of so many of his adventurous contemporaries. Performing in an airshow early in 1912, just four months after his transcontinental feat, he crashed and died.

Well before World War I, aeronautical Texans began to receive international acclaim. The most outstanding was certainly an illiterate cowboy from (appropriately) Birdville, Texas—Samuel Franklin Cody. In 1861, the year Cody was born, Birdville was a dusty cowtown (it is now a Fort Worth suburb called Haltom City). The son of a Confederate soldier turned cattleman, young Cody learned to rope, ride, and handle a Colt .45 revolver. At the age of twelve, Cody was with a cattle drive on the Chisholm Trail when a Chinese cook taught the inquisitive youngster how to build and fly a kite. Throughout a bizarre and flamboyant career, aeronautics remained Cody's hobby and passion, eventually winning him a permanent niche in aeronautical history: Sam Cody was the first man to build and fly a powered airplane in Great Britain.

Before arriving in the British Isles, Cody married a Texas girl, Lela Davis, unsuccessfully prospected for gold in the Klondike, and joined a "Wild West Show," where his proficiency with horses, roping, and six-guns made him a star. His wife was intrigued by the growing popularity of such shows in Europe, where Buffalo Bill Cody (no relation to Sam) received great acclaim. In 1889, Sam Cody and his family sailed for London. Their troupe, billed as "The Great Codys," started with the standard Wild West format, but broadened into a melodrama, *Klondike Nugget*, developed out of Cody's experiences in the Yukon. That play and other performances became continuing successes in Great Britain, France, Switzerland, Italy, and North Africa. Between shows, Cody tinkered with various inventions and kites, including a series of man-lifting kites that caught the attention of the Royal Navy, which considered the possibility of using them for aerial reconnaissance at sea. In the meantime, a ship had towed a man-lifting kite, with Cody aloft, across the English Channel in 1903. Cody also received an invitation to lecture on kites at London's Royal Pavilion Music Hall. Through all of this, Cody remained illiterate; to the time of his death in 1913, even his signature remained an illegible scrawl.

Cody's work with the Royal Navy involved contracts. Realizing that there was money to be made from his avocation, Cody gave up melodramas in favor of aeronautics. He went to work for the British army at Farnborough, soon to become world famous as a center for aeronautical research. Cody's salary was set at 1,000 pounds sterling per year, with free fodder for the white horse he habitually rode about the grounds. From his long experience with kites, Cody developed a remarkably intuitive flair for aeronautical design. The specifics of engineering, drafting, and construction were attended to by the professional staff at Farnborough; other associates handled correspondence, which Cody dictated. Since the military was keenly interested in balloons for aerial observation, Cody turned his attention to dirigibles in 1907 and guided construction of a powered airship, the *Nulli Secundus* (second to none). But work with winged aircraft continued. Cody experimented with kites powered by small engines and conceived the design for a full-scale aircraft, using a biplane configuration not entirely unlike some of this larger kites.

Finally, on October 16, 1908, Sam Cody made the first powered airplane flight in Great Britain, piloting a machine called *British Army Aeroplane No. 1.* The engine was a 50 hp Antoinette, previously used in airship trials in Farnborough. Although the plane was badly damaged in a crash landing, Cody was unhurt and continued to play a leading role in early British aeronautics, as both flier and designer. As he continued to set new records, his wife also won acclaim. During July, 1909, Cody took her along on one flight, and she became the first woman in England to fly as a passenger.

Samuel Cody died in 1913 while flight testing a float-equipped plane that he wanted to fly across the Atlantic. The British buried him with out-of-the-ordinary pomp and circumstance for an unlettered foreigner from a remote place like Texas, but Cody's achievements and bigger-than-life persona had endeared him to a nation with a reputation for harboring eccentrics. Although Cody had become a British citizen only a year before his death, the government extended him a striking posthumous distinction, as the first civilian to be buried with full military honors in a military cemetery. A reported 50,000 Britons lined the streets for the funeral procession, which featured innumerable military personnel, mounted riders, and a group of bagpipers— Cody would have loved it.

No monument in the United States exists to honor Cody, a unique pioneer of early flight. A special memorial does exist, however, in England. During Cody's work at Farnborough, he habitually used a tree near the field as a convenient tie-down anchor for his planes. Years later, the RAF ceremoniously put up an iron fence to protect "Cody's Tree," even though it was long dead, with only the trunk and a few leafless branches. When this remnant finally began rotting away, the RAF erected a full-sized metal casting of the moldering trunk and branches; still protected by the iron rail-

ing, the memorialized tree remains standing near the airfield, marked with an inscribed plaque:

S. F. CODY MEASURED THE THRUST OF HIS AEROPLANE IN 1908–1909 BY TYING IT TO A TREE WHICH STOOD HERE. NEARBY HE MADE HIS FIRST TESTS WITH HIS POWERED AEROPLANE ON 16TH MAY, 1908, AND HIS FLIGHT OF 1,390 FEET ON 16TH OCTOBER, 1908—THE FIRST SUSTAINED FLIGHT IN BRITAIN.

Around the turn of the century, the tempo of the feminist movement quickened, and women sought more equality in the business environment, ownership of property, and voting rights. As women began entering the professions long dominated by males, it was inevitable that they would eventually take to the air as well. During 1908–1909, women in Europe moved quickly from the passive role of passenger to the active role of pilot. By 1910, Mademoiselle la Baronne de Laroche from France had become the first certified woman pilot in the world.

In America, Harriet Quimby was the first woman to qualify for a pilot's certificate, in 1911. Early the next year, she became the first woman to fly an airplane across the English Channel. A number of women became active at about the same time, but among the best known were the flying Stinsons: brothers Eddie and Jack and sisters Marjorie and Katherine.

The Stinsons were originally from Mississippi, but moved to Texas before World War I, settling in San Antonio. With the encouragement of their mother, the sisters learned to fly in Chicago and at the Wright School in Dayton, becoming two of the earliest—and youngest—female pilots in the country. Katherine became the fourth licensed woman pilot in 1912; two years later, at the age of twenty, Marjorie became the youngest. With the advent of World War I, the family organized the Stinson School of Flying in 1915, and Marjorie became a flight instructor, teaching over 100 Canadian male students how to fly. Katherine followed an even more publicized career as a stunt flier. In 1913, during a show in Helena, Montana, she became the first woman to fly the U.S. Mail; in 1917, she set a new long-distance record for both men and women, piloting her fragile plane from San Diego to San Francisco, a 610-mile flight that took her up to 9,000 feet to clear some mountain passes. Katherine had also become an internationally known figure. During 1916–1917, at age twenty-five, she had completed a triumphant flying tour of China and Japan. In a traditionally male-dominated society, the diminutive, 101-pound female pilot was a phenomenon. Dozens of young women applied to flying school as a result of her tour; female fan clubs filled her hotel rooms with mementos and flowers. On returning to America, Katherine joined other women fliers in fund-raising flights and recruitment tours during World War I. Both sisters eventually retired from active flying in the postwar era.

By the 1940s, Jack Stinson had become the president of his own flying school on Long Island, New York, and Eddie had formed the manufacturing company that produced so many outstanding light plane designs. Stinson Field, in San Antonio, is still an active airport, a fitting legacy for an outstanding aeronautical family.

The Military: Its Birth and the Texas Contribution

The U.S. War Department, in a rather frenetic effort to assemble a viable heavier-than-air aviation division during the initial hectic days shortly after the outbreak of World War I in August, 1914, found itself in a dilemma—its air service was not only ill-equipped and understaffed, it was also of little use. In 1905, the War Department's first reaction to the awesome military prospects of powered flight had been embarrassingly cool. Though in the tactically superior position of being able to benefit first from Wilbur and Orville Wright's monumental discovery, it had repeatedly rejected their overtures.

A year earlier, convinced that Wilbur and Orville had succeeded where so many others had failed, the British had attempted to buy the Wright airplane for use in the military. Wilbur and Orville turned down the British bid and elected to hold out for a U.S. War Department offer. Unfortunately, their patriotism merited only a letter of rejection from the Recorder of the Board of Ordnance and Fortification: "That Messrs. Wright be informed that the Board does not care to formulate any requirements for the performance of a flying machine or to take any further action until a machine is produced which by actual operation is shown to be able to produce horizontal flight and to carry an operator. . . ."

Interestingly, when the Department's myopic rejection was written, the brothers had successfully completed over 150 flights in full view of reporters, photographers, and innumerable city folk and had perfected their machine to the point where passengers and limited cargo were being carried with a regularity comparable to that of most other conventional forms of transportation.

Two years later, the War Department, still dragging its feet and doing its best to ignore the arrival of the twentieth century, found itself facing the fury of the politically influential Aero Club of America. This organization, officially born on November 30, 1905, with headquarters in New York City, consisted of over 300 aero-pioneers and aviation supporters, many of whom were wealthy and not adverse to using their considerable influence to obtain certain worthy objectives. Consequently, when it became apparent that the War Department had failed to develop enthusiasm for the flying machine, select Aero Club members, as an act of conscience, took the initiative and went directly to President Theodore Roosevelt with a demand that some action be taken to acquire the Wright brothers' airplane for use as a military weapon.

The ball was now in the Wrights' court; with the Aero Club's support, the brothers returned to Washington, D.C., to sell their invention. This second meeting, of course, proved significantly more fruitful than the first—though the response implied that funding for an initial airplane acquisition by the War Department remained temporarily unobtainable, another meeting on December 5, 1907, firmly convinced the chief of ordnance that a legitimate flying machine had, in fact, been invented.

The army's Signal Corps division, under whose jurisdiction things aeronautical then fell, shortly thereafter released Specification No. 486, based on performance figures outlined by Wilbur Wright. These called for an aircraft with the ability to: carry a pilot and passenger with a combined total weight of no more than 350 lbs.; fly 125 miles; have a minimum speed capability of 40 mph; be assembled and disassembled in a minimal amount of time; and operate from varied terrain.

Though extraordinarily modest by contemporary standards, the Wright-authored specification created quite a stir when it was officially released on December 23, 1907. There were, it seemed, still a few nonbelievers. Numerous media torchbearers editorialized with War Department condemnations proclaiming foolhardiness and waste. And many congressional critics simply argued that the specification demanded the impossible.

Not surprisingly, the embryonic U.S. aviation industry did not agree. In fact, there were no less than forty-one responses to the War Department request, and twenty-two of these were later considered worthy of detailed analysis. Cost estimates for getting the proposed aircraft from drawing board to hardware varied from a low of $500 to a high of just over $10 million.

The competition was eventually narrowed to three contenders: J. F. Scott, who asked for $1,000 and 185 days to complete his aircraft; A. M. Herring, who needed $20,000 and 180 days to complete his; and, of course, Orville and Wilbur Wright, who needed $25,000 and no less than 200 days to complete theirs.

The War Department now found itself in a dilemma. All three aircraft appeared to have promise; unfortunately, there was only sufficient funding to undertake construction and flight testing of the machines of the two lowest bidders. In effect, this eliminated the Wright aircraft, which, not surprisingly, was really the machine the War Department wanted in the first place. In desperation the Department took its problem to the president, who, upon learning of the army's predicament, promptly informed its representatives that a "special fund," available only to the president, had sufficient money left over from the Spanish-American War debacle to permit the Wright aircraft purchase.

Prior to the haggle over funds—and actually prior to the original decision to explore the potential of the airplane—the War Department's Signal Corps office had taken the bold step of formulating a primitive aviation section under Office Memorandum No. 6, dated August 1, 1907, which stated: "An Aeronautical Division of this office is hereby established, to take effect this date. This division will have charge of all matters pertaining to military ballooning, air machines, and all kindred subjects. All data on hand will be carefully classified and plans perfected for future tests and experiments. . . ."

The Wright Model A *Military Flyer,* also known as S.C. No. 1 (Signal Corps aircraft No. 1), was eventually to become the only one of the three contract contenders to reach the hardware stage. Delivered by trailer to Fort Myer, Virginia, on August 20, 1908, it was quickly made ready for testing. During the nearly three weeks of flight trials that followed, a world endurance record of nearly one hour was set, and the first military observer, Lt. Frank Lahm, was safely and unceremoniously transported.

Unfortunately, the Fort Myer trials were abruptly terminated on a rather sour note. On September 17, Orville Wright and a military observer by the name of Lt. Thomas Selfridge, following their fourth circuit around the Fort Myer compound and while cruising at an altitude of several hundred feet, ran into catastrophic difficulty. A slight propeller blade deflection, caused by a fatigue crack, led to blade contact with a bracing wire and, seconds later, structural failure and a total loss of control. In front of numerous horrified observers, the *Military Flyer* broke apart in mid-air, slowly pitched over, and hurtled to the ground. Selfridge, sadly, died several hours after impact and thus had the doubtful honor of becoming the first U.S. military person killed in an aircraft. Orville was grievously injured.

The War Department offered a delay in the trials, and Wilbur immediately accepted. Returning to Dayton, while Orville recovered, Wilbur and a small team of assistants began a second *Military Flyer* (using the surviving parts of the first). Under the terms of the delay, the Wrights could still meet their contractual obligations if they could complete the trial requirements within a specified time.

The return to Virginia on June 20, 1909, after nine months of intensive construction work and flight testing, was triumphant. During the following weeks, flights over an hour long reaching altitudes above 4,000 feet were achieved without effort, and during the speed runs the average calculated velocity was over 42 mph. Perhaps most importantly, large crowds were on hand for almost every trial event. During the cross-country speed flight, for instance, no less than 7,000 people, including President William Taft, witnessed the flawless takeoff and landing.

Among those observing for the U.S. Army as an assignee to the Office of the Chief Signal Officer and a member of the board for the Fort Myer trials was Lt. Benjamin Foulois (pronounced *Fuhloy*). In 1908, Foulois

had participated in tests of the first army dirigible. Unimpressed with the military possibilities of lighter-than-air craft, he had accepted the invitation to observe the Wright trials with grave reservations.

By their end, however, and most certainly after a ride as a passenger on the last Fort Myer flight, Foulois walked away convinced that the airplane was where his, and the army's, future lay. In later years, while reminiscing about his first flight, Foulois said, "I would like to think that I was chosen [for that flight] on the basis of intellectual and technical ability, but I found out later that it was my short stature, light weight, and map-reading experience that had tipped the decision in my favor. . . ."

The final report describing the Fort Myer trials confirmed that the Wright *Military Flyer* had indeed successfully met the army's specified performance and other requirements. Accordingly, a contract for $30,000 (which included a $5,000 bonus for exceeding the 40 mph speed requirement) was let to the Wright Aeroplane Company of Dayton, Ohio, and the Wright aircraft, now officially designated S.C. No. 1, was turned over to the U.S. Army Signal Corps to become the first official U.S. military heavier-than-air flying machine.

Lieutenant Lahm, the first observer, and Lieutenant Foulois became the first U.S. military aviators under the terms of the War Department/Wright agreement. Before full-scale flight training could begin, however, Foulois was sidetracked and sent to Europe as the U.S. delegate to the International Congress of Aeronautics in Nancy, France. Consequently, a third aviator, 2nd Lt. Frederic Humphreys, joined the new Signal Corps aviation department and, along with Lahm, was assigned to a newly created training site near Maryland Agricultural College just outside College Park, Maryland. On October 8, 1909, U.S. military flight training was initiated there. Under the tutelage of Wilbur Wright, and with a little more than three hours of dual instruction each, both Lahm and Humphreys soloed on October 26. On November 5, the Wright S.C. No. 1 was damaged in a minor accident; during the ensuing repair period, the winter bad weather arrived. The cold, wind, and rain temporarily shut down flight operations for several months.

Weather (and terrain) played significant roles in the fragile but rapidly expanding world of pre–World War I aeronautics. Wilbur and Orville, in choosing a site for their initial full-scale manned glider and powered aircraft tests beginning in 1900, had spent months corresponding with weather station directors throughout the United States in an eventually successful effort to locate a place that provided the wind and terrain conditions considered necessary for a successful flight test program.

A windy, relatively flat beach on an obscure finger of coastal North Carolina was chosen, due almost totally to recommendations from the chief of U.S. Weather Bureau operations, Willis L. Moore. During November and December of 1899, Moore and Wilbur Wright traded correspondence and information on weather requirements for glider and manned aircraft experiments. On September 9, 1900, Wilbur wrote to his father, Bishop Milton Wright:

> In order to obtain support from the air it is necessary, with wings of reasonable size, to move through it at the rate of fifteen or twenty miles per hour.... If the wind blows with proper speed, support can be obtained without movement with reference to the ground. It is safer to practice in a wind, provided [it] is not too much broken up into eddied and sudden gusts by hills, trees, &c. At Kitty Hawk, which is on the narrow bar separating the Sound from the Ocean, there are neither hills nor trees so that it offers a safe place to practice. Also the wind there is stronger than any place near home and is almost constant so that it is not necessary to wait days or weeks for a suitable breeze. It is much cheaper to go to a distant point where practice may be constant than to choose a nearer spot where three days out of four might be wasted....

The last few words, pertaining to lost flight time, were also to play a key role in a preliminary War Department decision to find a more suitable site than Maryland for flight training in 1909. The U.S. government owned several large tracts next to a military compound known as Fort Sam Houston in San Antonio, Texas, a city and state with climate and terrain that were considered by many to be ideal for flying. In late 1909, this site was the War Department's unequivocal choice for a flight training center.

Fort Sam Houston was, in fact, a good place to learn the skills required to control an airplane safely. The terrain was flat, the weather was generally balmy—if rather windy—and there were growing indications that unrest in Mexico merited an aviation observation unit in the area.

In October, 1909, Lt. Benjamin Foulois had returned to the United States in time to squeeze in some fifty-four minutes of preliminary flight instruction from the Wrights just as the aforementioned accident and weather closed in on the Maryland operation. By this time, the Wright brothers had technically fulfilled the terms of their contract; after repairing the damaged aircraft, they returned to Dayton, Ohio, to pursue development of improved versions. This, coupled with the return of Lahm and Humphreys to their regular billets, left Foulois as the sole U.S. military aviator and the Wright S.C. No. 1 as the only heavier-than-air U.S. military aircraft.

In December, the War Department ordered Foulois to take the Wright aircraft to Fort Sam Houston. The directive, from Brig. Gen. James Allen, chief Signal Corps officer, as Foulois would later recall, was simple: "Your orders, Lieutenant, are for you to evaluate the aeroplane. Just take plenty of spare parts—and teach yourself to fly."

Foulois, a small crew of nine enlisted men, and seventeen crates full of aircraft parts and pieces arrived by train and truck at Fort Sam Houston in early February, 1910. After completing a small storage shed and reassembling the S.C. No. 1 aircraft and erecting the launch catapult (developed by the Wright brothers to shorten the distances required for takeoff), Foulois, though grossly undertrained, made his initial solo flights on March 2. He flew three times that day, ending his preliminary aerial excursions with a rather pronounced crack-up. After minimal repairs, he continued to fly, test the aircraft, and improve his piloting technique over the following months. He corresponded regularly with the Wrights, developed important modifications to the aircraft (including the addition of wheels to the original skis), became the first to use a seatbelt in an aircraft (a leather strap furnished by the local battery saddler), and verified the practical application of an aircraft to military operations by carrying out aerial mapping, photography, and observation of troops. By September, he had completed no less than sixty-one flights over Texas soil, logging a total flight time of nine hours.

During this period, there was a marked lack of support for the army's one-pilot, one-aircraft air force. Because of the S.C. No. 1's fragility—and Foulois' propensity for contacting the ground in unconventional attitudes—an average of three weeks of repair was required for each week of flying time. The War Department, in a magnanimous gesture of unparalleled proportions, provided Foulois with a staggering $150 to keep his craft airworthy during the last quarter of 1910. This figure was far from sufficient; Foulois quietly spent $300 of his own money to subsidize the Fort Sam Houston program.

By 1911, the attributes of the powered aircraft, due primarily to activities unrelated to Foulois' unheralded efforts deep in the heart of Texas, began to overcome the doubts expressed by many members of Congress and the Senate (best summarized in the immortal query of one unnamed Congressman: "Why all this fuss about airplanes for the army? I thought they already had one"). Accordingly, in 1911, the War Department took the liberty of assigning more officers to flying duty and committing itself to the expenditures necessary to buy additional aircraft to train them. The fiscal year 1911 War Department budget, in fact, included the first specific U.S. military appropriation for aviation—a rather modest $125,000, with $25,000 to be made available immediately.

Chief Signal Officer Allen immediately ordered five new aircraft with the initial funding: three Wright Type B and two Curtiss Model D biplanes. The first to be delivered was one of the Curtiss Model Ds, shortly afterward officially designated S.C. No. 2. This aircraft, ordered on March 13, 1911, cost $6,000 and was delivered to Washington, D.C., within a few days of contract signing. Several weeks later, it (or an aircraft exactly like it) was delivered to San Antonio and assigned to Foulois and his small group of Fort Sam Houston pioneers.

By now, Foulois had been joined by three officers from the Glenn H. Curtiss flying school on North Island, San Diego, California. Lt. Paul Beck, Lt. John Walker, Lt. George Kelly, and a growing contingent of ground support personnel now comprised a provisional aviation company, with Beck being the senior ranking officer in command.

A Wright Type B, designated S.C. No. 3, arrived shortly after the Curtiss aircraft and, in combination with the venerable S.C. No. 1, served proudly as the mighty aerial arm of the U.S. military services—with home base in San Antonio. On April 22, 1911, the two new arrivals served as tail guard of a 10,000 troop column assembled for review by Gen. William H. Carter.

It is interesting to note that another Wright Type B had been loaned to the Signal Corps prior to the arrival of S.C. No. 3. This machine, privately owned by *Collier's* magazine publisher Robert F. Collier, was one of the first civil aircraft ever acquired by a private citizen. A strong proponent of military aviation and well aware of the army's financial plight, Collier had elected to lease his newly acquired Wright aircraft to the Signal Corps for the grand sum of $1 per month. It was delivered to San Antonio on February 21, 1911, and, shortly afterward, was moved to Fort McIntosh near Laredo, Texas, while the Signal Corps demonstrated the practicability of using an aircraft to work with ground troops. It was returned to Collier following the arrival of the Signal Corps' own Wright Type B several months later.

Following official acceptance of the new Wright and Curtiss aircraft on April 11, S.C. No. 1 was officially withdrawn from service and deactivated. It was then shipped back to the Wrights, who eventually turned it over to the Smithsonian. It is presently displayed in the massive National Air and Space Museum facility in Washington, D.C.

Eugene Ely and Frank Coffyn, representing the Curtiss and Wright companies, respectively, served as instructors for the fledgling Signal Corps during these first few months of actual military operations at Fort Sam Houston. Interestingly, several months prior to his arrival in San Antonio, Ely had become the first pilot ever to land and take off from a ship. Coffyn was no less renowned, due to his exploits while demonstrating the abilities of Wright aircraft.

Accidents during this period were not uncommon. Most involved relatively minor repairs, although on occasion landings in mesquite trees, which dotted the local terrain like chicken pox, demanded significantly more time-consuming rebuilding. Fort Sam Houston during this period was a major army training facility. In May, 1911, it was also in the middle of a rather extensive training exercise that required the services of many thousands of enlisted men. On May 10, at 7 a.m., Lt. George Kelly, one of several pilot trainees working with the small Signal Corps detachment under Foulois, took off on a training flight in S.C. No. 2. This was the first flight of the Curtiss aircraft following an unscheduled mesquite-assisted landing and a day in the repair shop.

After some five minutes of flight, Kelly returned to Fort Sam Houston and attempted a landing. Wind conditions were not good; on his first approach, the aircraft was seen to hit the ground nose wheel first at a high speed and rebound into the air. A climb to thirty feet found Kelly heading toward the camping area of the 11th Infantry. He was apparently in trouble; in an attempt to avoid crashing into the crowded campground, he banked steeply, stalled, and abruptly dove to the ground. Kelly, thrown nearly twenty feet from the aircraft, had a fractured skull. He died several hours later in a Fort Sam Houston hospital and was later buried in the San Antonio National Cemetery. The post-accident investigation determined that a structural failure, caused either by the initial hard landing or by poor repair technique from a previous event, had induced a control loss that Kelly was unable to overcome.

The fallout from the accident proved to be quite severe: the point of ground contact, in the middle of the Fort Sam Houston reservation with its thousands of troops, caused the commander of the Maneuver Division, Gen. William H. Carter, immediately to prohibit further flying from the drill grounds. This, in turn, caused the army to discontinue the Fort Sam Houston operation altogether and return the Signal Corps contingent to College Park, Maryland. S.C. No. 2 was, in the meantime, repaired by civilian mechanics and shipped to College Park along with S.C. No. 3. Military flying in Texas had suddenly come to a halt.

A hiatus of no less than two years was to occur before military aviation returned to Texas. In the interim, Lieutenant Foulois was recalled to troop duty with the infantry, and military aviation was permitted very restricted growth with very limited congressional appropriations.

On March 5, 1913, three days after it had been authorized a small expansion by an act of Congress, the Aeronautical Division issued Field Order No. 1, establishing what was to be the First Provisional Aero Squadron. During this interim period, the nine aircraft attached to the Squadron were divided between two elements known as Company A and Company B— representing the first examples of "squadron assignments" ever in U.S. military aviation. The word "provisional," indicating an ephemeral quality not particularly agreeable to proponents of military aviation, was officially removed when the unit was formally recognized by War Department General Order No. 75, dated December 4, 1913. Formal approval of the First Aero Squadron was granted by the chief signal officer on January 7, 1914. At that time, some 114 U.S. Army personnel were at least temporarily assigned to aeronautically related slots.

The surviving Wright Type B (S.C. No. 3), the repaired Curtiss Model D, three Burgess Model Hs, and at least four other Wright and Curtiss aircraft were assigned to the newly formed First Aero Squadron. The Burgess machines were the first "enclosed cockpit" military aircraft to operate in Texas; the earlier Curtiss and Wright designs had both provided only rudimentary seating for the pilot and passenger on the leading edge of the lower wing.

On February 25, 1913, Capt. Charles Chandler, the acting commander of the Signal Corps aviation section, received orders to move all aircraft and related personnel and equipment from the Signal Corps training facility near Augusta, Georgia, to a newly dedicated facility near Texas City, Texas. This action was a response to increasingly tense U.S. relations with Mexico. The revolution and consequent takeover by Gen. Victoriano Huerta (following the assassination of President Francisco Madero) were causing headaches in Washington, complicated by the fact that the United States had not yet recognized Huerta's government. In addition, the U.S. government was allowing sales of munitions to such Huerta opponents as Gen. Venustiano Carranza and Francisco "Pancho" Villa; this, coupled with the failure to recognize his government, angered Huerta greatly.

Though it had now been almost two years since the Kelly accident, Fort Sam Houston's commander had not forgotten how close the hurtling Curtiss biplane had come to killing some of his troops. Accordingly, when army aviation was ordered to return to Texas, he insisted that a new site for flight training be found. This time, a beach front location near Texas City proved acceptable. Though not as convenient to the U.S./Mexican border as San Antonio, it was significantly more accommodating to seaplanes, which the Signal Corps was beginning to consider for possible addition to its minuscule aircraft inventory.

Unfortunately, the second stay in Texas, primarily in support of the Second Army Division, which was undertaking training maneuvers in the area, proved as tenuous as the first. Although it sounds contradictory to the original decision to move south, the weather in Texas City turned out to be not as accommodating as that of San Antonio, particularly for training purposes; this, coupled with a temporary calming of Mexican/U.S. relations and growing interest in seaplanes, prompted a partial move of the First Aero Squadron to a relatively new aviation training facility in San Diego.

In July, 1914, Congress enacted a law providing permanent personnel for army aviation. This, at last, firmly established the small aviation section of the Signal Corps and permitted a maximum of 60 officers and 260 enlisted men. The growing threat of war in Europe and the chronic problems with Mexico provided impetus for this increased army interest. Additionally, Congress had been made aware of the fact that several European powers had expended considerable sums in building up their military air forces. Germany, for instance, the world leader, already had in excess of 500 front-line aircraft. The U.S. inventory, by comparison, consisted of 20 machines—none of them considered technologically state-of-the-art or competitive from a performance standpoint.

Numbers notwithstanding, it was with some sense of anticipation that the United States elected to utilize military airpower for the first time in an attempt to neutralize the political ramifications of the folk hero status of Pancho Villa. Villa, who had recently been unceremoniously removed from office following a two-year stint as dictator of Mexico, was now commanding an outlaw band of Mexican nationals that was hell-bent on creating havoc for the Mexican government in power. The Carranza administration, though no less corrupt than Huerta's, was recognized by the U.S. government as the official ruling body of Mexico. Villa was of course antagonized by the U.S. show of Carranza allegiance and was quick to vent his displeasure in the form of blatant disregard of the customary territorial immunities provided by national boundaries. During one of several raids conducted across the U.S./Mexico border, on March 8, 1916, Villa entered the town of Columbus, New Mexico, and slaughtered seventeen U.S. citizens. This prompted the U.S. government to order the War Department to send Gen. John J. "Black Jack" Pershing, who was then commanding the Presidio of San Francisco, and a sizable military expedition south in an attempt to capture the legendary *bandito*.

Earlier, while Villa was warming up his campaign south of the Rio Grande, the First Aero Squadron had been temporarily assigned to Fort Sill, Oklahoma. On April 13, 1915, preliminary responses to the Villa uprising had come in the form of a First Aero Squadron detachment assignment to Brownsville, which resulted in several reconnaissance flights over Villa emplacements. This was the only aerial support provided to the U.S. ground forces that were then forming until the arrival of the bulk of the First Aero Squadron at San Antonio, some months later. During the move to Brownsville, four officers and fifteen enlisted men made the trek through Texas by truck and aircraft. They arrived on August 18, sweaty, but relatively unscathed.

By this time, a new aircraft, the untested Curtiss JN-2, newly assigned to the First in small numbers, was proving to be a problem. Poorly designed, grossly underpowered, and prone to control losses in relatively mild maneuvers, it was disliked by both pilots and ground crews. The Brownsville climate proved to be yet another liability, as the humidity and heat affected the JN-2's wood construction and caused difficulties with delamination. Modifications to the JN-2 coupled with the arrival of the improved JN-3 eventually overcame most of the First's concerns, but not before several pilots were seriously injured in accidents.

In 1914, the War Department decided to create a permanent home for the First Aero Squadron away from the unit's Signal Corps Aviation School facility in San Diego. Funding for the new facility was appropriated in April, 1914, and officially released in 1915. Fort Sam Houston was again chosen as the location, but this time a target range (Remount Depot No. 2), some four miles to the north, was declared the flying field.

On November 19, 1915, the remaining aircraft and personnel of the First still operating with the detachment at Fort Sill, Oklahoma, headed south to Fort Sam Houston. This was the first cross-country flight of a service unit in the history of U.S. military aviation. Because of the dearth of airports and support facilities between

Fort Sill and San Antonio, the unit's ground support equipment and enlisted men preceded the aircraft to predetermined stopping points located every eighty miles between the Oklahoma and Texas posts.

Shortly after its arrival back in San Antonio, the First, which was once again under the guiding hand of the newly promoted Capt. Benjamin Foulois, was sequestered for service in the rapidly growing anti-Villa campaign in Mexico. This initial combat assignment, coupled with the fact that all eight Curtiss JN-2s (ordered in January, 1915, and delivered to San Diego while the First was there) had arrived, gave the unit the minimal equipment and personnel needed to create a legitimate aerial observation force.

Villa, in the meantime, had assembled a rather small air force of his own. Operated by a select group of American mercenaries, this consisted of a Wright biplane of unknown type, a Christofferson-type Curtiss pusher, and a venerable Martin Type T. These three aircraft provided limited reconnaissance capability for the Villa forces and were utilized sparingly.

Following the attack in Columbus, New Mexico, Brigadier General Pershing, at the command of the War Department, began organizing a force of some 15,000 troops, whose objective was the elimination of Villa as a political power. Along with the mobilization taking place just outside Columbus, the First Aero Squadron also was ordered to the New Mexican town on March 15, 1916. Under the command of Foulois, ten pilots, eighty-four enlisted men, and eight aircraft were assigned to the anti-Villa task force.

The First's inadequate equipment proved a major liability during the campaign period that followed. On the initial operational sortie, for instance, on March 19, from Columbus to the advanced base at Casas Grandes, Mexico, one aircraft was forced to return, one was seriously damaged during a forced landing at night, and the remaining six were forced to land because of impending darkness (the aircraft were not equipped for night flight). Later, it was discovered that the mountain ranges in the area, with peaks of 10,000 to 12,000 feet, were significantly higher than the maximum altitude capabilities of the aircraft. Additionally, the strong wind blasts emanating from these ranges were too powerful for the powerplants or airframes to master, and the never-ending dust storms created maintenance and operational headaches never previously imagined.

The first month of operation from Columbus was to prove the most significant of the campaign. In fact, by April 20, only two craft were considered airworthy, and these were returned from Casas Grandes to Columbus, where they were dismantled and scrapped. Replacement aircraft had arrived in the meantime, but these eventually proved no more capable than their predecessors.

Throughout the Villa campaign, which lasted into 1917, First Aero Squadron accomplishments were minor, from a tactical standpoint. Relatively modest flights in an effort to transport mail, orders, and miscellaneous small support items were accomplished in good weather, but more demanding responsibilities usually proved impossible. In retrospect, it is apparent that the flight crews and maintenance personnel of the First Aero Squadron under Benjamin Foulois functioned admirably in an environment rendered unworkable by climate and equipment. Forced prematurely into a situation that quickly proved untenable, they nonetheless proved highly disciplined and dogmatically devoted to the cause of military aviation.

Quarter Share No. 3 ~~6~~

$ 1. 25.   San Antonio, T,, June 27th 1865.

Six months after the sale of a U. S. patent right for an airship, invented by me, I promise to pay to *Dr. Herff*
ONE DOLLAR and TWENTY FIVE CENTS, together with his share of One Fourth of the amount received by such sale, expenses deducted, or two months after the term for which a U. S. patent will be granted to me, together with a yearly payment of his share of One Fourth of the profits accrued by the sale of such airships, as the case may be, value received.   *J. Brodbeck*

As these shares indicated, Jacob Brodbeck was quite serious about his flying machine and its profitability as a business venture. It is not known how many shares, if any, were sold to investors, and little information survives concerning Brodbeck's financing scheme.

At the San Antonio Fair Grounds, about 1904, onlookers waited to see a rare balloon flight. This vehicle had a propeller (right) and a steering apparatus (left), indicating that it was controllable in flight. Lines attached to sand bags on the ground kept it stable during static display periods.

Maj. Gen. Benjamin Foulois shortly before his death on April 25, 1967.
A quiet yet persistent proponent of airpower, he is now considered
the father of U.S. military aviation.

Fred DeKor, of Houston, was typical of the pre-WWI "bird-
men" who made exhibition flying a professional career. The
rugged Curtiss "Pusher" was often the aircraft of choice.

During the 1914 Abilene Fair, an airman (probably Fred
DeKor) gave a flying display in a Curtiss "Pusher" that was
probably the first of its kind in this west Texas community.

The original Wright Type B "Military Flyer" was delivered to Fort Sam Houston in 1910. Lt. Benjamin Foulois is seen (second from right) leaning on the Wright biplane's lower wing during a photo session on the Fort Sam Houston compound shortly after the aircraft was delivered.

In 1909, while Wilbur was in France demonstrating a Wright biplane to the French government, Orville embarked on his mission to Fort Myer, Virginia, to attempt to convince the U.S. military services that the flying machine could be of significant use in combat scenarios.

The Fort Myer, Virginia, trials proved financially rewarding for the Wrights as they were eventually able to consummate an agreement with the U.S. government calling for the acquisition of one Wright aircraft for use by the Signal Corps.

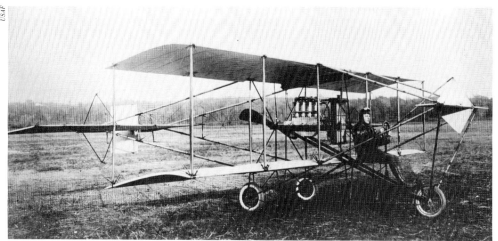

A Curtiss Model D "Pusher" was the second aircraft type acquired for military use in the U.S. Technologically the Curtiss aircraft was mechanically and aerodynamically more advanced than the Wright machine, having fixed tricycle landing gear and independent control surfaces.

The Wright Type B was eventually equipped with wire wheels and air-inflated tires and flown conventionally from prepared takeoff and landing surfaces. A maximum of two crew members was normally carried, with both sitting on the leading edge of the wing just ahead of the engine.

Accommodations for Benjamin Foulois and his fledgling aviators were minimal at the Columbus, New Mexico, base of operations created for Gen. "Black Jack" Pershing and his troops during his infamous Pancho Villa campaign of 1916.

The underpowered Curtiss JN-2 was a notoriously difficult aircraft to fly and maintain. Due to a terribly inhospitable climate, almost all JN-2s in service with Foulois' squadron were declared non-flightworthy before the end of the Villa campaign.

The Curtiss JN-2s were of wood and fabric construction and were powered by small Curtiss OX-type water-cooled V-8 engines. Underpowered and inappropriately utilized, they proved of little value in the heat and sand of the Mexican desert environment.

Field maintenance procedures during the Villa campaign were only marginally effective in combating the ever-present desert dust storms and unrelenting heat. Personnel also suffered in this environment, though their devotion to the cause of military aviation remained remarkably strong.

Training aircraft were delivered from the various production facilities direct to Kelly Field's training bases in a disassembled state aboard railroad flatcars. Once at the field, they were off-loaded, assembled, flight tested, and immediately delivered to the base's operational training units.

The Curtiss JN-4, affectionately nicknamed ''Jenny'' by those who flew and maintained it, was a developed and significantly more successful version of the earlier JN-2. Love Field's JN-4s were an integral part of the service's air training operations in Texas in 1918.

These Kelly Field Curtiss JN-4s were effectively written off following a head-on collision during training maneuvers in 1918. The cadet crew members involved apparently survived, receiving only minor injuries.

Many hundreds of aircraft were destroyed in accidents that occurred at the various Texas training facilities activated during WWI. Most involved Curtiss JN-4s such as this Kelly Field example seen following an unscheduled stall/spin demonstration in 1918. The fate of the crew member(s) is unknown.

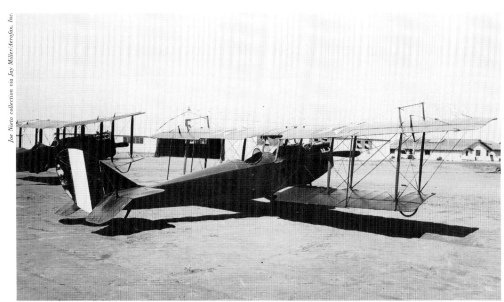

Post-WWI flight training, though significantly reduced in volume from that of WWI, retained the services of the venerable JN-4 as the primary training aircraft. Powered by either the Curtiss OX or Hispano-water-cooled V-8 engine, the JN-4 was capable of 90 mph in level flight.

The British-designed and manufactured S.E. 5 was one of the most effective Allied pursuit aircraft of WWI. The type was acquired for use by the U.S. air services, though only a few actually entered combat during the war. S.E. 5s were somewhat less docile than JN-4s as evidenced by this example's unusual post-landing attitude.

The JN-4's rather fragile structure was not particularly suitable for the training role for which the aircraft was intended. This Love Field JN-4, flown by "Lt. Anderson," was one of the less fortunate examples to accommodate the U.S. Air Service's training mission. Though "Lt. Anderson's" fate is not recorded, the odds are fair that he did not survive the mission.

The JN-4 was the most-produced U.S. military aircraft of WWI. Love Field JN-4s were typical of the breed in service—being flown from sod fields and piloted by neophyte aviators with high aspirations.

Field maintenance in the early 1920s, such as that taking place on this DH-4, was accomplished with few concessions to comfort.

Two Italian Caproni Ca.5 bombers were temporarily based at Kelly Field in 1921, for never-consummated use as testbeds under the direction of Gen. "Billy" Mitchell.

Cows were notorious consumers of dope and lacquer impregnated aircraft fabric. Aircraft left unprotected in fields overnight rarely survived unscathed.

As part of an agreement reached with its Allies during WWI, numerous British, French, and Italian combat aircraft were brought to the United States for technical evaluation and study. Among them was this immense Handley Page O-400 bomber, which was tested at Kelly Field during the early 1920s. The O-400 represented the state-of-the-art in bomber design at the time.

Post war work for the Air Service included flying the mail. Conversions for this mission included this Curtiss R4L modified by Love Field's Aviation Repair depot.

One of the more common post war aircraft found in Air Service use was the British-designed de Havilland DH-4. During the war it was manufactured in the U.S. by Boeing and Airco.

The two Texas-based Italian Caproni Ca.5 bombers were flown on simulated combat sorties on several occasions during their short tenure at Kelly Field. The photo on the left is an exceptionally rare air-to-air view of the Caproni while it was overflying downtown Dallas during a test mission. Both bombers were eventually scrapped in the early 1920s.

Institute of Texan Cultures

*San Antonio's Stinson Field, named after the famous flying Stinson family, became a nationally
recognized center for aviation activities and flight instruction following WWI. It survives to
this day, serving San Antonio as a public domain airport and a flight instruction facility.*

USAF/Kelly AFB History Office

*The Duncan Field Depot Engineering Department was often called upon to refurbish the various aircraft types
(French-built SPADs are shown) operated by the U.S. Air Service. Because almost all aircraft during this period
were of wood and fabric construction, restoration to flightworthy condition was not usually a difficult task.*

Love Field was relatively far from any populated areas during its immediate post-WWI training center days. A lull in activity slowed the field's growth considerably during this period, but its proximity to Dallas kept flight training activity at a respectable level.

Duncan Field, which eventually was to be absorbed by the rapidly expanding Kelly Field complex, was a major aircraft overhaul facility during and immediately following WWI. Both permanent and temporary facilities were built to accommodate the support requirements generated by the demands of WWI.

Love Field's repair depot was very active throughout WWI. Virtually any aircraft could be accommodated in the depot's sizable hangars, including nonindigenous types such as this British-manufactured S.E. 5 biplane fighter.

Love Field also served as an engine repair depot, and a large variety of engines could be accommodated. Engine test stands served as ground test stations for the various engines used by U.S. military aircraft.

Spare parts supply depots, such as the Duncan Field operation near San Antonio, were a mandatory accoutrement of the military logistics system developed during WWI. Literally thousands of parts were stored in these facilities, which were located at several Texas military airfields.

After the war, Love Field's Aircraft Repair Depot served the maintenance needs created by the Air Service's involvement with mail delivery. Among the types repaired at the facility in 1919 was this "Liberty" powered Curtiss R4L, developed specifically for airmail transport.

War bond drives were sustained by parades and meetings. The various military services often participated in these events, supporting the cause by showing Allied hardware used in the war or enemy hardware that had been captured. This French SPAD XIII pursuit, representative of similar SPADs flown on the front by American pilots, was provided by Kelly Field for a 1918 San Antonio parade.

Retha McCulloh, after soloing in 1928, became the first Texas woman to get an American-issued pilot's license. High boots, jodhpurs, goggles, a leather helmet, and a leather jacket were standard dress for an aviatrix of the era.

2. Between the Wars

From Aerial Antics to Airlines

Between the wars, aviation literally raced ahead. New records for speed, endurance, and distance were established and then wiped out as promoters and adventurers posted better figures. Texas received its share of headlines, since many long-distance flights utilized the southwestern route first taken by Cal Rodgers in 1911. There were other records, too, some made in Texas, and others made by Texans. Because so many aviation stories related to the state, whether the planes and pilots made the local, national, or international news, Texans could not help but be aware of the rapid progress of flight technology.

During the 1920s, the army and navy made several highly publicized flights that made headlines and dramatized aviation for residents of Texas. In 1919, a pair of army pilots flew a Martin bomber across the state in the process of completing an "around the rim" circuit flight of the United States, covering 9,823 miles in just over three months. In 1924, two of the army's Douglas *World Cruiser* biplanes made the first aerial circumnavigation of the world, covering 26,345 miles in a series of record-breaking flights between April and September. Heading west from Seattle, Washington, two remaining planes of the original quartet passed through Dallas, Sweetwater, and El Paso on their way back to their starting point. On December 21, 1926, five Loening OA-1A amphibians took off from Kelly Field, San Antonio, on the first leg of a Pan-American Goodwill Flight that touched twenty-two countries before making their final stop in Washington, D.C., on May 2, 1927. Texans took a special interest in the event, not only because of the San Antonio departure, but also because one of the five planes had been christened the *San Antonio*. The flight was also important in helping promote Latin American air routes in the future.

Texans, like citizens all over the world, were captivated by Lindbergh's historic solo flight across the Atlantic on May 20–21, 1927. Youngsters across the state participated in spontaneous celebrations and events honoring the milestone flight. While many of them constructed model planes and dreamed of Lindbergh's exploit, many other aviators decided to imitate the feat.

In the aftermath of Lindbergh's epochal flight, James D. Dole, president of the Hawaiian Pineapple Company and member of the National Aeronautic Association, offered prizes of $25,000 and $10,000 to the first two pilots to fly nonstop from America to Honolulu. Although 1,400 miles shorter than Lindbergh's 3,600-mile flight to Paris, it was much more demanding: it was entirely over water, and the Hawaiian Islands would be missed entirely if fliers erred by as little as 3½ degrees to either side. The Dole Race, staged in the summer of 1927, attracted numerous hopeful entries, not all of them prepared for the task ahead. One entrant, William P. Erwin of Dallas, seemed qualified. An American ace of World War I, he was backed by a group of business friends who purchased a Swallow monoplane and called it the *Dallas Spirit*.

Of thirteen accepted entries, three were eliminated by accidents in prerace trials; two more were eliminated by federal inspectors. Of the remaining eight, only four made successful departures on starting day, August 16, 1927. The *Dallas Spirit* was not among the starters, having been grounded due to a long tear in its fuselage fabric. Only two planes reached Hawaii, and a massive search, including thirty-nine navy vessels, went into action to spot the two missing aircraft. Rewards for discovery of the planes and crews reached $40,000.

Bill Erwin decided to make a special effort to locate the missing planes. He had been planning to fly on to Tokyo and Hong Kong after reaching Hawaii. There was also the possibility of a world flight, and international newspapers had already arranged to syndicate his personal experiences. Disappointed in the Dole Race, Erwin volunteered to fly to Honolulu on a route not covered by current efforts. With a navigator, he took off on August 19 to the cheers of 20,000 well-wishers. About seven hours later, a garbled radio message from Erwin about mechanical problems suddenly ended in silence. The *Dallas Spirit*, along with the two previously lost planes, vanished into the rolling Pacific. The multiple fatalities of the Dole Race prompted careful management of intercontinental ventures of the future. Cities and newspapers became more circumspect in offering prize money; governments were cautious in sanctioning flights originating in their jurisdiction. But long-distance flights continued, and fliers inevitably died.

The 1920s and 1930s included dozens of "record" speed, distance, and endurance events. Some of them were legitimate efforts to enhance aeronautical development. Many more were publicity schemes. Although interest in aviation progress could be found in a contest sponsored by the *Fort Worth Star-Telegram*, an aura of promotion surrounded the effort of Roy Robbins and James Kelly in their endurance record of May 29, 1929. Their short-lived record, flying a Curtiss *Robin*, was soon eclipsed by other headline hunters. In the meantime, Robbins continued his aviation career and became a well-known corporate pilot, as well as something of a legend in Texas Aviation. There were also trans-Atlantic linkages, such as the September, 1930, flight from Paris to Dallas by Dieudonne Coste and Maurice Bellonte to collect a $25,000 prize put up by Col. William E. Easterwood.

Perhaps the most famous Texan to hold world records was Wiley Post, born in Van Zandt County, on November 22, 1898. The Post family lived on a farm near Abilene before moving to Oklahoma about 1907. As a young man, Post took courses at an automotive school, studied radio, and finally went to work in the oilfields. Airplanes fascinated him, and he eventually paid $25 to a barnstormer for a ride. His fascination intensified one day in 1924 while watching an airshow put on by a group called the Texas Topnotch Fliers. On an impulse, the adventurous Post decided to take over for an injured parachute jumper. While still roughnecking in the oilfields, he became an airshow regular, making dozens of jumps over the next two years. He also learned how to fly. After losing any eye in an oilfield accident, Post adopted the rakish eyepatch that became a trademark. With money left over from his insurance settlement, he paid $1,200 for his first plane.

In 1927, Post used his Curtiss *Canuck* to elope with Mae Laine, of Sweetwater. He did some barnstorming and flew for various oilmen on business trips. One, F. C. Hall, had been beaten to an oil lease by a fast-driving rival, so he hired Post. Hall bought one of the fastest planes of the era, a Lockheed *Vega*, christened the *Winnie Mae*, after his daughter. Post began to acquire a national reputation, competing in various speed events with Hall's permission and winning the National Air Race in 1930.

But Post was already thinking in international dimensions. He wanted to set a new record for girdling the globe. The record had been set in 1929, when the German dirigible *Graf Zeppelin* made the trip in only twenty-one days. It was a dramatic eclipse of the time of nearly six months required for the world flight by the army in 1924. Post acquired a new *Winnie Mae* (the original had been sold to an airline), lined up sponsors, and convinced Australian-born Harold Gatty to fly along as navigator. He also persuaded the State Department to secure special permission for him to fly across the Soviet Union, not yet officially recognized. After a year's

preparations, Post and Gatty took off from New York City on June 23, 1931. Following stops in England and Germany, the *Winnie Mae* droned across western Russia and into Siberia, making five stops before touching down in Alaska. From there, Post and Gatty winged across Canada, landing twice more for fuel before reaching New York on July 1. The weary but jubilant *Winnie Mae* crew had flown 15,474 miles in 8 days, 15 hours, and 51 minutes, a new world record and only the third world flight in history.

The restless Post soon began planning a solo world flight. The *Winnie Mae* was carefully refurbished and equipped with improved radios and an autopilot, which would allow him to nap occasionally en route. Departing from New York City on July 15, 1933, Post claimed a new record on the first leg by flying nonstop to Berlin. Most of the equipment, including the autopilot, worked well, although a radio went dead at the worst time, as he was trying to find his way through swirling clouds near Fairbanks, Alaska—20,000-foot Mount McKinley loomed somewhere below. Spotting a fortuitous break in the overcast, he dived down to the Alaskan mining town of Flat. Exhausted, Post ran into a ditch at the end of the short airstrip, bending a propeller and collapsing the landing gear. After some radio calls, mechanics and a new propeller were flown in; Post was up and away the next day. On the final segments, he struggled to overcome fatigue. The autopilot worked, but he was afraid of falling asleep for too long. His solution to the problem was ingeniously simple. He held a wrench and tied some string from his finger to the handle. When he fell asleep, the wrench slipped from his grasp; startled awake, he scanned the instruments, checked the course, and dozed off again. On July 22, 1933, Post landed in New York, 7 days, 18 hours, and 49 minutes after leaving, having shaved nearly a full day's time from his own earlier record with Gatty. Over 50,000 New Yorkers crowded the airfield to welcome him back.

Post's next goal was to win the MacRobertson Race from England to Australia. To beat the competition, he realized he would have to fly at 30,000 feet or more, where the *Winnie Mae* could outrun other planes flying in the denser atmosphere of lower altitudes. Moreover, he calculated on picking up favorable high-altitude winds that could give him an additional 100 mph. Since the airplane couldn't be pressurized, he designed a pressure suit, built by the B. F. Goodrich Rubber Company. Although the suit was not perfected in time for the race to Australia, Post successfully tested it at 40,000 feet, and subsequent trials validated his original idea of finding high-speed winds at high altitudes.

The *Winnie Mae* went to the Smithsonian Institution; Post was already planning new aerial adventures. In the summer of 1935, he left for Alaska with close friend Will Rogers, the famous columnist and beloved humorist, who was gathering new material for his syndicated articles. Post wanted to equip the hybrid Lockheed monoplane, called the *Orion-Explorer*, with floats to operate from Alaska's lakes and rivers. Because the original pontoons were late in delivery, he used a larger pair, salvaged from another plane. As a result, the *Orion-Explorer* was a bit tricky to handle, but they set off from Seattle. Post landed on a small lake in Alaska to ask directions to Point Barrow. On takeoff, the engine stalled; the nose-heavy airplane plunged into the water, killing both men. Post was buried in Oklahoma. Mrs. Post settled in Dallas.

At the same time that Post was completing plans for his global solo, a young Texan named James Mattern hoped to upstage him. A native of San Angelo, Mattern had been an airline pilot until 1932, when he and a navigator tried to fly a Lockheed *Vega* around the world, crash-landing in Russia when a hatch cover tore loose. A year later, Mattern was ready to try again—alone. Even though he lacked some of the essential equipment, such as an autopilot and a radio direction finder, he confidently took off in June, 1933, in another *Vega*. Poor weather and fatigue dogged the effort from the beginning. Finally, a frozen oil line over Siberia brought Mattern down for good, in the region of the Anadyr River. The plane was totally destroyed; Mattern found himself with a broken ankle, all alone in the frozen, bleak Siberian wilderness. After thirteen days of isolation, the desperate Mattern finally managed to start a brush fire. Some Eskimos spotted the unusual spiral of smoke and rescued the injured flier.

Mattern's failures and Post's success were not lost on Howard Hughes, who set out in 1938 to break Post's record. Hughes spent three years planning the attempt. He flew and analyzed three different planes, finally choosing the new Lockheed Model 14, a twin-engine airliner. A crew of engineers and mechanics went to work on the plane, removing the passenger seats to allow room for additional fuel tanks. When members of the press finally got aboard, they saw so many different navigational aids and examples of modern radio equipment that they called it "the Flying Laboratory."

The Hughes flight was no go-it-alone effort like those of Mattern and Post. In addition to Hughes, as pilot, the big twin-engine Lockheed carried a crew of four. Arrangements were made for a chain of ground stations and radio-equipped ships to maintain continuous communications. Spare parts were sited all along the scheduled flight path and at six stops en route. With Hughes at the controls, the Lockheed 14 landed at New York's Bennett Field on July 14, 1938, 3 days, 19 hours, and 17 minutes after leaving the same airport. Post's record had been cut in half; Hughes' new record remained unbroken for nearly a decade. Unlike the daring ventures of his predecessors, Hughes' flight was a logical and methodical effort. Nothing went wrong; there were no dramatic crackups or near disasters. In many ways the Hughes journey marked the conclusion of individual heroics, replaced by carefully articulated corporate projects. An era had ended—although there was one grace note, represented by the improbable success of "Wrong-Way Corrigan."

While the *Spirit of St. Louis* was taking shape at the Ryan Aircraft Company in San Diego, a smiling, hard-working kid named Douglas Corrigan helped build it. Corrigan was born in Galveston, on January 22, 1907. His father's business as a carpenter and contractor took them to Aransas Pass and eventually to San Antonio, where they lived until 1919. The family then moved to California, where young Douglas got a job in the Ryan shop. Lindbergh, who often prowled the premises during his plane's construction, met Corrigan, remembered him after the *Spirit's* famous journey, and shook his hand. Corrigan never forgot.

Years later, Corrigan kept nagging the Bureau of Air Commerce for permission to fly the Atlantic in an aging Curtiss *Robin*. The Bureau repeatedly said no. It did, however, grant permission for a transcontinental flight, and Corrigan flew his *Robin* nonstop from California to New York in the summer of 1938. Reporters who were covering the imminent departure of Howard Hughes' meticulously planned and equipped global flight were quite taken with the bareheaded kid with a ready smile and Irish sense of humor. While Hughes flew around the globe, Corrigan tested his creaky *Robin* and worried about his gas tanks. He allayed the suspicions of government flight inspectors with a request to make a return flight to California. On July 17, 1938, Corrigan took off, made a sweeping bank—and headed east, out over the Atlantic. Fog obscured his view nearly all the way, and he consistently claimed that his error resulted from misreading a compass. In any case, he landed at Baldonel, Ireland, the next day. The Irish were jubilant that one of their own had made such a flight, and they took special delight in repeating Corrigan's puckish explanation: "I left New York yesterday morning headed for California, but I got mixed up in the clouds and must have flown the wrong way."

In the glare of publicity, officials ignored Corrigan's brash violation of the rules. In England, Ambassador Joseph P. Kennedy entertained his fellow Irish American. Back in the United States, the director of the Bureau of Air Commerce, one Dennis Mulligan, jokingly admitted, "It was a great day for the Irish."

Corrigan became a well-paid hero. He wrote his own autobiography, *That's My Story,* and played himself in a motion picture, *The Flying Irishman.* Wisely, he retired from derring-do aviation, using the royalties from his book, film, and personal appearances to buy an orange grove in California, where he quietly faded from sight. Others were not so lucky. At least five other amateurs died the next year trying to imitate Corrigan's impromptu flight to fame and fortune.

The postwar decades ushered in the rise of a new sector of civil aeronautics, now referred to as general aviation. (In the early postwar years it was called utility aviation to distinguish it from scheduled air transport.) The general aviation sector involved an imaginative variety of activities: sport flying, aerial surveying, barnstorming, business travel, crop dusting, and instruction. Its earliest practitioners were usually military veterans who picked up a cheap war surplus JN-4 *Jenny* and became barnstormers. These flying gypsies became fixtures at county fairs, circuses, political rallies, or any gathering that provided crowds willing to pay to watch aerobatics or actually risk a ride in an airplane. En route from one show to the next, an itinerant gypsy might try to drum up fee-paying passengers by stunting over a small town, then landing in a convenient pasture to await prospective customers.

Some of the early stunt fliers, but not all, lived a long life. Ormer Locklear, for example, enjoyed a highly publicized, but brief, career as a wing-walker, a stunt he helped popularize. Locklear was born in Greenville in 1891. Because the little town was near Fort Worth, Locklear was able to see some of the earliest aviation events in the state, including an international show with Garros and Simon in 1910, followed by Cal Rodgers' junket in 1911. These appearances encouraged Locklear to build a crude glider. He became known locally as a bit of a daredevil, a reputation considerably enhanced in 1916, when Harry Houdini hired Locklear to race his motorcycle down Main Street in Fort Worth while Houdini, trussed up and trailing in the dirt, managed to break out of his bonds.

When America entered the war in 1917, the adventurous Locklear became a flying cadet at Barron Field near Fort Worth. During a training flight, so the story goes, he clambered out of the cockpit onto the nose of a flying plane in order to replace a radiator cap. Another time, he crawled out to the engine to replace a loose plug wire. Others had essayed modest tricks in a flying plane; Locklear turned it into an art. In 1919, he joined forces with a promoter, William H. Pickens, who had organized prewar aerial shows with Lincoln Beachey and later managed sports figures like gridiron hero Red Grange and Finnish track star Paavo Nurmi. For a thirty-minute performance, Locklear's fee started at $1,000 and went up to $3,000. Sensational headlines followed him across the country as he cavorted across the wings of a JN-4, hung by his knees from the struts, and scrambled from one plane to another in mid-air. He perfected the stunts that became standard for barnstormers everywhere.

Inevitably, Locklear wound up in Hollywood, a lean, mustachioed aviator who became a fixture at splashy parties at Charlie Chaplin's house, at Cecil B. De Mille's mansion, and at Pickfair, the elegant estate of Douglas Fairbanks and Mary Pickford. He appeared in *The Great Air Robbery* (Universal, 1919) and starred in *The Skywayman* (Fox, 1920)—his last film. During shooting of a night scene, Locklear followed the script, which called for a stall followed by a spin, but he never came out of the dive. Skeets Elliott, a long-time flying buddy, died with him. Hollywood staged a funeral march that remained unmatched until Valentino died six years later: a 24-man band from the Los Angeles Police Department, 200 cars, assorted military units, and an honor guard from the American Legion. Tom Mix was a pallbearer. Overhead, planes scattered rose petals. In Fort Worth, over 50,000 loyal fans and friends turned out to receive Locklear's casket for burial. The producers rushed prints of *The Skywayman* to theaters; the hasti-

ly completed film featured Locklear's final—and fatal—stunt.

Even though flying was widely portrayed as a high-risk activity, many of those eager to become pilots were not easily discouraged. This included women as well as men. Bessie Coleman was one of many native Texans who wanted to fly. Born to a poor black family in Atlanta, Texas, in 1896, she overcame barriers of both racial and sexual prejudice. Lack of money forced her out of college, and she eventually went to Chicago, where she became the proprietor of a chili parlor. The chili business made money; by the time Coleman was in her mid-twenties, she had the means to travel and enjoy life as she chose. After watching some barnstormers and stunt pilots, she wanted to take flying lessons. Few American flight schools accepted women, and none of them wanted a black woman. Coleman withdrew her savings and sailed for France. When she returned in 1921, license in hand, she was prepared to "give a little coloring," she said, to aviation. Her dream was to train other aspiring black pilots, and she became involved in the airshow circuit to raise money. After beginning in the Chicago area, Coleman moved to Houston, Texas, and became a regular performer in aviation meets throughout the South, where she attracted large crowds of both black and white spectators. She had almost all the money needed to start her flying school when, during the preparations for an airshow in Florida in 1926, she crashed, ending her life and her dream.

Slats Rogers, on the other hand, survived many aerial stunts, as well as bootlegging through Texas. He lived to a ripe old age, spinning out his last years as the proprietor of a steakhouse in McAllen.

Others chose a more conventional route into the aviation business. In San Antonio, Edgar Tobin became a dealer for Alexander Eaglerock Aircraft. Tobin was an early pioneer in the challenging business of merchandising private flying to the general public. But other activities attracted his interest, and he developed an even more successful business in aerial photography. The rapid growth of surveying in the booming Texas oilfields propelled Tobin Aerial Surveys into early prominence in the new industry of aerial photogrammetry. Tobin's business took the company's planes all over the United States, as well as to foreign countries, making photographic surveys for oil wells, pipe lines, highways, urban planning, industrial development, and a wide range of activities useful to an expanding urban society. There were competitors. Fairchild Aerial Surveys, originating in the Northeast, established a regional office in Dallas and soon negotiated surveying contracts that covered some 30,000 square miles in 1933 and extended into Mexico. Aerial surveying had become an integral part of the Texas petroleum business as well as serving other sectors of business and industry throughout the state. In time, many barnstormers settled down to steady jobs as surveyors, corporate pilots, or crop dusters. To support this market, fixed base operators, or FBOs, set up shop. They offered charter services and instruction, equipped their shops with tools for repair and maintenance, and sold gas, oil, and parts.

Following Lindbergh's flight, the proliferation of flying schools and intensified interest in flying drew many more Texans into aeronautics. One was Retha McCulloh (Mrs. E. C. Crittenden), a petite schoolteacher from Temple. After graduating from high school, she attended Baylor University and then accepted a job in Beaumont, where she taught arithmetic to fifth and sixth graders. Following a flight with a local barnstormer in September, 1928, she decided she wanted to be a pilot. The instructor charged $20 per hour for lessons, but the flight school paid her $20 per hour as a publicity move. "Even my fifth-grade math class figured it came out about right," she laughed. All was not right with the Beaumont School Board, who thought it was not becoming for a teacher in the public schools to take flying lessons. But the board finally relented, and McCulloh made her first solo, in a Waco biplane, on October 22, 1928. After a trip to Houston for the medical exam, license no. 5260 was issued to Retha McCulloh in February, 1929. The same year, she became a charter member of the ninety-nines, a group of women fliers in the United States. Amelia Earhart had been one of the organizers and served as its first president. McCulloh had the stylish wardrobe necessary for open cockpit biplanes of the era: khaki gabardine riding pants, high leather boots, and a leather jacket with a karakul collar. She flew for three years, giving it up after the birth of her first son. State licensing authorities extended her certificate for one year, to 1934, because she was the first pilot to have a baby.

In 1928, the Texas Aero Corporation, located in Temple, became the first organization in the state to have a government license for the manufacture and sale of new aircraft. George Williams, who had been active in the area before World War I, designed several aircraft for the firm, which also had financial support from George's brother, E. K. The pasture that George Williams used for flying near the family home became an active airfield after World War I, when returning veterans continued their aviation activities there.

Roy Sanderford had been a wartime flight instructor in Mississippi and had also been stationed in San Diego. Before his discharge he had built up flying time in Curtiss trainers, French SPAD fighters, and British S.E.5 light bombers. Returning to Belton, he soon gravitated to Williams Field, as it was known, at Temple. During a contest for local political office, Sanderford gained a winning edge by campaigning in a World War I surplus *Canuck*, a JN-4 trainer manufactured in Canada. Although E. K. Williams never became a pilot, he often used planes for business trips. He also generated a lot of regional publicity by using a local pilot to deliver copies of the *Temple Telegram* to nearby communities.

At some point during this period, Williams Field became Woodlawn Air Port, a lively center for instruction, maintenance, and repair for sport and utility flying in the prosperous twenties. Williams and Sanderford also experimented with modifications to the *Canuck* trainers.

They devised a monoplane, mounting the wing above the *Canuck*'s fuselage. The redesigned wing featured a flat lower surface, and the new structure proved to be stronger than the original design. Flight tests yielded improved stability and performance, as well as reduced drag. With a better engine in the nose, this aircraft became the prototype of the Temple Monoplanes.

Among the aficionados who gravitated to the Woodlawn field was George A. Carroll of Killeen. An experienced mechanic and pilot, he was also a skilled welder. In 1923, he joined George Williams and others in building several new, improved prototypes of the Temple Monoplane. The characteristic design for sport planes of the era was an open cockpit ship, built as a wood framework covered by fabric. From Williams' design, Carroll developed a fuselage formed by welded steel tubing. Although the wing retained its basic twin-span wood design, Williams and Carroll built welded steel ailerons for it. They also added several other improvements, such as a wing truss that was an integral part of the fuselage structure. The most interesting innovation involved landing lights. In the standard design of the era, some lights were permanently mounted and some retracted into the wing, but they illuminated the landing path in only one position. The Temple Monoplane carried adjustable lights that could be beamed straight down, allowing a flier to reconnoiter a dark field more conveniently. When landing, they could be adjusted through a ninety-degree arc, allowing the pilot to select the position best suited to existing field conditions and lighting—in retrospect, a small thing. But in the 1920s, any pilot convenience was something of a novelty, especially one that could be controlled from the cockpit.

Encouraged by the interest shown in the Temple Monoplane, the Williams brothers decided to go into production. In 1927, the Texas Aero Corporation was formally established with George Williams as president and brother E. K. as chairman of the Board of Directors. George Carroll served as vice-president, and Roy Sanderford became secretary-treasurer. In August, the company moved into a combined hangar and manufacturing facility. In the fall, the company was listed as one of sixty-four American firms approved for the manufacture of aircraft. Having completed three prototypes by this time, the Texas Aero Corporation was ready for operations.

The Temple Monoplane received its approved type certificate on June 22, 1928. The company's primary production model was the *Commercialwing*, delivered with a fireproof mail compartment. The first plane went to Continental Airways of Cincinnati, Ohio, and was used on routes between Cincinnati and Cleveland, Columbus, and Louisville, Kentucky. This early success prompted the Texas manufacturer to develop several other models. The design and construction of a four-place, enclosed cabin monoplane was noteworthy, since most sport planes of the era conformed to the open cockpit biplane style. Designated as model C-4, it took to the air in October, 1928. Although the four-place passenger cabin was spacious and appointed with blue velour upholstery, the pilot flew the plane from an open cockpit behind the wing, since aviators of the era often preferred to fly with the wind on their faces. At a time when instruments were few and generally unreliable, many early birds felt that flying with the body exposed to the nuances of the airstream was the only way to pilot a plane.

Other aircraft types followed. The *Sportsman* appeared early in 1929, available as an open cockpit two-place plane or an enclosed cabin version. During a tour of the United States, Lady Mary Heath, a well-known British aviator, made a flight in the enclosed *Sportsman* and is reported to have exclaimed, "This is the best performing airplane in its class today!" The company justifiably repeated this accolade at every opportunity, although Lady Heath flew numerous planes of the *Sportsman* class during her American sojourn and managed to proclaim something flattering about every one of them. The most unusual plane produced at Temple was a tri-motor. Evidence suggests that it was developed specifically for aerial photography. The engines were only moderately powerful, since each of the Velie motors put out about 60 hp. But the plane had a wingspan of 50 feet, allowing it to reach an altitude of 18,000 feet for wider photographic coverage. Only one plane was built, delivered to the geology department of the Texas and Pacific Coal and Oil Company in San Antonio.

The pace of activity created a need for larger facilities. Temple Aero wanted to increase production of the mail planes and take advantage of the apparent market for its sport and utility models. In April, 1929, the original company, capitalized at $150,000 only two years earlier, was reorganized at $1 million. Plans called for the Temple operations to continue, while a new facility at Love Field in Dallas emphasized manufacturing. The stock market crash in the fall of 1929 ended the Dallas plans, although a second effort secured new hangar and maintenance facilities at Meacham Field in Fort Worth. Texas Aero bid a contract for carrying airmail between Dallas and Fort Worth, San Antonio, and Houston, but lost out to Bowen Air Transport, which also took over the hangar at Meacham Field.

Texas Aero retreated to Temple, where additional discouraging events followed. The Depression hit other companies that had signed contracts for the *Commercialwing*, and orders were canceled. The Texas concern managed to hang on by concentrating sales efforts on the *Sportsman* and by training a dwindling number of student pilots. The final blow came on August 15, 1930, when George Williams and a flight student died in a crash. By the fall of 1930, the cumulative effects of the Depression and the death of Williams brought an end to Texas Aero, the first aircraft manufacturer in Texas.

Although the demise of Texas Aero signaled the end of one chapter in Texas aviation history, other manufacturers attempted to make their mark. The most successful stories evolved from the massive production

requirements of World War II. Still, there were other hopeful companies, even in the discouraging years of the Depression. The town of Center, located in the timber region of east Texas, appeared to be an unlikely spot for an aircraft manufacturing plant—especially in 1933. It seemed an even more unlikely choice as the new home of the States Aircraft Company of Chicago, Illinois. But the economic pressures of the Depression resulted in many strange stories, and the hegira of States Aircraft from the region of Lake Michigan to the region of the Toledo Bend Reservoir, on the Texas-Louisiana border, represented only one of many curious circumstances.

J. B. Sanders, a banker in Center, had bought a Hisso *Travel Air* in Chicago, and a pilot named Bud Downes was hired to fly the plane to Texas. Downes also acted as a test pilot for States and planned to give flying lessons to Sanders. When he arrived in Center, he mentioned to Sanders that States Aircraft, like many other builders, was in deep financial trouble. The high-winged monoplane built by States had a tubular steel fuselage but used spruce for ribs and spars, as well as plywood to cover the leading edge of the wing. Perhaps Sanders saw a way to supply the wooden components of the plane from materials and craftsmanship available in the timber region of east Texas. Certainly, the Chicago aviation firm would be a bargain. In any case, Sanders bought the company and put Center in the business of making planes—or so everyone hoped.

The original States monoplane had been designed in 1929 by Frederick H. Jolly. Small and compact, the plane had a high wing and two open cockpits in tandem. A typical model, equipped with a Kinner engine, cruised at 100 mph and landed at about 35–40 mph. In 1932, a flying service and repair company run by a Chicagoan, Adam Bialorski, acquired the business. When Sanders bought the operation, Bialorski remained a stockholder, along with Joe Isvolt, an experienced States builder who drove the first truckload of parts and equipment to Center. Like pilot Bud Downes, Bialorski decided to make the move to Texas, giving the new firm a core of seasoned builders and pilots.

The States Aircraft Company of Center, Texas, organized on September 8, 1933, also received an approved Repair Station Certificate from the Bureau of Air Commerce. Temporary work got under way in a rented building, formerly an auto garage and service station. The back door opened on a horse pasture; a blacksmith shop and auction barn were neighbors across the dirt alley. "High tech" had arrived in Center.

Meanwhile, a new airport and a manufacturing facility were taking shape on J. B. Sanders' farm on the outskirts of town. The factory building came from a lumber company that had closed its doors. The steel building, 100 feet by 300 feet, was moved piece by piece from its original site, fifteen miles away. When it was set up again at Center for States Aircraft, two-thirds of the structure was left over, to be used for hangar space. In addition to one other licensed mechanic, the company depended on part-time assistance. One such worker was a high school sophomore, Leo Childs, a tall, friendly kid who seemed to have a special knack for working with planes. He picked up a mechanic's license and thus began a career that carried him through changing phases of aeronautics, including working at NASA's Johnson Space Center.

Until States began selling planes on a continuing basis, the company eked out an income by doing maintenance and overhaul work. The roster of aircraft that passed through the hangar door at Center was an interesting catalog of aeronautical activity in the region. One of the first jobs involved a Pietenpol monoplane. A homemade job built from a kit and powered by an engine from a Ford Model A, it had to be rebuilt after a crash. It was followed by a Waco that needed its wings recovered and variety of other planes: a Spartan sport plane with a three-cylinder engine; an Alexander Eaglerock; a *Travel Air* powered by a Wright Whirlwind; a pair of Curtiss *Robins*; and the inevitable Curtiss *Jenny*, powered by a rebuilt OXX-6 engine. At the same time, the States Aircraft crew was working on its first Texas-built product, a States Model B-4, with a Kinner K-5 radial engine. It was completed in March and flown to Beaumont for a public introduction arranged by the Beaumont Wing-Over Club.

The next big day for States Aircraft came in May, when the airport was dedicated. Sanders was able to get a $12,000 grant from the Civil Works Administration to develop a proper airfield. Encompassing 160 acres, the field boasted two runways (2,400 feet and 2,700 feet), along with hangar space, gas and oil, telephone, and lounge areas. The town acquired two large aerial markers, and pilots could have a car waiting by circling over the city before landing. The opening-day hoopla featured the visit of the commanding officer of Barksdale Air Base, who brought in a squadron of Boeing P-12 pursuits to embellish an airshow that advertised stunt fliers and parachute jumpers, including a Miss Eris Daniels.

Although States Aircraft continued to do maintenance and repair, the market for new planes proved to be elusive during the Depression. By 1937, when operations came to a close, only four planes had been built. The heavy woodworking equipment eventually was bought by a toy manufacturer in Tennessee. The hangar was remodeled into a skating rink and then converted into winter quarters for a traveling carnival. Eventually it was torn down, and the land was put back into farming.

Many employees went on to other careers in aviation. Bud Downes flew for American Airlines and eventually became chief pilot for Trans-Texas Airways (later Texas International, which merged with Continental). Leo Childs, after graduating from high school in 1936, studied engineering at Texas A&M before joining Lockheed on the West Coast. His subsequent career weaves a thread through much of the story of Texas aviation. Joe Isvolt worked for American Airlines, then spent thirty years at Pensacola Naval Air Station. Still others became airline pilots, military pilots, and aviation managers. States Aircraft Corporation may have

had a short life in Texas, but its legacy was a rich one.

Compared to the post-1945 era, the number of openings for airline pilots between the wars was limited. Still, a slow but steady growth of airline companies provided opportunities for pilots as well as mechanics and other personnel. Air travel also added a significant dimension to transportation in a state characterized by formidable distances. For the nation as a whole, the Air Mail Act of 1925, or Kelly Bill, began the process of turning over government airmail routes to private contractors and marked the origins of commercial airlines. Only a handful of the original companies survived more than a few years, as smaller lines merged with competitors to survive or were simply taken over by larger rivals. An incomplete roster of lines based in Texas, as well as some interstate lines with Texas destinations, serves to illustrate a colorful but transient era of aeronautical development.

The first commercial line to serve the state was National Air Transport, one of the major coast-to-coast organizations incorporated to take advantage of the Kelly Bill. On May 12, 1926, a National plane departed Love Field and headed for Chicago with the first airmail; passenger service was added in the fall of 1927. Within the state, Southern Air Transport System of Fort Worth stands out. Southern was actually a collection of three operating divisions, including Texas Flying Services, Gulf Air Lines, and Texas Air Transport. Collectively, these divisions serviced various mail routes with Stearman J-5s, Pitcairn *Super Mailwings*, and *Travel Airs*. Passenger runs depended on *Travel Airs* and Curtiss *Robins*, as well as Fokker *Super Universals* on more heavily traveled routes. TAT itself was formed by Temple Bowen, a scrappy veteran of bus lines in Fort Worth. Founded in November, 1927, TAT operated a mail route from Galveston to Dallas, later adding Brownsville, San Antonio, and El Paso.

Another early line with connections to Texas was Southwest Air Fast Express (SAFE), which ran Ford Tri-Motors from Dallas and the northern part of the state to Sweetwater and Wichita Falls. The segment was actually part of a combined coast-to-coast service by planes and trains, the latter taking over on night portions of the route. After an overnight train ride from Sweetwater to El Paso, passengers boarded planes operated by Standard Air Airlines, flying from El Paso to Los Angeles. One of Standard's planes was a Fokker F-7A, christened *The Texan* and distinguished by a prominent slogan on its fuselage, "Los Angeles–El Paso." All of these—Southern Air Transport, SAFE, and Standard—eventually became part of the system that emerged as American Airlines.

During the late 1920s and early 1930s, a series of small airlines bravely unfolded their wings, often encouraged by optimistic chambers of commerce, only to find that survival meant surrender to larger, better-financed operations with better-balanced routes. Examples include Amarillo Airport Corporation (Amarillo/Tulsa), Weddell-Williams Air Service of New Orleans (New Orleans/Houston and Dallas), Western Air Express, based in the Midwest (Denver/El Paso, Wichita Falls, and Dallas), and Reed Airlines, a small operator based in Lawton, Oklahoma, which tried to survive on traffic north to Oklahoma City and south to Wichita Falls. By the mid-1930s, all had disappeared.

The difference between success and failure was often a mail contract, as Temple Bowen discovered. In the fall of 1930, after he had sold his interest in Texas Air Transport, he organized a brand-new operation, Bowen Air Lines. Bowen hoped to get an airmail contract, but lost out to American. Since American and Bowen competed for passengers on several of the same routes, the feisty Bowen was especially aggressive. His airline flew speedy Lockheed *Vegas*, as opposed to American's slower Ford Tri-Motors. Bowen was incensed when the Post Office Department began using promotional material that urged people to "Fly with Air Mail." Bowen thought the slogan gave American Airlines, his fiercest rival, free and unfair advertising. All the Bowen Air Lines planes received a new legend, emblazoned on the fuselage, "Fly Past the Air Mail," which they often did. Bowen Air Lines hoped for success through high-speed schedules on heavy-traffic routes between the Dallas–Fort Worth area and Houston, as well as Oklahoma City and Tulsa. The company was one of the first to fly the Lockheed *Orion*, a low-wing monoplane whose powerful engine and retractable gear gave it an unheard of speed of 200 mph. But Bowen, like so many other small companies, could not compete with larger airlines fortified by airmail revenues.

The clientele for which these airlines competed came primarily from the thriving petroleum industry. From Wichita, Kansas, down through Oklahoma and across Texas, a rapidly expanding economy based on oil created a new transportation market. Along this axis, from the Midwest to the Gulf Coast of Texas, lay many cities that had not become rail centers during the railroad construction era. Lacking convenient traditional transportation and communication links, communities throughout the oil boom region turned to air travel. Moreover, the terrain and climate, as always, proved favorable for aviation. Although not all of the hopeful airline entrepreneurs survived more than a few years, some, like Paul and Tom Braniff, succeeded.

In the spring of 1928, the Braniffs began with the Tulsa–Oklahoma City Airlines, a shrewdly chosen route that was, significantly, backed by a pair of local oil companies interested in improved transportation. With no mail contract, the fledgling operation flew a pair of Stinson *Detroiters*—each accommodating a pilot and 6 passengers—and carried a remarkable 3,000 passengers before the year was out. Late in 1930, after various name changes and added service to Wichita Falls, Fort Worth, and Dallas, Braniff Airways became the official title; by 1934, the company won a significant—and profitable—mail contract from Dallas to Chicago by way of Oklahoma City and Kansas City. In that same year, Braniff made Love Field its principal operations and maintenance base; it moved the home office to Love Field in 1942.

The growth of airline travel meant the growth of airports. As new ones were opened, or old ones were improved, the ceremonies often became front-page news stories, especially during the 1920s and 1930s. The early years of air transport paralleled the heyday of distance records and high-speed flights. Aeronautics had a heroic quality that drew huge crowds to the takeoffs and landings of each new record seeker. An aura of excitement colored events like the opening of new airports, where the curious could see examples of the planes making the headlines, gawk at the headline maker, and even dream of taking an airline trip. Even if one did not fly, using the airmail was a vicarious form of participation. The dedication of Brownsville International Airport in 1929 combined all of these news-making qualities. It not only launched a new international mail and passenger service but also made Brownsville a major station of the young but already awesome Pan Am. In addition, people had a chance to see the legendary Lindbergh.

Planners brought in the city police, the sheriff's department, the border patrol, and the Boy Scouts to handle the traffic and the crowds. Lindbergh launched the service on March 9, with a northbound flight from Mexico City. He arrived in Brownsville to confront a throng of 25,000 spectators, including aeronautical luminaries like Amelia Earhart and headliners like Frank Hawks, holder of the transcontinental flight record. The *Brownsville Herald* boasted about the size of the airfield crowd, "believed the largest ever assembled in the Lower Rio Grande Valley." The paper also noted the presence of air transports from both Mexican and American companies: "One of the novel spectacles Sunday morning was seven of the huge tri-motors drawn up in phalanx form at the airport." Continuing its litany of significant events of the momentous weekend, the paper reported, "pilots and air transport managers pronounced this the greatest number of the leviathans of the air to be assembled at one time at any port in the United States." The new line connected with Texas Air Transport between San Antonio and Brownsville. From Brownsville, Pan Am scheduled daily arrivals and departures linking Texas to Mexico City with connecting routes through Central America to the Panama Canal.

Pan Am's station in Brownsville was a significant post for some three decades. It marked a major juncture where Central American passengers and mail changed carriers for destinations throughout the United States. The Brownsville station represented the high standards of Pan Am services, and its repair and maintenance procedures were viewed as models for the industry. Until World War II, Brownsville could boast that some of the most advanced transports in the world made it a regular port of call. By the time the Brownsville station was deactivated, on October 31, 1962, other long-range equipment, including jets, could make nonstop trips to Mexico City from major population centers like Dallas–Fort Worth, Houston, and San Antonio. Brownsville's historic role as an aeronautical way station had been ended by the inevitable progress of aviation technology.

In addition to Pan Am, South American lines

developed services to other countries beyond Panama. Pan Am's own long route was a challenging one. In an article for the prestigious journal *Aviation* (February, 1933), the magazine's assistant editor, S. Paul Johnston, summed it up:

Consider the topography of the P.A.A. routes from Brownsville to Tampico, to Mexico City, to Tapachula to Managua, thence down the continental funnel to Panama. There are no railroads to follow, no continuous pattern of towns and villages with ready communication facilities, no interested and far-seeing governmental agencies to provide lighted airways and weather information services; instead, hundreds of miles of trackless jungle and rugged, snow-capped ridges 15,000 ft. above the sea, tremendous areas between population centers where habitation is figured on the basis of a fraction of a human being per square mile, weather which varies in a single hour's flight from the dank atmosphere of the lowlands to the blinding fogs and blizzards in the mountains, and last, but not least, the negative influence of a string of politically dissociated Central American republics. It is against such odds that the Western division of Pan American operates. Therein lies the rationalization of the super-meticulous attention given to the flying equipment at Brownsville.

The care included repair and maintenance of engines, propellers, and airframes, as well as floors, windows, and seats, but the formidable terrain put a premium on mechanical reliability, and that is where the Brownsville operation excelled. Johnston rhetorically wondered if all the extra attention was justifiable on a dollars-and-cents basis, but concluded that the steamy tropical forests and snow-covered passes made Pan Am's thorough maintenance "an utterly invaluable form of insurance."

Over the years, Pan Am became a significant technical resource for the evolution of Mexican aeronautics. The first paved runways in Mexico, built in 1930, were constructed with the guidance of Pan Am personnel; communications and meteorological facilities followed. At Brownsville and other Pan Am stations, company instructors trained hundreds of pilots, mechanics, and technicians from Mexico in techniques that Pan Am had tailored for Latin American climate and topography.

Many segments required pilots to fly through clouds, especially since there were few safe alternate airports, but the Tampico to Mexico City leg was notorious for recurrent cloudy conditions, which often obscured 11,000-foot mountain ranges en route. Beginning in 1928, pilots were forced to develop rudimentary skills in instrument flying, and a special instrument flying syllabus was instituted at Brownsville when the airport opened in 1929. Pan Am acquired a Fairchild FC-2 and fitted out the rear seats with a complete set of dual instruments and controls. With canvas and plywood screens cutting off the students' view of the outside world, the instructor could simulate many of the predicaments to be expected along the route. Between Mexico City and Tampico, pilots were told to expect clouds or fog, or both, at least 50 percent of the time. Thus, the experience of instrument flying in the Fairchild, like the habit of meticuluous maintenance, was a practical example of trip insurance. In addition to specialized flight instruction, Pan Am also used a Barany chair, spinning students around to create disorientation, then using an associated panel of instruments to demonstrate conclusively that the instrumentation was trustworthy, even though the subjects' senses were not.

The technology and techniques perfected in the early days of Ford Tri-Motors enhanced Pan Am's operations out of Brownsville during each succeeding generation of airliners. In 1934, the company introduced the DC-2, followed by the much improved DC-3 in 1937. Pressurized aircraft were especially attractive over mountainous routes, and Pan Am was among the first to use them in 1940, introducing the four-engine Boeing 307 *Stratoliner* on the Brownsville to Mexico line. In the postwar era, long-distance transports and new gateway cities, like New Orleans and Houston, meant the decline of traffic through Brownsville. In October, 1960, for example, Boeing 707 jets began carrying Pan Am passengers nonstop to Mexico City. Two years later, Pan Am deactivated its Brownsville station for good, leaving a rich heritage in the history of inter-American air transport and instrument flying.

During the late 1920s and early 1930s, the airlines had acquired a hodgepodge of different types. As various routes grew longer and became stabilized, airline executives moved to standardize their equipment. In 1934, American Airlines advertised some fifty-one planes for sale, including twenty-three Stinson Tri-Motors, sixteen Pilgrims, and eight Stearmans. American especially wanted to consolidate its fleet and to introduce new planes that incorporated the advanced refinements of the past few years. The company retained its fleet of Curtiss *Condors*—something of an anachronism, with their biplane configuration—but the *Condors* were specially equipped for American's transcontinental sleeper service. The airline buttressed the *Condor* fleet with a plane reputed to be the most advanced high-speed airliner of its day, the Vultee V-1. These metal-skinned eight-passenger speedsters were not only fast but quiet, with additional soundproofing for passenger comfort. The Vultees were heavily used on American's routes from Texas to the Great Lakes. But the single-engine Vultee was also the last of its type. Boeing and Douglas were on the verge of revolutionizing the air transport industry with a pair of new airliners that incorporated all the recent advances, added some new ones, and featured two powerful engines that more than doubled the passenger capacity of aircraft like the *Orion* and the Vultee V-1.

The Boeing 247 went into service in 1933, serving primarily on northern transcontinental routes operated by United Airlines and its predecessors. It carried ten passengers, along with two pilots and a stewardess, and featured a number of recent innovations such as de-icing equipment and engine cowlings based on research conducted by the National Advisory Committee for Aeronautics. The Douglas DC-2, which began commercial flights in 1934 with TWA, was not only faster, but carried fourteen passengers, incorporated the technical refinements of the Boeing 247, and added others, such as flaps for better control during takeoff and landing. The DC-2 proved to be a striking success, and American lined up with other operators to purchase it. In the meantime, the government's cancellation of the airmail contracts led to a reorganization of American Airways as American Airlines, Incorporated, on April 11, 1934. Due to his managerial expertise with Texas Air Transport and Southern Air Transport, predecessors of American Airlines, C. R. Smith became president. During the next four decades, he not only made American into one of the most successful airlines in the United States, but also became one of the most respected airline experts in the world.

Cyrus Rowlett Smith, universally known as "C. R.," entered the airline business through the financial side of the industry. Born in Minerva, Texas, on September 9, 1899, he was raised in Amarillo and Whitney. He decided to attend college at the University of Texas in Austin, where he majored in business administration. Between 1921 and 1928, he worked as an accountant for Peat, Marwick, and Mitchell, and as an assistant treasurer for the Texas-Louisiana Power Company. In 1928, he became secretary and treasurer of Texas Air Transport, then vice-president and treasurer of Southern Air Transport after it acquired Texas Air. As American Airways grew, Smith became vice-president of its Southern division from 1931 to 1934, then president of the reorganized American Airlines. As one of the nation's most knowledgeable airline executives during World War II, Smith agreed to enter the air force to head the Ferry Command, later the Air Transport Command. In the postwar era, he headed American until his retirement in 1968. After a tour as secretary of commerce during the first administration of Lyndon Baines Johnson, Smith returned to American in 1973–1974, serving as interim chairman of the board and chief executive. He retired permanently in April, 1974.

When Smith took over American in the spring of 1934, one major challenge was the problem of phasing-in new equipment like the DC-2. In the process, Smith and his managers recognized the need for an even more advanced transport, and their proposals were a major factor in the development of the DC-3, a classic airplane in the history of aviation. In December, 1934, the DC-2 made its debut on American's East Coast routes, where competition was fierce, especially on the schedules to Chicago. For its long-distance transcontinental service, American kept the Curtiss *Condor*, on the assumption that its sleeper services cut down passenger fatigue. Like everyone else, Smith was impressed with the DC-2's performance, but he wanted a larger plane with the *Con-*

dor's space for overnight berths. Smith and his chief engineer telephoned Donald Douglas in California to explain their goals and asked about a stretched DC-2. At first, Douglas demurred. But Smith got a $4.5 million loan from the Reconstruction Finance Corporation, a New Deal loan agency carried over from the Hoover administration. With Smith's promise to buy twenty bigger transports, Douglas was ready to start the new project. Thus, the classic DC-3 owed much to federal largesse.

The plane was originally called the Douglas Sleeper Transport, or DST, with space for fourteen berths. It was rolled out on December 17, 1935, and christened the *Flagship Texas*, no doubt in honor of C. R. Smith's role. A dayplane version, the DC-3, had twenty-one seats. The American order called for eight DSTs and twelve DC-3s. The DST models were delivered first, and American operated them as dayplanes on its New York/Chicago route in the spring of 1936. Delivery of the DC-3 models began in August, releasing the DSTs for their original role in sleeper service on transcontinental routes.

With great fanfare, American launched its new sleeper service on September 18, 1936, advertising 16 hours eastbound and about 18 hours westbound, against prevailing winds. These were through flights, eliminating a change of planes in Dallas, where passengers typically transferred to *Condors* for the western part of a transcontinental trip. Dallas remained a principal link in the route, which included Memphis, Dallas, and Tucson.

With the DC-3, airlines at last had a plane that made money carrying passengers, ending total dependence on mail payments for a profit. More powerful engines gave the DC-3 a performance superior to that of the DC-2. With twenty-one seats rather than fourteen, the DC-3 boasted a 50 percent increase in payload, but additional aerodynamic refinements kept the increase in operating costs to only 10 percent. C. R. Smith's original order resulted in an airliner of unrivaled success. Within six years, 80 percent of domestic airline service in the United States was flown by the DC-3.

Other major airlines began to tap the Texas market. The original New Orleans/Houston route had been flown by Robertson Airplane Service. Robertson was taken over by Weddell-Williams Transport Corporation, which was in turn taken over by Eastern Airlines on December 31, 1936. At about the same time, Eddie Rickenbacker became general manager. As a war hero and America's "ace of aces," Rickenbacker gave Eastern a special image of aeronautical prowess. Before long, Eastern's new Douglas transports brought the latest in modern aviation to the Gulf Coast region.

Braniff Airlines also improved its service in Texas. Flying Lockheed *Vegas* on its attractive Dallas/Chicago route, the airline ran through active commercial cities and petroleum centers like Fort Worth, Oklahoma City, Kansas City, Tulsa, and Wichita. When Braniff bought out Long and Harmon early in 1935, Dallas/Amarillo schedules were added; the demise of Bowen Airlines brought Houston, Brownsville, and other Texas cities into the system. In June, 1937, Braniff joined the growing ranks of companies equipped with DC-2 transports. Another airline, Chicago and Southern, reached into the Gulf Coast market, flying to Houston from Memphis on March 1, 1941.

The comfortable accommodations and rapid service offered by modern transports like the DC-3 made coast-to-coast flights particularly appealing. For Texans, the options of transcontinental airline flights led to additional options for intercontinental air travel as well. After the flights of Wiley Post and others in the mid-1930s, many Texans probably dreamed of girdling the world by air, even though they realized they lacked the skills and experience for such a daunting journey. If they could not pilot their own planes, perhaps they could fly with somebody else. About 1935, Bolivar Falconer, of Marlin, realized he could establish a historical precedent in this way: he could be the first to circumnavigate the world as a commercial airline passenger.

In 1885, Falconer, a native of Mississippi, moved with his parents to Marlin, where relatives had been planters along the Brazos. Falconer graduated from Marlin High School in 1887 and attended college for two years in Mississippi before returning to Marlin, where he became a postal clerk. High scores on a Civil Service exam in 1890 took him to the War Department in Washington and to a lifetime career in the civil service, from which he retired in 1931 as senior examiner of the U.S. Civil Service Commission. In the meantime, he picked up a degree in mathematics from Harvard, a degree in neurology from George Washington University, and an M.D. from Georgetown University. A stint in the Philippines, 1929–1930, seems to have whetted Falconer's appetite for travel; within five years after his retirement, he circled the globe four times by steamship and railway. Making a trip by air seemed the next logical step.

The growth of airline routes serving Texas and the United States was paralleled in many countries overseas, especially in Europe. Although all parts of the world did not enjoy the frequent scheduling and reliability of airlines in America and Europe, air routes began to form a network around the world. Since limited range and passenger safety were essential factors in planning routes, the airlines tailored their schedules to routes above land and within easy range of safe airports. Flights over open water were kept to a minimum and as short as possible. For these reasons, passenger services over the broad reaches of the Atlantic and Pacific were long in coming.

A pair of breakthroughs between 1935 and 1936 made intercontinental passenger flights a reality. Beginning in 1935, Pan Am began flying mail from San Francisco to the Philippines, using a four-engine flying boat built by Martin—the famed M-130 *China Clipper*. In 1936, Pan Am began passenger service over the route, making the Pacific passage in about six days, with stops at the islands of Hawaii, Midway, Wake, and Guam. The same year, trans-Atlantic passengers could choose to fly across via the *Hindenburg*, a mammoth German Zeppelin. In

1936, the giant dirigible made ten round trips between Germany and the United States, cruising at a sedate 78 mph over the Atlantic. With the Atlantic and Pacific legs of a global journey now in place, Falconer was ready for his unique odyssey.

Falconer departed on May 8, 1936. With the help of the American Express Company, he put together an itinerary that took him from Dallas to New York aboard the *Southerner*, an American Airlines DC-3. The trans-Atlantic leg was made by Zeppelin dirigible, on the *Hindenburg*. Arriving in Frankfurt, Germany, Falconer backtracked somewhat, taking a German airliner to Amsterdam, but the entire trip across Europe, through the Middle East, and on to the Orient used KLM, the national airline of the Netherlands. At Penang, in Malaya, he changed to a plane of Imperial Airways, departing on May 25 and arriving in Kowloon the next day. Falconer had to board a steamer to Manila, where he ran into a time-consuming snag. Before leaving New York, Falconer had been told that Pan Am passenger service across the Pacific would begin in June. But rough weather and heavy seas had prevented shipment of materials to Wake and Guam for the construction of hotels. As a result, Falconer spent five months waiting in the Orient, touring Japan, Korea, and the Chinese mainland.

Falconer finally departed the Philippines on October 31, aboard a Martin *Clipper* flown by Captain Edwin C. Musick. There were ten other passengers, including three women, one of whom was a young reporter for the Hearst papers, Dorothy Kilgallen. There was another delay of sixteen days in Honolulu before the passengers reached Los Angeles, where Falconer caught an American Airlines sleeper plane, arriving in Dallas on November 20, 1936. The trip covered 26,000 miles, took sixteen flying days, and cost $3,355, excluding Falconer's five-month enforced delay in the Orient. Comparing the journey to his previous travels, Falconer observed that "the great advantage of the Zeppelins and airplanes over ships is their speed." He felt that the greater size of the Zeppelins made them much more comfortable than planes.

Falconer wrote a didactic little book about his record trip, *Flying around the World*, privately published in 1937. Much of the text is comprised of historical asides and snippets of advice on what to see, including one's old friends. Basically, he sums up his judgment of the significance of the trip in one sentence: "As the cost of traveling in the air is about twice as great as traveling on water no one will be apt to travel by air unless his time is limited or he desires the novelty of air travel." He concludes with one last piece of advice: "In taking a pleasure trip around the world by air one should arrange to stop off at many places in order to see the country in a more leisurely way."

Progress between the wars had been remarkably rapid. By 1932, all federal airways, including those in Texas, were lighted, and several radio-wave stations were under construction. Although most of the news stories about aviation in the state came from larger urban areas like Dallas, Fort Worth, San Antonio, and Houston, dozens of other municipalities and commercial groups developed aviation facilities, bringing the total to 147 airports. Love Field, in Dallas, was one of 6 major fields across the nation, and the Dallas Aviation School had become one of the largest training centers in the United States, graduating as many as 250 students per year. While many of these new pilots found it difficult to get a job during the Depression, a considerable amount of aviation activity persisted. Figures published in 1932 listed 874 licensed pilots, along with 430 aircraft, although 150 of them were unlicensed.

While a precise breakdown of early figures is problematic, it is likely that Texas aeronautics enjoyed a degree of stability due to business flying related to the oil, gas, and petrochemical industries in the state. The long distances in Texas made flying feasible and worthwhile. By 1936, the federal Civil Aeronautics Authority had consolidated its organization and strength throughout the United States. Within Texas, the CAA reported 133 licensed airports, as well as 728 licensed pilots and 449 licensed aircraft. The pace of aviation activity began to accelerate with the threat of world war. In 1940, Texas reported the same number of airports, but the number of planes rose to 610 and pilots numbered 1,002. A new state agency, the Aviation Defense Board, not only recognized the growing role of aeronautics in the state's economy, but also symbolized recognition of an impending world conflict, already under way in Europe.

The Military: Wartime and Peacetime

With the drums of war beating ever louder on the eastern side of the Atlantic, and the First Aero Squadron's debacle in Mexico exposing gross deficiencies in the military's aviation branch, Congress in 1916 finally acknowledged that something had to be done about U.S. military aircraft and aviators—and most importantly, military aviation policy. To underscore the seriousness of its intentions, Congress allocated for military aviation the then staggering sum of $13,281,666 in August, 1916.

The U.S. aviation industry, because of the starvation diet on which it had been forced to subsist for so very long, was unable to assimilate the sudden influx of capital. For years it had lagged behind world airframe and powerplant technology development; now that the need for high-performance pursuit and bombing aircraft was acknowledged, the wherewithal to produce such technologically advanced war machinery simply did not exist. Prior to the War Department's urgent request, research and development in the aeronautical sciences had been kept to a minimum. Almost all of the high-performance and state-of-the-art advances were taking place in Europe, where support for the various aviation industries was provided in the form of large funding allocations and sizable aircraft orders.

In April, 1917, the army's aviation section had 131 officers and 1,087 enlisted men. In total, there were fewer than 250 aircraft and balloons on inventory, and not one of these was considered comparable in performance or technology to the most modern combat types found in Europe. Out of 366 aircraft on order from 9 different manufacturers in 1916, only 64 had been delivered; it was obvious that the industry's capacity to produce, like the quality of the aircraft it was making, was severely limited.

The European Allies, in effect, rescued the Air Service from its decade-old quagmire of abuse and underfunding. When the United States entered the war on April 6, 1917, the Allies promptly placed their technical expertise, including aeronautical technology, at the disposal of U.S. industry. A hungry and immature U.S. aviation industry unhesitatingly took advantage of the European industry's largesse. This, coupled with the fact that European Allied commanders had expressed the opinion that initial U.S. aid to the war effort should be in the form of a powerful U.S. air force to share responsibilities on the hard-pressed western front, forced Congress dramatically to increase the funding priorities for military aviation.

On May 26, the reality of just how inadequate the U.S. aircraft industry's production base was became apparent when French Premier Ribot asked the United States to provide no less than 4,500 combat aircraft for use on the western front by June 30, 1918. Additionally, Ribot noted that training aircraft, which were needed in far greater numbers than combat types, would bring the total production requirement to an absolutely staggering (in consideration of U.S. aircraft production capacity at the time) 22,625 machines!

Just as unbelievable was the fact that the Air Service agreed with Ribot's figures and committed itself and the U.S. aircraft industry to meeting the production figure goal. This was made still more absurd by the fact that the only aircraft company in the United States with even modest production capacity was the Curtiss Aeroplane Company; all other manufacturers, with the possible exception of the Wrights, were unknown and unheralded builders with small staffs and limited floor space. The Air Service, in effect, not only committed itself to serious monetary expenditures, but also to building, from scratch, a huge and aggressive aircraft industry in the United States.

Unfortunately, the aspirations of the Air Service far outstripped the production capabilities of the aircraft industry. In a frantic effort to achieve the objectives outlined in the agreements with Premier Ribot, France, England, and Italy each agreed to support the embryonic U.S. production effort by supplying aircraft, drawings, and engineering and production personnel. The logistics of moving both across a vast stretch of water—while overcoming language, engineering, and technological barriers—in the end proved more than the industry could absorb. Though orders for aircraft poured in by the thousands, completed airframes only trickled out factory doors, and powerplants remained all but unobtainable. Aircraft, more often than not, were being assembled in factories that were themselves still under construction! In many instances, foreign aircraft built in the United States for use in the war were shipped overseas without engines. Allied production, it was assumed, would accommodate the incomplete U.S. machinery.

Texas' role in the Great War, once a major plan began to evolve, concerned two areas of significance. First and foremost, it became the heart of the Air Service's flight training element; second, it became a key cog in the logistics wheel.

Weather, as in past Air Service decisions concerning Texas, once again came to the fore when it came time to bring the Great War's business south. The state's flat, relatively uninhabited, sun-baked plains proved ideal for training fledgling aviators. It was considered apocryphal that a terrestrial protrusion, no matter how small, would invariably get in the way of a neophyte pilot. Few such obstructions existed in Texas...

San Antonio—already having served as one of the birthplaces for U.S. military aviators and also having the strategic advantage of the relatively sophisticated Fort Sam Houston airfield facility—quickly became the heart of Air Service training, not only in the state, but also in the nation. To accommodate the demand placed on the War Department by the agreement with Premier Ribot, additional training facilities sprang into existence almost overnight.

When the United States entered the war in 1917, there were only three significant dedicated flying schools in the country. The oldest and largest was in San Diego, California; there was a relatively new school in Mineola, Long Island, New York; and there was a small school at Essington, Pennsylvania. (There were also small schools in Chicago, Illinois, and Memphis, Tennessee, but these proved short-lived due to generally poor weather conditions at the former and the small size of the field at the latter.) Like the Maryland school that had preceded them, however, the Mineola and Essington operations proved exceptionally vulnerable to the inclemencies of winter weather. Although not necessarily affected by weather, the San Diego school was rapidly proving to be more suitable for seaplane training than for landplanes, and there was a concentrated effort to reserve the San Diego school for regular army officers only—leaving Air Guard and other service personnel to go to whatever other training facilities were available.

With war pressures forcing the processing of significant manpower, flight training facilities began to sprout up all around the San Antonio area. The most significant of these was in the form of a large tent encampment with its associated concentration of aviation

enlisted men near what was eventually to become Dodd Field. Fort Sam Houston was already proving inadequate in terms of facilities and space; therefore, a new flight training site was somewhat arbitrarily chosen approximately five miles southwest of what was then the heart of San Antonio.

Temporarily referred to as Kelly No. 1, in honor of the man killed in the Curtiss Model D accident at Fort Sam Houston in 1911, this site quickly grew in importance and consequently became Camp Kelly on June 11, 1917, and—under General Order No. 49 of the Headquarters, Southern Department—Kelly Field on July 30, 1917. Kelly Field was officially opened on August 11, 1917.

In September, 1917, a seven-week course for supply officers and adjutants was begun, though it was transferred out less than five months later. This was paralleled by the initiation of an engineering officers' school and its transfer to Massachusetts Institute of Technology. In the meantime, the primary flying school gained momentum with an influx of personnel and equipment. Additional acreage adjoining the original Kelly No. 1 was acquired (as Kelly No. 2); this was later used for a primary flying school as well as other aviation training.

By December, 1917, there were over 1,100 officers and 31,000 enlisted men assigned to Kelly No. 1 and Kelly No. 2. As quickly as they were processed through flight training, they were moved to flight training facilities in other parts of the country, where they served as instructors in their own right.

In January, 1918, an "advanced" or instructors' flying school was opened at Kelly No. 2; during the same period, 595 primary students were receiving instruction at Kelly No. 1. In March, 1918, yet another school, for aircraft and engine mechanics and chauffeurs, was opened, with a capacity for 1,000 personnel. With the organization of training installations at other stations, the pressure at Kelly was gradually relieved, and fewer enlisted men were processed there. By October, 1918, the number had dwindled to 680 officers, 17,000 enlisted men, and 563 cadets (at the two airfields).

By the end of the Great War on November 11, 1918, Kelly No. 1, the primary school, had cranked out 1,480 officers (with "only 25 casualties") and Kelly No. 2, the advanced school, had qualified 298 pilots as flying instructors. The field had grown almost overnight from a mesquite patch to the largest flying field in the world and had served as a reception and testing center for recruits, training pilots, ground officers, and enlisted mechanics. Approximately 250,000 men were given trade tests and organized into aero squadrons at Kelly; all fliers trained during World War I came to the field at one time or another, including historically significant aviators such as Edward Rickenbacker, Frank Luke, Raoul Lufbery, and William Mitchell.

Kelly, of course, was not the only Texas military aviation facility during this period. Included in the list of notables were San Antonio's Brooks Field (specializing, like Kelly No. 2, in flying instructors, but also utilized for balloon training), Camp Wise (specializing in observation balloon training), and Stinson Field, Houston's Ellington Field (specializing in "bombing pilots"), Benbrook's Carruthers Field, Everman's Barron Field, Dallas' Love Field (noted as being in Hawes, Texas), El Paso's Fort Bliss, Waco's Rich Field, Wichita Falls' Call Field, Port Arthur's Naval Air Station (used for balloon training), Austin's Penn Field (specializing as an Air Service school for radio officers and operators), and near Fort Worth, Taliaferro Field.

Taliaferro Field was actually a collection of several airfields: Taliaferro No. 1, Hicks Field (located about ten miles north of what was then Fort Worth), Taliaferro No. 2, Benbrook Field (on the west side of the city), and Taliaferro No. 3 (also known as Everman Field, located about ten miles to the south of the city). On November 14, 1917, a large contingent of Royal Flying Corps (Canada) personnel ceased flight training operations in Canada and moved to the Taliaferro facility. Three days after termination of operations in Canada in April, 1918, flight training was resumed in Texas. The Canadian operation had logged some 67,000 flying hours and produced some 1,960 U.S. and Canadian pilots.

Complementing this effort in Texas and other states was a ground school program created by Hiram Bingham, a Yale professor commissioned in the Signal Corps who played a key role in the training program by starting a series of ground schools for cadets at six leading American universities. Among these was the University of Texas (the others being MIT, Cornell, Ohio State, the University of Illinois, and the University of California). By the end of this program, these six schools—and two others added later (Princeton and Georgia Tech)—had received almost 23,000 cadets and graduated more than 17,500.

In order to support the rapidly expanding network of training facilities in Texas, the Air Service elected to set up supply depots in Houston and San Antonio (and elsewhere across the United States). These facilities, with a complement of about a dozen officers and a few hundred enlisted men, received, stored, and issued all supplies and equipment to the various airfields throughout the country.

Additionally, three aviation repair depots were responsible for the repair and maintenance of aircraft, one of them located at Love Field in Dallas. Love Field, mysteriously named after Lt. Moss Lee Love, a pioneer army flier killed in a California air crash not known ever to have passed through Dallas, was originally built in 1917 as an army advanced air training center. The initial installation was a line of hangars and sheds located along the northern edge of the field and overlooking Bachman Lake. When the war rolled to a halt, military activity at Love Field was terminated. Shortly afterward, a group of Dallas businessmen bought most of the land on which Love Field stood and partially turned it into an industrial park.

At the end of the war, as production of aircraft wound down and demand all but ceased, many of the remaining airframes and engines were placed in temporary storage at the depot facilities at Kelly Field in San An-tonio and Camp Logan in Houston.

The Great War, in effect, officially placed Texas on the map as *the* spot in the continental United States in which to train neophyte aviators. The terrain, climate, expansive flatlands, and minimal populace were particularly suited to the needs of flight instruction and the idiosyncrasies of state-of-the-art flying machines; importantly, state economic conditions, coupled with readily available land, made the flying climate undeniably hospitable.

Upon the signing of the armistice on November 11, 1918, the military services initiated a massive reduction program with the primary objective of returning the services, as quickly as possible, to a peacetime footing. In reality, this was not easily accomplished. The late entry of the United States into the war had demanded a rather rapid gathering of momentum, which was just beginning to peak as the war somewhat suddenly drew to a close. Contracts for thousands of airframes, for instance, though rapidly canceled (the figures include 13,000 aircraft and over 20,000 engines), had in many instances been consummated. Accordingly, the aircraft were completed and delivered even though they were no longer of any use. Partly as a result of this, and partly as a result of surplus aircraft and engines from active inventories, a once barren civilian aviation marketplace was suddenly flooded with military surplus flying machines. This all but eradicated the embryonic U.S. civil aircraft industry and at the same time gave rise to barnstorming and national public infatuation with flying.

Military aviation activity, particularly in the state of Texas, though once again hobbled by governmental economic constraints, retrenched during this period in order to take stock and assess its future prospects. The postwar period was fraught with pitfalls, not the least of which was a horrendous Air Service safety record best summarized by an observer who noted that the number of deaths in the army's aviation branch was *4,200 percent* higher than the average for all other army branches combined. In 1921, for instance, 92 percent of the accidental deaths in the army occurred in the Air Service alone.

Following the war, certain flying fields, depots, and peripheral stations, including Kelly Field, were selected for permanent retention. A report released on April 21, 1919, showed that, within a matter of less than five months following the official cessation of hostilities, only a few hundred officers, cadets, and enlisted men remained assigned to Kelly.

In May, 1918, the Air Service for the first time became separate from the army. This proved short-lived, however; by 1920, Congress had made it an army component once again. By 1926, total personnel assigned to the service was down to a postwar low of 10,000. The Air Corps Act effectively changed the manpower and equipment problems that had resulted from the postwar retrenchment, however, and through limited congressional appropriations made permanent provisions for some 1,650 officers and 15,000 enlisted men.

Thanks to the newness of the art, record-setting flights were an almost daily occurrence in the postwar period from 1918 to 1920. Many of these records, such as Col. G. C. Brant's Houston to Belleville, Illinois, flight of 720 miles in 453 minutes in a de Havilland DH 4, though often short-lived and relatively insignificant, were nonetheless daring and usually accomplished in a pioneering spirit. Others, such as Ralph Block's flight from Houston to Mineola, Long Island, while carrying two paying passengers (Mrs. Seymour Cox and her nine-year-old son) on a cross-country record for civilians, were almost too mundane to record.

In December, 1919, the Training and Operations Branch of the Air Service elected to initiate regular pilot instruction once again. War Department General Order No. 7, dated January 30, 1920, designated two stations as primary "pilot schools." These were March Field, California, and Carlstrom Field, Florida. Kelly Field, for some reason lost to history, was not mentioned; in fact, it was officially declared by General Order No. 18 of March, 1920, to be an Air Service mechanic school.

While Kelly's primary mission now became the instruction of mechanics, it continued to support miscellaneous aircraft-related activities such as the border patrol. The still unsettled southern U.S./northern Mexico border required constant surveillance. Maj. William Mitchell, a historically significant Air Service officer of great renown and foresight, started an aircraft-borne patrol in an attempt to police the area from Brownsville, Texas, to San Diego, California, in 1919. Flying twice daily in each direction, the patrols were assigned the task of spotting illegal border crossings and discouraging marauding bands.

During the nearly two-year period that flight training was absent from Kelly Field, the only aviation events of any note, other than the continuation of mechanic training, were a new unofficial world-record parachute jump of 19,861 feet over San Antonio, by Lt. John H. Wilson on May 8, 1920, and a new speed record between Kelly Field and McAllen, Texas, by Lt. Everett Davis in a de Havilland DH 4B. The latter flight, covering 256 miles, lasted 100 minutes.

The slow rebirth of an Air Service training program kept a flicker of hope alive for the various Texas fields in Houston, Dallas, San Antonio, and elsewhere during this period. The flicker grew into a flame in 1921, when pursuit and bombardment advanced training was transferred to Kelly Field from other training facilities around the country. This was followed in 1922 by transfer of the army's observation school to Kelly and later by the instigation of attack training at the field.

In June, 1922, the training program was again revised, with the end result being the abandonment of the Carlstrom and March Field facilities and relocation of their primary training programs at Brooks Field, Texas. Having officially opened its doors in December, 1917, Brooks Field began functioning as a primary school in 1922, graduating no less than 3,422 students by May 6, 1940.

Also in 1922, all of the widely scattered "advanced" training schools were pooled at Kelly Field. This resulted in a complete training facility in the immediate vicinity of San Antonio. Kelly, at this time, was also the site of experiments conducted by Prof. J. G. Butler of the Department of Agriculture, wherein an airplane, piloted by Lt. F. B. Booker, was used in an attempt to determine the origins of wheat rust spore in the United States.

On May 4, Kelly Field also served as the point of departure for Lt. James Doolittle and Lt. Leland Andrews for their speed-record-setting cross-country flight from Texas to California. Leaving San Antonio and heading west, they covered the 1,200 miles to the Pacific Coast in 13 hours and 25 minutes. On June 18, the army demonstrated its bombing capabilities to some 30,000 observers when the schooner *Navidad* was purposely sunk off the coast of Galveston near the Fort Crockett complex. Army Air Service pilots from Ellington and Kelly fields participated in the maneuver. On June 20, in a humanitarian act of some historical merit, Army Air Service pilots from Kelly Field participated in a relief program along the Mexican border. Torrential rains in the mountains around Monterrey had caused an overflow of the Rio Grande, and supplies and equipment were moved into the area by the Kelly Field crews.

On July 3, James Doolittle and Leland Andrews again departed Kelly Field, this time heading east. Leaving their Texas departure point at 5:15 a.m., the pair, in their de Havilland DH 4, stopped only two times en route, at Ellington Field and Florida's Pensacola naval air facility, and did not terminate the flight until landing at Jacksonville, Florida, some 1,025 miles later, at 5:40 p.m.

The pooling of advanced training at Kelly Field officially got under way on June 28, 1922. On that date, the Air Corps Advanced Flying School was officially opened and the War Department, under General Order No. 39, declared Kelly Field to be a permanent military flying field. Training activities in the Air Corps during this period were generally broken down into six months of "primary" at Brooks Field, followed by six months of "advanced" work at Kelly. The advanced phase was subdivided into about 2½ months of basic instruction, utilizing de Havilland DH 4 aircraft, and 3½ months of specialized work in pursuit, bombardment, observation, or attack, employing current models of the representative aircraft types. Concurrently, "special observers" were trained in rear seat observation.

Modest record-breaking flights continued through the early 1920s. In 1922, Capt. W. P. Hayes and MSgt. C. W. Kolinsky flew a de Havilland DH 4B from Kelly Field to New Orleans, Louisiana, a distance of 560 miles, in 4 hours and 30 minutes; on August 7, Lieutenant Hine and Lieutenant Webber returned to San Diego, California, from a 4,000-mile mapping trip that included a stop in El Paso; and Lt. James Doolittle broke all records for flight across the United States by covering the distance between Jacksonville, Florida, and Rockwell Field near San Diego, California, in 22 hours and 35 minutes—having stopped in San Antonio en route for 1 hour and 15 minutes in order to refuel.

Airship activity in Texas continued at a relatively low level due to the marked general lack of interest in lighter-than-air craft in the army. Brooks Field served as the primary lighter-than-air facility in the state, and, on September 17, 1922, participated in a cross-country maneuver involving the army's C-2 airship, which flew from Scott Field, Belleville, Illinois, to Brooks in 15 hours and 50 minutes. On another record-setting flight beginning on October 7, 1924, the U.S.S. *Shenandoah*, one of the world's largest dirigibles, flew a 9,000-mile mission, logging 258 hours of flying time. Fort Worth was the midway point on each segment of its two-way flight across the continental United States.

In 1923, the army again demonstrated its cross-country flying ability when six aircraft, under the command of Capt. Thomas G. Lamphier, flew from San Antonio to San Juan, Puerto Rico, and back. The overwater portion of this mission was considered extremely dangerous at the time, and the flight's success heralded new confidence in the ability of an airplane to operate over large bodies of water.

In 1924, Kelly again served as a parachute testing ground when Cpl. C. E. Conrad jumped out of an unsupercharged de Havilland DH-4B piloted by Lt. L. S. Andrews at a record altitude of 21,500 feet. A speed record followed on April 23, when Lt. E. M. Powers, flying a Thomas-Morse pursuit, averaged 174.7 mph over a 45-mile course. Yet another record was set on August 8, when a nonstop flight from San Antonio to Kokomo, Indiana, taking 8 hours and 20 minutes and covering 1,118 miles, was completed by Lt. W. R. Peck.

In 1925, Texas' unobstructed terrain again played a role in a decision to utilize Kelly Field as a test site. Cpl. Harlin Utterback, on April 1, jumped from a circling aircraft at an altitude of 3,000 feet in the first voluntary night parachute jump. A flashlight permitted him to see the ground immediately prior to contact.

During the maturation processes in the army's air training program, several changes directly affected the developments at Kelly Field and Air Corps training in general. Among these was a decision in January, 1926, to reorganize Kelly, officially making it the Air Service Advanced Flying School in accordance with Personnel Order No. 306, War Department, Office of the Chief of Air Service. The school was subdivided into School Headquarters, the Academic Division, the School Troop Division, and the Services.

Next came the adoption of the closely related medical function. The School of Aviation Medicine, in June, 1926, was transferred from Mitchell Field, Long Island, to Brooks Field, Texas. There it became a permanent and integral part of the training system.

Another innovation was the conception and organization of the Air Corps Training Center, consisting of the Primary Flying School and the School of Aviation Medicine at Brooks Field and the Advanced Flying School at Kelly Field. The purpose of this activity was to provide a single local center for the coordination and control of all training matters. It was authorized on August 16, 1926, and its headquarters were subsequently

located at Duncan Field, adjacent to Kelly Field.

Perhaps the most serious change was renaming the old Air Service the Air Corps. This was among the many suggestions presented by the Morrow Board, which had been created in 1925 to analyze the status of the military air services and to give them direction and purpose. Paralleling the efforts of the Morrow Board was the Lassiter Board, which, though formed in 1923, made its official presentation to Congress at almost the same time as the Morrow Board.

Unfortunately, the Morrow Board report proved decidedly more cautious than that of the Lassiter Board, and a conservative mood in Congress eventually gave a victory, of sorts, to the former. Basically, the Lassiter Board had concluded that the military air services should be made a separate and distinct element in the War Department, totally independent of the army and navy. The Morrow Board, on the other hand, concluded that the military air services should remain integrated with the army and navy, and that the Air Service should only be given a new name in order to provide it an element of "prestige." Congress accepted the Morrow Board conclusions, and the Air Corps Act of July 2, 1926, officially changed the name of the Air Service to the Air Corps, "thereby strengthening the conception of military aviation as an offensive striking arm rather than an auxiliary service."

In spite of the innovations being wrought in basic training and operational air service dogma, the fundamental fact remained that there was no money available for the acquisition of new aircraft. By July 1, 1924, the Air Corps inventory showed a total of 1,364 aircraft, of which only 754 were in commission. Of the latter, 457 were observation types, 59 were bombers, 78 were pursuits, and 8 were attack types. During most of the 1920s, the total offensive strength of the Air Service in the United States consisted of one pursuit, one attack, and one bombardment group. There also was one pursuit and one bombardment squadron in each of the three overseas departments. Congressional military air service appropriations in 1924 were just over $12 million. Most of the research being conducted during this period was under civilian auspices, primarily in the form of manufacturers who were working within the guidelines of military specifications.

From July 7, 1922, through December 30, 1940, 3,945 pilots were graduated from Kelly Field, making it the alma mater of most of the Air Corps pilots trained prior to World War II. The aviation supply activities at Kelly continued to grow as well. Facilities for repairing aircraft (the Aviation Repair Depot) were moved to Kelly from Dallas' Love Field, in March, 1921, and consolidated with the existing supply depot to form the San Antonio Air Intermediate Depot.

During the 1920s, the existence of the Depot played a key role in the rationale behind a number of historically significant flights originating, in one form or another, from Kelly Field. The most noteworthy of these was the almost-forgotten Pan-American Goodwill Flight, which explored most of the periphery of Latin America.

This mission could trace its origins back to a decision by Maj. Gen. Mason Patrick, then chief of the Air Service, to convince Congress and the War Department of the Air Service's usefulness by demonstrating its capabilities through actual deeds. Following planning sessions under the auspices of the State Department, the Pan-American Goodwill Flight team and equipment, under the command of Maj. H. A. Dargue, were assembled at Kelly Field. Assigned to the mission were five Loening OA-1A aircraft and ten crew members. On December 21, 1926, the aircraft departed Kelly, not to be seen again in the northern hemisphere for over four months.

During the mission, Dargue and his fellow pilots and crew members took care of all ceremonial functions, all maintenance, and all peripheral and related mission chores. At most of the stops along the route, the lumbering Loening amphibians were the first aircraft the locals had ever seen. Weather forecasting en route was nonexistent, and communication from aircraft to aircraft was by hand signal.

Unfortunately, the flight was not completed without incident. On approaching for landing at the Argentine Air Service Field near Palomar, Buenos Aires, two of the five Loenings collided, killing one crew and destroying both aircraft. Eventually, the three remaining Loenings made it back to the United States and, on May 2, 1927, landed at Bolling Field near Washington, D.C., officially completing the flight. A total distance of 22,065 miles had been flown, exploring much of the unknown perimeter of both Central and South America. Some fifteen days later, the historical significance of this pioneering mission would be buried under an avalanche of publicity surrounding Charles Lindbergh's successful attempt to cross the Atlantic Ocean by air.

Kelly Field also played an important, though not nearly as legitimate, role in another mid-1920s event. In September, 1926, Paramount Pictures convinced the War Department to permit the Air Service to participate in the filming of its forthcoming movie *Wings*, starring Buddy Rogers and Richard Arlen. Once consent was obtained, a number of World War I–vintage aircraft were flown to Kelly Field from various parts of the country, including several de Havilland DH 4s, a few SPADs, and several Fokker D-7s, brought to the United States as booty following the capitulation of the Germans in November, 1918, and considered to be the most important combat aircraft of the war. Filming of the movie's air-to-air scenes was done almost exclusively in the airspace surrounding San Antonio.

On June 20, 1930, another major training facility, Randolph Field—named after William M. Randolph, who was killed in 1928 while assigned to the field Site Selection Committee—was dedicated some eighteen miles northeast of San Antonio. The new base, having been approved for construction by President Calvin Coolidge on February 18, 1928, was the end result of a long-term study calling for the consolidation of all nationwide military pilot training. Costing some $4 million

to build, it was touted as "the greatest flying training field in the world."

Though Randolph was only half finished on June 20, 1930, some 15,000 people gathered for the opening day ceremonies (construction, based on the original contract agreements, would not be completed until 1932) and were entertained by the maneuvers of no less than 233 aircraft—which represented effectively the entire extant U.S. Army aircraft inventory at that time—and a nine-man mass parachute jump. Dan Moody, then governor of Texas and one of the distinguished guests, remarked, "all that we are to become may depend on the men who are trained at this field." In less than a decade his words would prove all too prophetic.

The headquarters of the Air Corps Training Center were transferred to Randolph on October 1, 1931, and relocation of primary/basic training activities from Brooks Field outside San Antonio and March Field in California was completed by October 25. The School of Aviation Medicine was also moved to Randolph during this period.

Brooks and Kelly fields were not abandoned, but instead became the centers for tactical observation and advanced training (observation, bombardment, pursuit, and attack), respectively. Concomitantly, training at Randolph began in November, 1931. This so-called peacetime training system—primary and basic in an eight-month period at Randolph, and four-month courses at Kelly prior to commissioning—lasted until mid-1939.

During these years a number of specialized training aircraft were utilized at the various Texas fields. Students being qualified in the observation specialty flew in single-engine biplanes, Thomas-Morse O-19s, and Douglas O-25s and O-38s, all of which started arriving in volume during FY 1930. Twin-engine Keystone B-3A biplanes, converted from LB-10As in FY 1930, were assigned for bombardment training, along with Keystone B-6As. Although Thomas-Morse MB-3As were still employed for pursuit instruction during the early 1920s, new Boeing P-12s, one of the most significant and successful biplane fighters ever manufactured in the United States, soon became available at Kelly. Boeing P-12Bs and P-12Ds, both with 525 hp engines, were flown by pursuit students. Curtiss A-3s and A-12s were used as attack training aircraft during this period.

The effects of the Great Depression were quickly felt in the Air Corps, which, almost from its inception, had suffered from rather anemic congressional funding. Only forty primary trainers were obtained for use at Kelly, Randolph, Brooks, and other training facilities during a six-year period from 1930 through 1935. The active life of Consolidated PT-3 and PT-3A trainers had to be extended greatly because of this; by 1936, when the first group of twenty-six state-of-the-art Stearman PT-13s arrived, there were still some thirty-five PT-3s in the Air Corps inventory.

It was airmail, interestingly enough, that led to a reappraisal of the Air Corps and its chronic mid-1930s funding problems. In February, 1934, Postmaster General James Farley revoked the right of civil airlines to transport mail on the grounds that existing mail contracts were both illegal and abusive. To keep the airmail service intact, he made immediate arrangements for the Air Corps to transport the mail. The timing was imprudent. With poor equipment, antiquated aircraft, and little experience, novice Air Corps pilots attempted to meet schedules that were impeded by weather, poor maintenance, and logistical headaches too numerous to mention.

The weather proved the most immutable element with which the Air Service pilots had to contend, leading to no less than nine deaths during the first three weeks of the airmail operation. Public reaction was immediate and vocal. For the first time, or so it appeared, the public had been made aware of the inadequacies of the army's aircraft, training techniques, and personnel. The army had at last been embarrassed into solving the longstanding Air Corps funding feud.

Fallout from the bad weather experiences of the Air Corps also forced serious exploration of instrument flying technique. San Antonio's military medical facilities became intimately involved in the resulting test programs, most notably in the form of experimentation by two instrument flight proponents, William Ocker and Carl Crane, whose instrument flight techniques eventually helped pave the way for night and bad weather flying as we know it today. Their widely distributed publications on the subject served as the foundation for all contemporary instrument flight handbooks.

With the signs of war discernible across the Atlantic, the War Department, under the public mandate evolving from the airmail debacle of 1934, began a slow rebuilding of its military services, with special emphasis placed on the creation of a viable and sizable military air service. In 1938, the industry was producing 100 aircraft per month—its highest rate since World War I. Two years later, this figure was quadrupled and, less than two years after that, quadrupled again.

Fédération Aéronautique
Internationale
FRANCE

Nous soussignés pouvoir sportif
reconnu par la Fédération
Aéronautique Internationale
pour la France certifions que:

Mme Bessie Coleman
né à Atlanta, Texas
le 20 Janvier 1896
ayant rempli toutes les conditions
imposées par la F.A.I. a été breveté:

Pilote-Aviateur
à la date du 15 Juin 1921
Commission Sportive Aéronautique.
Le Président:

Signature du Titulaire
Bessie Coleman

N°. Du Brevet: 18.310.

A young black woman, Bessie Coleman, of Atlanta, Texas, was the first female from the state to receive a certified pilot's license. Coleman's license, awarded in France by the Federation Aeronautique Internationale, was issued on June 15, 1921.

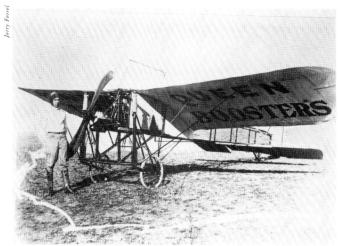

George Williams, of Temple, posed with the Bleriot copy he built and flew before WWI. The French Bleriot created by Louis Bleriot, was popular among homebuilders of the period.

Local subscribers to the "Temple Telegram," the newspaper published by George Williams' brother, sometimes received their copies dropped from this airplane while in flight.

The rapid progress of aviation in the 1920s caught the imagination of many youngsters. These sisters were ready to take flight in the sleek "Miss San Antonio".

One of the earliest aircraft dealers in Texas was Edgar Tobin. In 1928, he persuaded the St. Anthony Hotel in San Antonio to exhibit in its lobby one of his Alexander Eaglerock biplanes.

The Texas Aero Corporation, organized by George Williams in Temple, produced several aircraft models in the late 1920s. The "Sportsman" was built primarily for pleasure flying.

The Temple "Commercialwing," with a fireproof mail compartment, was Texas Aero's principal production model in 1929. It was considered an advanced design configuration for the era.

Representative of the many hundreds of aircraft designs that failed, the obscure "Helioplane," designed by San Antonio resident A. L. Hackenberger, was built in 1930.

Developed in the 1920s, autogyros achieved lift from large, rotating blades mounted above the aircraft, rather than wings. Frank Eng posed beside his Pitcairn at Stinson Field in 1939.

The original Temple Monoplane design, certificated in 1928, featured a framework of welded steel tubing with fabric covering. Most aircraft of the period were still of wood and fabric construction. An adjustable landing light is visible outside the wing struts.

The Lockheed "Vega" carried only a modest payload, but its speed gave it a sizable prestige factor. As flown by Braniff ("The B Line"), the vertical stabilizer provided a map showing the route from Chicago, to Kansas City, to Tulsa, to Oklahoma City, to Fort Worth, and to Dallas.

Wiley Post and his famous Lockheed "Vega", the "Winnie Mae", set numerous global speed records and several altitude records. Post's pioneering flights, utilizing the "Winnie Mae", made major technological and physiological contributions to the science of flight. The "Winnie Mae" is now permanently enshrined in the Smithsonian Institution's National Air & Space Museum.

Many Lockheed "Vegas" soldiered on for years, often flown by smaller commercial operators when the larger airlines acquired newer, more efficient transports. This particular aircraft, seen in a typical open field environment without paved runways, was operated in the early 1940s by Mauldin Aircraft of Brownsville.

The airfield at Brownsville became a major gateway to Central America when Pan American began flying its relatively long-legged Ford Tri-Motors.

This festive group greeted the arrival of one of Pan American's Douglas DC-2 transports at Brownsville during holiday ceremonies.

Pan American's imposing all-metal Ford Tri-Motors carried mail as well as passengers on various Latin American routes. The Tri-Motor was safe, rugged, and dependable and served as a pioneering air transport for many of the major U.S. airlines during the late 1920s and early 1930s.

LOS ANGELES
12 HOURS

PAA
PAN AMERICAN AIRWAYS

RIO DE JANEIRO
5 DAYS

BROWNSVILLE
TEXAS

NEW YORK
16 HOURS

PANAMA CANAL
20 HOURS

POPULATION
26,000

CHICAGO
11 HOURS

FAMOUS FOR
CLIMATE ~ CITRUS

MEXICO CITY
3 HOURS

From Brownsville, near the southernmost tip of Texas, air travel whisked passengers to American cities in a matter of hours. Rio de Janeiro, however, was still a five-day trip across some of the most rugged terrain of Central America.

When the Brownsville airport opened in 1929, thousands of spectators turned out to see the numerous aircraft, the spartan but substantial facilities, and several world renowned luminaries. Among the latter were famed aviation personalities Charles Lindbergh and Amelia Earhart.

Although many aircraft, like this Travel Air D-4000, were built in the 1920s for pleasure flying, they were also often used in a variety of utility roles. This example was operated by the Valley Dusters to dust agricultural crops for insect control.

After surviving for over three decades, this Travel Air of Mid-Valley Dusters came to an abrupt and untimely end in 1949. The fate of the pilot remains unrecorded.

States aircraft in Center acquired this large building (originally used by a lumber firm) as its airplane factory and repair center. A rare Spartan C2-60 two-seat sport aircraft (left) is seen next to an equally rare 40 hp Taylor "Cub."

A Galveston native, Douglas "Wrong Way" Corrigan, made a highly publicized tour of Texas following his successful solo trans-Atlantic flight in a Curtiss "Robin" in 1938.

In 1927, Marchese de Pinedo flew his Savoia Marchetti SM-55 seaplane, nicknamed "Santa Maria," from Italy to the United States on a goodwill tour that included Texas. The aircraft was destroyed in Arizona several weeks after the Texas visit when a cigarette ignited spilled fuel.

*The development of Brownsville into an international passageway into and out of the U.S.
created a need for support and maintenance capabilities. The first engine overhaul shop
is seen during its days in a small lean-to attached to one of the main hangars.*

*Brownsville's small engine overhaul facility was very well organized and almost spotlessly clean.
Engine overhaul stands and work benches were all state-of-the-art designs providing access
convenience and exceptional mobility.*

Joseph Nieto, whose photographs make up a sizable percentage of those appearing in the first chapters of this book, is seen at Stinson Field in 1927 sitting in the remains of a rare WWI-vintage Thomas Morse pursuit. Nieto was a notable collector of early aviation reference material.

The Curtiss "Robin," one of the more notable commercial aircraft available in the late 1920s, was originally available with two engine options: a Curtiss "Challenger" radial, or a Curtiss OX-5 V-8 (shown). Many "Robins" were operated in Texas during the 1920s and 1930s.

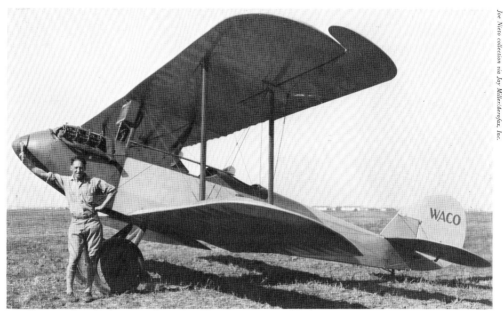

Open cockpit biplanes, such as this Waco 9, with the pilot in the rear seat and room for two passengers in the forward seat, were popular sport aircraft in the late 1920s and early 1930s. The Waco 9 was particularly popular in Texas due to its good flying characteristics.

Recreational flying became increasingly popular during the 1920s, though it was by no means a poor man's sport. This Travel Air Model BW, typical of the recreational aircraft of the period, was owned and flown by San Antonio sportsman J. Lapham.

Another popular three-place biplane of the 1920s and 1930s was the Swallow. Powered by the ubiquitous 90 hp Curtiss OX-5 water-cooled V-8, it was capable of cruising at just over 100 mph. Availability of spare parts coupled with cheap prices made the OX-5 popular.

During the early 1930s, the Lockheed "Vegas" of Bowen Airlines offered some of the fastest air service in the United States. Bailey Peyton (left), president of the San Antonio Chamber of Commerce, prepared for a business trip in 1933.

During the 1930s, enclosed cabin monoplanes such as this Conoco-operated Stinson Model R became more numerous as their attributes of increased comfort and improved performance overcame outdated safety concerns. The oil companies, because of their need and financial status, were pioneers in the use of aircraft to meet corporate transportation requirements.

With its clean, cantilever wing and tightly cowled radial engine, the Cessna "Airmaster" was a relatively fast, reliable aircraft optimized for business travel and efficient operation. Its design was advanced enough to permit it to win several speed contests for its class during the 1930s. Interestingly, its high-wing design set the precedent for almost all Cessna aircraft to follow.

C. R. Smith (right), the highly respected president of American Airlines, was a major figure in air transport history. Ralph Damon (left) was American Airlines vice president in charge of operations.

Originally produced in the 1930s, the Stinson tri-motor could carry ten passengers in exceptional comfort and safety over ranges approaching 700 miles. The tri-motor shown, one of only three extant, was refurbished and modified by American Airlines for a successful promotional tour in the early 1980s.

With Lockheed Model 10 "Electra" transports, Delta Air Lines became a significant carrier throughout the Gulf Coast region. The small "Electra" powered by two radial engines, was capable of relatively high performance and economical operation. It served as a precedent-setting design for Lockheed and helped pave the way for the later, and much larger, "Constellation" airliner series.

USAF/Kelly AFB History Office

Balloons rapidly lost ground to conventional aircraft following the successes of the Wrights in 1908 and 1909. Their popularity as sport aircraft remained strong, however. The start of the National Balloon Race in San Antonio in April, 1924, was a major public attraction at the time.

(G-375-467-1) (8-5-86 |P| (Line 12th Sqdn. Fort Sam Houston, Texas)

Military flight activity at Fort Sam Houston continued into the mid-1920s as confirmed by this view of the facility taken in August, 1926. As can be seen, the venerable Curtiss JN-4 remained a viable trainer even though it was now approaching the end of its first decade of service.

Use of the parachute was a relatively novel idea during the mid-1920s when this photo of two de Havilland DH-4s dropping "machine gunners" over Brooks Field was taken. The semi circular layout of Brooks Field is visible in the background. Most of the larger buildings are hangars. Note the lack of paved landing and takeoff surfaces.

Three Keystone LB-5s, temporarily assigned to Kelly Field, were used to explore the bombing capabilities of this relatively advanced biplane. The open expanses of the Texas Hill Country surrounding San Antonio provided ample target range areas for bombing practice.

Five Loening OA-1A amphibians participated in the army's Pan-American Goodwill flight of 1927. All five departed Kelly Field in December, 1926, and did not return to the United States for four months. Unfortunately, two aircraft were destroyed before the mission was completed.

Loening OA-1A, "San Antonio," was one of the five aircraft to participate in the Pan-American Goodwill flight and one of three to complete it. The mission, under the most trying of conditions, was amazingly successful in consideration of the minimal navigational aids provided.

Joe Nieto collection via Jay Miller/Aerofax, Inc.

Six Thomas-Morse O-19Cs are seen during formation maneuvers over Brooks Field in the early 1930s. This radial-engine observation biplane was typical of the limited production military aircraft then available to the military.

Joe Nieto collection via Jay Miller/Aerofax, Inc.

When the army's Air Service was charged with moving the mail, the aircraft assigned to the mission were mostly observation types. Among them (from front to rear) were the Curtiss R4L, the de Havilland DH-4, and the Curtiss JN-4—seen at Love Field's aviation repair depot in 1919.

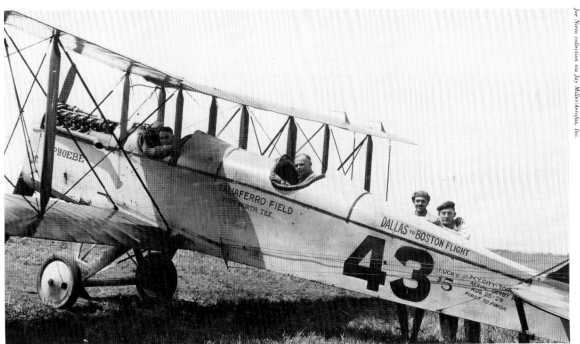

With the availability of inexpensive surplus military aircraft at the end of WWI, sport flying and air racing became popular pastimes. A de Havilland DH-4 from Fort Worth's Taliaferro Field was an apparent entry in at least several of the lesser-known races of the day.

The need for widespread logistical support for military aviation led to the development of several early cargo aircraft, including the Dougals C-1, shown. This aircraft and its successors played a key role in the development of the massive military aircraft logistical support facilities extant in Texas today.

Developed in the Netherlands, the civil Fokker F.VII transport was adopted by the army in 1925 under the designation C-2. Like the Douglas C-1, this aircraft and its several sister-ships were often seen operating in Texas while servicing military cargo transportation needs in the state.

The de Havilland DH-4, developed by the British during WWI, remained a viable element in the Air Service inventory until the late 1920s. The type was manufactured in the U.S. by the Dayton-Wright Co., the Standard Aircraft Corp., the Fisher Body Division of General Motors, the Boeing Airplane Co., and the Atlantic Aircraft Corp.

Four of the five pilots for the 1927 U.S. Army Pan-American Flight (from left to right), Maj. H. A. Dargue, Capt. I. C. Eaker, Capt. A. B. McDaniel, and Capt. C. F. Woolsey, stand next to one of the five Loening OA-1A amphibians used during the flight, which covered most of the periphery of both Central and South America.

Taken in 1932, this photo of Brooks Field shows the semi-circular arrangement of the hangars and the large dirigible hangar located in the middle of the landing and takeoff field.

With the closing of the aviation repair depot at Dallas' Love Field in 1921, San Antonio's Duncan Field became the site of the combined San Antonio Air Intermediate Depot.

During the 1930s, pilots received primary and basic training at Randolph Field north of San Antonio prior to reporting to Kelly Field for advanced training. Randolph eventually acquired the nickname "West Point of the Air" and was also to gain a reputation for being one of the most beautiful military airfields in the U.S.

Randolph Field served as a back drop for much of the footage shot for the MGM classic "West Point of the Air." The base's flat landing and takeoff fields, excellent weather, and available aircraft (Douglas O-2s are shown) proved ideal for the required action scenes.

For the film "Wings," several aircraft were modified to mount cameras instead of guns. The resulting footage was considered a major breakthrough for the film industry at the time.

A retired Thomas Morse MB-3 took on the guise of a wrecked German "Fokker" during the filming of "Wings". Most of the surrounding observers were actors and film crew members.

At Kelly Field in order to train bombardiers for the war effort, a miniature bombing range was built. Bombardiers perched high overhead and looked through mobile bomb sights in order to practice their bombing technique. This view is from overhead, looking down on the model target area.

Mrs. Henry Sueda via Kelly AFB History Office

Though only thirty Seversky BT-8s were built, the type represented a major breakthrough in trainer design. It was the first production monoplane trainer and also the first to be specifically built for the purpose of training instead of being a converted observation type or a beefed-up primary trainer. BT-8s were used to a limited extent at Kelly Field just prior to the outbreak of WWII.

Joe Nieto collection via Jay Miller/Aerofax, Inc.

By the end of WWI, Kelly Field was the largest military training facility in the U.S. Thousands of pilots and ground support personnel were housed in literally hundreds of buildings, many of which were tents and other temporary structures. Duncan Field's repair depot is visible in this view as the distant row of buildings in the upper right.

Joe Nieto collection via Jay Miller/Aerofax, Inc.

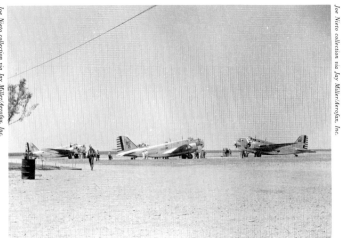

Joe Nieto collection via Jay Miller/Aerofax, Inc.

Pre war accommodations at Midland Field were marginal. Tents, providing poor protection from the hot sun and sandstorms, made up the bulk of the base's buildings.

Midland Field was one of numerous small training bases specializing in bombardier training. These outdated Douglas B-18s were used to train neophyte bombardiers.

WASP Anita Locklear, sister of the famed 1920s wing walker Ormer Locklear, is seen on the wing of a Fairchild PT-19A at Avenger Field. The WASP's contributions to the war effort were numerous and their work as flight instructors and aircraft ferry pilots was outstanding.

3. World War II

In 1939, with a heavy emphasis once again being placed on training and processing of recruits to handle the various aircraft-related chores of an Air Corps and navy on a near-wartime footing, Texas quietly returned to center stage. Although conventional military instructional processes continued at bases like Randolph, Kelly, and Brooks, additional responsibilities began to accumulate as the need for trained personnel increased.

From June through July of 1939, for instance, the Air Corps Training Center gave refresher courses at Randolph to civilian flying instructors in a concerted effort to support civilian flying school operations. The basic objective was to fill the need for primary flight instruction by contracting with the highly skilled pool of civilian flight personnel then available in the state. Because of the prevailing moderate climate, it was only natural that much of the Civilian Pilot Training Program (CPTP) should occur in Texas. Numerous small county, city, and municipal airports became involved, and hundreds of civilian flight instructors eventually produced thousands of capable, militarily suitable pilots.

The planned expansion of the Army Air Corps in 1939, in response to the rumblings of war in Europe, diverted primary training to other schools, while basic training continued at Randolph. By 1942, the number of Randolph graduates had increased from a 1930s average of 200 per year to well over 5,000. In 1943 and 1944, when the need for pilot instructors was most critical, Randolph's pilot training school became the Central Instructor's School; about 15,000 pilots learned flight instruction techniques there, while actual pilot training was diverted to the nearly thirty other training bases that mushroomed into existence at that time. Concomitantly, Kelly and Brooks fields became the nation's most important primary flight training facilities and, in fact, were the heart of the nation's pilot training program throughout World War II.

The navy, too, had become concerned about its aviation training programs and, like the Air Corps, had concluded that Texas offered a number of advantages unavailable in any other state. On December 1, 1938, a navy rear admiral by the name of Hepburn submit-

ted a committee report to Congress calling for a naval air station to be constructed on Corpus Christi Bay. The committee's decision was based on the area's sparse population, ideal weather conditions, and reasonably priced land.

By May, 1939, the committee's report had been accepted by Congress and a board had been appointed to select a suitable site for the main facility. The selection process did not take long; within a few months, Flour Bluff, a small fishing village about twelve miles south of Corpus Christi, was chosen.

Brown and Root, W. S. Bellows, Robert and Company, and the Columbia Construction Company were all picked to participate in the construction of the new naval air station. On June 13, 1940, the contract was approved; shortly thereafter, construction began on the 2,050-acre site. By Christmas, even with the considerable logistical problems that had to be overcome, the base was half completed.

Consequent to the birth of the main station, work on several satellite fields was also undertaken. Two of these, Rodd (858 acres) and Cabaniss (1,003 acres) fields, were started in September, 1940; a third, Cuddihy Field (789 acres), was initiated in November.

Though not fully completed, all four facilities were commissioned by the following summer, with the main station opening on March 12, 1941; Rodd Field on June 7, 1941; Cabaniss Field on July 9, 1941; and Cuddihy Field in September, 1941. The total construction costs came to $40 million.

Nine days after commissioning, on March 21, flight training was started at the main station with the arrival of the first group of fifty-two naval aviation cadets. The first graduation ceremony was held on November 1, 1941; by December, the graduating rate was some 300 new naval aviators per month.

Graduating rates increased considerably during the early days of the war, jumping to over 600 a month following the December 7, 1941, attack on Pearl Harbor. Eventually, by the end of World War II, more than 35,000 cadets had received their training at the Corpus Christi complex.

The naval training complex in the Corpus Christi area eventually included a total of twenty-five outlying practice fields consisting of more than 6,500 acres. In addition to Cabaniss, Rodd, Cuddihy, and later Waldron major auxiliary fields, there were two others that were attached to the Corpus Christi NAS operation but significantly more distant. One, about sixty miles northwest of the Corpus Christi area, was known as the Beeville Auxiliary Air Station, Chase Field (named after Lt. Com. Nathan Brown Chase, who was killed in an aircraft accident near Pearl Harbor in 1926), Beeville, Texas; the other, about forty miles west-southwest, was known as the Kingsville Auxiliary Air Station, Kingsville, Texas.

The other practice fields were mostly grass strips for landing and takeoff practice. A few, such as the airfield in Rockport, Texas, were specifically built for navy flight training but never expanded into legitimate facilities. Still others, such as the Corpus Christi Municipal Airport, were extant facilities put into use as a matter of convenience.

Many changes were now occurring within the Air Corps, not the least of which was the formation, on June 20, 1941, under Army Regulation 95-5, of the Army Air Forces. The AAF had its own staff, but, unfortunately, because of a politically motivated oversight concerning its relationship to the army's General Headquarters, it remained a subsidiary army service. As part of this restructuring, on July 1, 1942, the AAF Flying Training Command, headed by Maj. Gen. Barton Yount, was established in Fort Worth to supervise the three flying training centers then extant, subsequently called the Eastern, Central, and Western Flying Training Commands.

In 1942, an unprecedented need for Air Corps crews and aircraft led to serious shortages of both on the various battle fronts that had developed in Europe and Asia. Pilot training goals increased rapidly from 30,000 pilots per year to 50,000 in late 1941; by early 1942, this figure had risen to 70,000. By October, 1942, the annual need was no less than 102,000 pilots.

As the demand for pilots increased, the criteria for qualification were lowered. Various options in military status were made available to attract large numbers of cadets. In November, 1942, Congress lowered the draft age to include eighteen- and nineteen-year-olds. This cut into a population that had been an excellent source for Army Air Force aviation cadet recruiting. In December, President Roosevelt, by executive order, terminated all voluntary enlistment, thus forcing applicants for flying training to be in the army before they could apply to be cadets. All cadets had to be drawn from the monthly quota of men allocated to the AAF. Under this system, it soon became apparent that the pilot trainee goals, now calling for more than 100,000 pilots, could not be met.

Among the proposals submitted to strengthen the pilot ranks was a plan to utilize women as noncombatant pilots. Such a revolutionary idea quickly met with resistance. As the need for pilots increased, however,

the Ferry Command was permitted to recruit women who were already trained and accomplished pilots, although they would technically be civilian pilots under contract to the Command. Twenty-three women responded to the initial request to serve. All were under thirty-five years of age, with 500 hours or more of flying time, and were rated to fly aircraft of at least 200 hp. With these qualifications, they could be put to work immediately with only such training as was required to check them out in a new aircraft. They were referred to as WAFS (Women's Auxiliary Ferrying Squadron); their group, first referred to as the 319th Army Air Forces Flying Training Detachment (AAFFTD), and later as the 318th AAFFTD and the 2563D AAF Base Unit, Avenger Field, remained viable from September 10, 1942, until deactivation on December 20, 1944.

With the WAFS leading the way, it was only a matter of time before personnel commitments would dictate that the requirements for female military aviators should be lowered. There were, of course, a sizable number of female pilots in the general U.S. population, but most of them did not meet one or more of the requirements: the age limit of thirty-five, the minimum logged flying time of 500 hours, or the requirement for a type-rating in aircraft with 200 hp or more.

Jacqueline Cochran, a pilot of significant skill and accomplishment, was appointed director of the newly created Women's Flying Training Detachment—eventually to become more commonly known as the Women's Air Service Pilots, or WASPs. The purpose of this operation was to provide primary and basic flight instruction to qualified women for potential assignment to the Ferry or Air Transport Command. Though conceived at first as a "brushup" course for women with some flying experience, it was later expanded to a comprehensive flight training program of 210 hours.

Twenty-eight women arrived at Houston Municipal Airport for the first class on November 16, 1942. Serving as guinea pigs, this first class not only learned flying skills, but also paved the way, from a curriculum standpoint, for all other WFTD classes to follow. The curriculum, in fact, evolved as the class proceeded, and what started out as a course a "few weeks" in duration ended as a five-month sojourn in hell.

The training had been contracted out to a private company (Aviation Enterprises, Ltd.). Training took place in a variety of aircraft, including a required 25 hours in liaison types, 75 hours in commercial types, and 15 hours in basic and advanced Air Corps trainers. In addition, each pilot was required to have 20 hours in a Link trainer (a ground-type simulator) and 180 hours in ground school.

WFTD classes were complicated by the fact that accommodations were minimal and at some distance from the Houston airport, food was poor and at times unobtainable, and transportation between the airport and WFTD housing was abysmal.

The flow of trainees into the program was originally planned to be 122 students every 4½ months, for a total of 396 during the 1943 calendar year. This was later increased to 750, though the larger number quickly placed a great burden on the already overworked Houston airport operation.

The facilities at Houston were, in fact, proving increasingly inadequate. As the number of new trainees continued to grow, it became apparent to all concerned that something would have to be done, and soon. Accordingly, the Air Corps Gulf Coast Headquarters recommended that a new training site be selected.

At this time, through good fortune more than preplanning, a training facility in Sweetwater, Texas, became available. The operators of Sweetwater's Avenger Field, the Plosser-Prince Air Academy, had been indicted by a federal grand jury, and Gulf Coast Headquarters recommended that a new contractor be sought. Several were considered, including Plosser-Prince (which had, by this time, been acquitted!), but the old Houston airport contractor, Aviation Enterprises, Ltd., was chosen. This resulted in a slow phaseout of the Houston operation and a similarly paced buildup of the one in Sweetwater.

The first group of women pilot trainees to enter the Sweetwater facility was part of the 87-trainee class of 43-W-4. Now referred to officially as the WASPs, they arrived in the raw west Texas town on February 21, 1943. They were followed some two months later by the other class members who had initially been assigned to the remnants of the Houston operation. All classes from 43-W-4 on, transferring from Houston to Sweetwater, brought with them the various Houston-based training aircraft (Fairchild PT-19s, Consolidated BT-13s, North American AT-6s, and Cessna AT-17s) they were then flying.

Central Flying Training Command, upon request, submitted a new program for flight training—providing for 180 hours of flying—in April, 1943, which was approved. The flight time was to be distributed over a 24-week period in the following manner: primary, 55 hours; basic, 65 hours; and advanced, 60 hours. A class was scheduled to enter training every four weeks, thus permitting six classes to be instructed at one time.

In October, 1943, it was decided to increase the training period again from 24 to 27 weeks. Flying time was also increased to 210 hours, divided into 70 hours of primary, 70 hours of intermediate, and 70 hours of navigational training. Other changes, primarily in curriculum, would follow, but the 210 hours allocated would remain constant throughout the remainder of the program.

Sweetwater proved to be the ideal location for the WASP training facility. Flat, and having the usual balmy Texas weather, it permitted constant tight scheduling and rapid student progression through the curriculum. To the fledgling WASPs, it was not a haven for the faint of heart; rattlesnakes and other local "nasties" were significantly more common than they liked to believe. Additionally, Sweetwater and the surrounding territory were dry—and alcoholic beverages were forbidden on the base.

Approximately 60 percent of the women entering the

WASP program graduated. Once the course was completed, graduates were usually assigned to the Ferry Command or the Air Transport Command. Additional flying assignments sometimes followed. Instruction in duty aircraft or aircraft to be ferried was minimal, and WASPs often went to work highly dependent upon skills learned at Sweetwater. They flew virtually every major aircraft type in World War II.

Consequent to the war and the need for additional training facilities, a number of airfields were created specifically to meet Air Corps training requirements. In some cases, these facilities were simply civilian fields commandeered by the army; in others, they were specifically built for instruction purposes. Such facilities were scattered all over the state; some of the more prominent included Marfa, Pyote, Sheppard, Webb, Amarillo, Midland, Laughlin, Dyess, Reese, Foster, Connally, Laredo, Perrin, Goodfellow, Stinson, and Bergstrom army airfields.

Naval aviation in Texas also continued to prosper during this period. The Corpus Christi training complex was one of the navy's busiest, and there appeared to be few regrets in the hierarchy concerning the 1940 location decision. Hensley Field, established as a training field for reserve pilots by the City of Dallas in August, 1929, also became a naval aviation training center at this time. A 160-acre tract was ceded to the main Hensley Field facility on May 15, 1941, to be used as a training and elimination base for civilians entering naval aviation. This responsibility changed somewhat on January 1, 1943, when the facility was declared to be a naval air station. Its mission also changed, from elimination to naval aviation cadet training. In addition to the naval aviation cadets, officers and enlisted men of the regular navy, the Marine Corps, and the Coast Guard (and the associated reserve components of each) received their first flight training at Dallas NAS. Also, at one time, a number of Free French aviation cadets were enrolled as student aviators there; for a few months, the Dallas facility served as a storage depot for surplus aircraft and engines.

On July 1, 1946, the mission of Dallas NAS became Naval and Marine Air Reserve programs. At this same time, the Air Corps component, on the Hensley Field side of the Dallas reservation, converted its training operation to an Air National Guard facility. Several units were later considered resident at the base, including navy fighter squadrons VF-201 and VF-202, fleet air logistics squadron VR-59, various operational control and support units, numerous intelligence units, Marine Aircraft Group 41, the 136th Tactical Wing of the Texas Air National Guard, and various Army Reserve and National Guard units.

Dallas Naval Air Station was, and still is, a shore installation of the commander, Naval Reserve Forces. It is under the operational and administrative command of the commander, Naval Air Reserve Force, with headquarters in New Orleans, Louisiana.

In addition to flight training, many Texans became involved in the Civil Air Patrol (CAP). Organized on

December 1, 1941, only days before America entered the war, the CAP was formed to allow nonmilitary pilots to fly and to implement national security. D. Harold Byrd, a Dallas oil executive, helped create the CAP and became commander of the Texas Wing. Formed under the Office of Civilian Defense, the CAP was essentially a volunteer organization whose members flew a hodge-podge of light planes. They performed courier services, forest patrols, and surveillance along American borders and coastlines. Although the CAP in Texas looked for enemy submarines along the Gulf Coast, there was also extensive aerial patrolling along the border with Mexico, where German, Italian, and Japanese agents were reportedly active. All along the border area, from Texas to California, intelligence sources received persistent reports of unusual air activity related to espionage, and the Texas Wing of the CAP flew long patrols to spot clandestine aircraft and to discourage unauthorized air traffic. Among other things, intelligence sources were worried that American currency was being smuggled into the United States to finance subversive activities by Axis agents. In Texas and elsewhere, the CAP contributed valuable service; in the postwar era, it continued as an invaluable search and rescue group that saved dozens of lives.

Another noteworthy World War II endeavor involving Texans was Maj. Gen. Claire Chennault's "Flying Tigers." This mercenary flying group, formed by Chennault to help the Chinese in their near-futile efforts to fend off Japanese invaders during the Sino-Japanese War of 1939–1940, performed admirably with outdated aircraft and minimal supplies. One of the best known and most highly respected members of this elite group was San Antonio's David Lee "Tex" Hill—who eventually scored no less than twelve air-to-air victories before returning to the U.S. for further combat duty in the country's indigenous air force.

Besides serving as a primary training site for neophyte military aviators, Texas also contributed to the war effort by blossoming into a haven for the aerospace industry. With a hefty labor market and a rather diminutive tax burden, the early World War II business environment in Texas provided the aerospace industry with a nutritious diet that promoted rapid growth and healthy profit margins.

In 1940, when President Franklin Roosevelt stated that the U.S. aircraft industry would produce 50,000 aircraft for the war effort, the resulting shock waves could be felt across every state in the union; 50,000 aircraft was a staggering number, and, in a flashback to World War I, most industry observers declared it impossible to achieve.

Under the auspices of the Defense Plant Corporation chartered under Section 5d of the Reconstruction Finance Corporation Act of 1940, aircraft manufacturers began searching for sites for the new plants that would be needed in order to manufacture the large quantities of aircraft required. Texas—once again because of its relatively mild weather and its newly discovered economic advantages, and also because of its location

(which would serve to decentralize, from a target standpoint, the highly concentrated East and West Coast aircraft manufacturing complexes)—suddenly became a hotbed of aircraft industry activity.

Although Texas patrons had tried for years to entice aircraft manufacturers to move south, their efforts had been in vain. Entrenched on the East and West Coasts, the manufacturers had refused to admit that Texas' economic and climatic advantages outweighed the logistical problems—and that the latter could easily be overcome with a modest infusion of time and money. Finally, when manufacturers were forced to consider other options by the exigencies of the rapidly expanding European war, the merits of operating a business on Texas soil became all too apparent. Almost overnight the state went from having no aircraft industry at all to having one of the three largest aircraft production centers in the United States (the other two being in California and New York).

Starting the ball rolling was a visit to Dallas, in late 1939, by officials from San Diego, California–based Consolidated Aircraft Corporation. Following a review of available plant sites, a tract west of Hensley Reserve Airfield, then owned by the City of Dallas and leased to the War Department, was chosen as the location of a new Consolidated plant. Contingencies remained, however, not the least of which was a proposed merger between Consolidated and the Hall Aluminum Aircraft Company. Unfortunately, the Hall merger did not occur, and the proposed Hensley Field project remained in limbo.

At this point, North American Aviation, Inc., another California-based industry giant, suddenly stepped into the picture. North American also had initiated plans to set up plants in another state. J. H. "Dutch" Kindelberger, then president of North American, arrived in Dallas just as Consolidated received word that the Hall merger proposal was failing. Determining in short order that the Hensley Field site picked by Consolidated was also ideal for the proposed North American plant, he arranged to have Consolidated released from its contract obligations and to have North American take over Consolidated's options.

In September, 1940, the Defense Plant Corporation approved a contract calling for the construction of a major new aircraft production facility to be located at Hensley Field, just southeast of downtown Grand Prairie, Texas. This facility was to be leased to North American and utilized by the company to build military aircraft.

Grand Prairie, in 1940, was a town of some 2,000 inhabitants, most of whom were only vaguely aware of the military aircraft industry, and few of whom realized the import of the forthcoming North American aircraft production facility. North American proposed that the majority of the people hired to work in the new plant be indigenous to the state, with only a small percentage of the work force coming from the company's Inglewood, California, operation. On September 28, 1940, Ernest Beech, chief executive officer of North American, broke ground on the new plant in a retired cotton field just northwest of Mountain Creek Lake.

Numerous problems surrounded the construction of the new facility, not the least of which was the challenge of building housing to accommodate the thousands who would be moving to the area to work. One partial solution to this dilemma was "Avion," a million-dollar housing development of 300 homes built under the sponsorship of the Federal Works Administration. In one instance, one house in the Avion project was built from scratch on a prelaid foundation in an incredible 58 minutes and 50 seconds.

North American's Hensley Field plant was a model establishment for its day. Constructed of concrete and steel, it became the first windowless, fully air-conditioned and artificially lighted aircraft production facility in the United States. The main production building provided 855,000 square feet of floor space, and additional square footage was available in peripheral structures designed to service the needs of the main production line. There was a power-generating plant, a million-gallon water reservoir, a sewage treatment plant, air-conditioning cooling towers, a paint storage building, foundries, and aircraft storage buildings. When it was dedicated on April 7, 1941, only seven months had passed since the ground-breaking ceremony. The cotton field had disappeared forever.

Between 1941 and 1945, more than 20,000 aircraft, including P-51 *Mustang* fighters and T-6 *Texan* trainers, rolled from North American's Grand Prairie plant. In one thirty-day period, no less than 728 aircraft were produced—a mark never bettered in the United States before or since. By the end of the war, North American's Texas operation had more than 39,000 employees working in three 8-hour shifts—24 hours a day.

Consolidated, even after yielding its claims to the Grand Prairie site to North American in 1939, continued its search in Texas, still concentrating on the Dallas–Fort Worth area. Knowing that Consolidated was still in the market for a Texas facility, both the Dallas and Fort Worth chambers of commerce inundated the company with brochures, goodwill emissaries, and general propaganda. In August, 1939, Amon Carter, the publisher of the *Fort Worth Star-Telegram*, initiated a propaganda blitz that probably remains unparalleled in the history of the city. Carter's determination to get the Consolidated plant in Fort Worth unquestionably played a key role in the company's eventual pro–Fort Worth decision.

Initial studies by Consolidated had indicated that there was significant merit in setting up shop on Mountain Creek, some twelve miles from the heart of Dallas. The Fort Worth propaganda blitz soon overwhelmed those who supported that option, however, and, in late 1940, the War Department proposed that Consolidated oversee the construction of a new aircraft production facility near Fort Worth. In February, 1941, the District U.S. Engineers Office allocated $10 million for the new plant's construction, and Fort Worth then tacked on $3 million in the form of land purchase bonds.

On April 18, 1941, ground-breaking ceremonies, in the middle of a spring shower, were conducted with the help of Brig. Gen. Gerald Brant and Amon Carter. During the nine months following, the Austin Company of Cleveland, Ohio, in concert with the Army Corps of Engineers, worked day and night building the immense factory. On April 17, 1942, one day short of a year since ground-breaking, the first Consolidated B-24 *Liberator* rolled out the north end of the nearly mile-long production building. This aircraft was the first of over 3,000 produced in Air Force Plant 4, as it became known officially, by Consolidated's Fort Worth Division between April, 1942, and VJ Day in 1945.

One of Texas' lesser-known contributions to the war effort were the petroleum products generated by its petroleum products industry. During World War II refineries in Texas set numerous records in the production of high-octane aviation fuels and high-temperature lubricants. These were transported by train, boat, and aircraft to combat zones throughout the world where they were utilized by Allied combatants in virtually every form of combat vehicle in service.

Perhaps the least-known petroleum industry product was helium gas which was extracted from production sights around Amarillo and used to fill the dozens of U.S. Navy blimps tasked with the mission of anti-submarine warfare. These blimps on occasion escorted convoys in both the Pacific and Atlantic Oceans.

In the postwar era, the continued presence of major airfields and the production of a new generation of military aircraft represented major legacies of the wartime experience in Texas.

The "Taj Mahal," as the main administration building at Randolph Field has been nicknamed, is a classic example of early-1930s military architecture. It remains in active use to this very day and is still the tallest and most imposing structure on the Randolph Field compound.

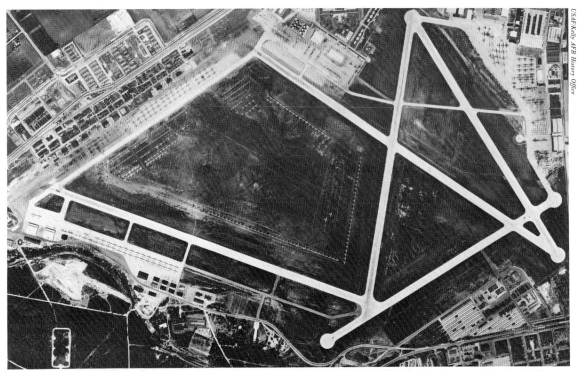

An aerial view of Kelly Field at the height of the war in September, 1944. Visible on ramps and in the fields surrounded by the base are several hundred military aircraft, including trainers, fighters, bombers, and cargo types—many of which were awaiting ferry clearances for delivery to the various fronts.

During WWII, repair depot installations could be found at most of the training bases located around the state. Many resembled, in one form or another, this sub depot at Ellington Field. Visible on the ramp are several rare WWII aircraft types including Beech AT-10s, a single Curtiss AT-9, and a single Douglas O-46.

During WWII, sub depots, such as this one at Laughlin Field outside of Laredo, were primarily responsible for the procurement and storage of aircraft parts and supplies. Most of the aircraft visible on the ramp are Lockheed B-34 "Venturas" used for coastal patrol work by the army.

Unquestionably the most easily recognized U.S. military biplane trainer of WWII, the Stearman PT-13/-17 series, usually referred to simply as the "Stearman," was the most common primary trainer used by the Air Corps from 1939 to 1945. Many thousands entered the Air Corps inventory before the end of the war.

Five Stearman primary trainers, representing the markings of several of the Allied forces which used them, formate over Texas during WWII. The ubiquitous "Stearman" was used to train tens of thousands of pilots for the war effort.

Post war use of the "Stearman" for both business and pleasure included crop dusting and sport flying. Heavy use of the aircraft as a crop duster contributed to a rapid consumption of what was originally a massive supply of engines, spare parts, and airframes.

Though less well known in the training role, Ryan's PT-22 was no less needed in the war effort. Unlike the biplane "Stearman," the PT-22 was a monoplane configuration. A restored PT-22 owned by Bill Wicks of Midland is seen in flight over west Texas.

Joe Nieto collection via Jay Miller/Aerofax, Inc.

One of the lesser-known WWII advanced trainers was the Beechcraft-designed AT-10. Many of the twin-engine all-wood AT-10s found their way to Texas training fields during WWII. Of the 2,371 AT-10s eventually built, some 600 were manufactured by Globe Aircraft of Dallas.

Perhaps the best-known advanced trainer of WWII was North American's AT-6 "Texan." Many thousands were manufactured at plants located in both California and Texas. Well over 2,000 AT-6s remained in service with the air force after WWII.

Rockwell International

Over 4,000 AT-6s were manufactured by North American's Dallas division during WWII. These aircraft, following roll-out, were immediately flight tested and then delivered, usually by air, to their user base. The AT-6 was a tandem two-seat radial engine monoplane of all-metal construction. It was one of the first operational training aircraft to be equipped with retractable landing gear.

USAF

North American's AT-6 was used by the navy as well as the air force. Navy variants were usually referred to as SNJs. Pilots found the aircraft docile, rugged, and dependable. Post war use of the aircraft spread beyond the military training mission with many serving as testbeds and target drones. The AT-6 had a gross weight of over two and one-half tons and a maximum speed of 210 mph.

Rockwell International

The AT-6 found a renewed life after its lengthy and very respectable military career. Operating expenses became palatable for private sector operators, and large numbers of AT-6s were integrated into the sport aviation community. Several hundred AT-6s are now regularly flown by private owners. They are often seen performing at airshows and fly-ins.

Rockwell International

The inimitable North American P-51 "Mustang," considered by many to be the single most important U.S. fighter of WWII, was manufactured by North American in Texas and California. With a maximum speed of over 430 mph, it was one of the fastest production aircraft of the war.

Jay Miller/Aerofax, Inc. collection

Though not manufactured in Texas, many of Republic's P-47 "Thunderbolts" passed through the state during the course of the war. The "Thunderbolt" differed from the "Mustang" in having an air-cooled rather than a liquid-cooled engine.

At the beginning of WWII, Fort Worth's Consolidated plant built a sizable number of specially configured B-24s, known as LB-30s, for the British government under Roosevelt's Lend-Lease program. Some LB-30s were never delivered and were retained for use by the air force.

*One of the lesser-known Consolidated products of the war was the pressurized four-engine B-32 bomber.
Competing with Boeing's superior B-29 it had a short production run and a limited operational career.
Out of a total of 1,588 B-32s on order at the end of the war only 115 were completed.*

*Consolidated's best known WWII product was the B-24 "Liberator" bomber. It was often compared to its Boeing
stablemate, the B-17. Though not as well liked as the B-17, it was produced in significantly greater numbers.
With over 18,000 completed, it in fact became the most produced U.S. combat aircraft of WWII.*

Consolidated's B-32 was an attempt to take the B-24 airframe and make it into a state-of-the-art pressurized bomber. Of the 115 B-32s eventually completed by Consolidated less than half reached the front before the end of the war. This airplane's production history was dictated by the success of its main competitor, the Boeing B-29.

Avenger Field was one of the less hospitable training facilities in the air force, but the WASPs did not seem to mind. Arguments with rattlesnakes and scorpions were not uncommon, but these rarely affected schedules. Like their male counterparts the WASPs were trained in Consolidated BT-13s and North American AT-6s.

Spartan's diminutive C2-60 low wing monoplane, powered by a 3-cylinder Jacobs radial engine, was one of the least-known products of the Oklahoma-based Spartan Aircraft Company. This particular C2-60, the only flyable example remaining, is owned by Bert Mahon of Justin.

The Waco GXE was a more powerful version of the Waco 10. Powered by a Curtiss OXX-6 water-cooled V-8, it could carry three passengers at a cruising speed of just under 100 mph. This GXE, owned by Max Krueger of San Antonio, is considered the finest example extant.

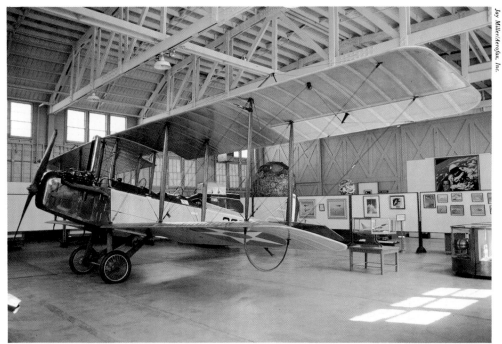

The Edward H. White Memorial Museum, located at Brooks AFB, has a large selection of aerospace memorabilia including this pristine WWI-vintage Standard J-1 trainer. Other artifacts include full-scale space hardware, vintage aircraft engines, and aerospace medical gear.

Samples of three of Grumman's most famous "cats" are operated by the Confederate Air Force at Harlingen. Included (from the front) are an FM-2 "Wildcat," an F6F "Hellcat," and an F8F "Bearcat." All are radial engine fighters of WWII–vintage.

In the early 1970s, Braniff International Airlines hired famed artist Alexander Calder to paint several of the company's aircraft, including this Boeing 727-200 seen during a stopover in Austin. The company reaped a publicity bonanza from the rather gaudy paint schemes.

The deregulation of the airline business and the resulting economic events generated a renewed interest in the commuter airline industry. One of the older commuter airlines in the state, Rio, operates a sizable stable of de Havilland DHC-6 "Twin Otters" such as this one seen at Abilene.

Southwest Airlines has developed its service around only one aircraft type, the Boeing 737. The smallest of the Boeing airliner family, the 737 has proven to be reliable and economical to operate. The latest model 737, the -300, has recently been added to Southwest's fleet.

Texas International Airlines, part of Texas Air Corporation and now officially known as Continental Airlines, operated the Boeing 737's main commercial competition, the Douglas DC-9. Comparable in performance to the 737, it proved popular with both passengers and crews.

When Dallas/Fort Worth International Airport first opened its doors in 1973, it was visited by a BAC/Aerospatiale "Concorde" supersonic airliner. This aircraft, co-operated by British Airways and Air France, remains the only operational supersonic airliner in the world.

Mooney's innovative Mk.22 "Mustang," the world's first pressurized single-engine light aircraft, was unfortunately a commercial failure. Less than thirty aircraft were completed at the company's Kerrville facility before the program was canceled due to lack of orders.

Jay Miller/Aerofax, Inc.

"Space Shuttle" training requirements dictated the development of a full-scale "Shuttle" simulator. Two highly modified Grumman "Gulfstream IIs" were acquired for this mission and based at NASA's Ellington AFB facility.

Jay Miller/Aerofax, Inc.

The Swearingen "Metro" was a twin-turboprop design optimized for commuter airline operations. Extremely fast, but somewhat difficult to fly, it was to play a key role in the mid-1970s decision by Fairchild Industries to acquire Swearingen.

The sport and aerobatic airplane market in Texas has been excellent due to the generally good flying weather and uncluttered airspace. This highly modified de Havilland DHC-1 "Chipmunk" owned by Jim Hall of Midland is typical of the aerobatic types seen.

Though ungainly in appearance, the Aero Space Lines "Super Guppy," currently owned by NASA and based at its Ellington AFB facility, has shown itself to be an ideal transport for oversize aerospace hardware, the entire nose is hinged so that it can be opened for cargo.

Jay Miller/Aerofax, Inc.

The ready availability of epoxies, resins, fiberglass, and other state-of-the-art construction materials has lead to the cottage industry development of numerous highly sophisticated homebuilt aircraft such as this Austin-based single-seat Rutan "Quickie."

Jeff Burke

Olney-based Air Tractor, founded by noted ag-plane designer Leland Snow, produced some of the world's best crop dusting aircraft before selling production rights to other companies. Ag-pilots found Snow-designed aircraft rugged and relatively easy to fly.

Aero Commander produced a Leland Snow designed ag-plane called the "Thrush Commander" for a number of years, eventually selling their rights to another manufacturer. This particular "Thrush Commander" was owned by Connie Edwards of Big Spring.

The Texas Air National Guard has operated a large number of aircraft throughout its fifty year history, including the supersonic McDonnell F-101B "Voodoo" interceptor, shown. The F-101B has now been replaced by the McDonnell F-4 "Phantom II."

The General Dynamics F-111 variable-sweep-wing fighter remains one of the most controversial combat aircraft ever to see USAF service. A Cannon AFB-based F-111D is seen over New Mexico shortly after being refueled by a Boeing KC-135A.

Jay Miller/Aerofax, Inc.

Vought's versatile A-7 "Corsair II" is in service with the air force, the navy, the Air National Guard, and several foreign air forces. An Oklahoma Air Guard A-7D is seen during a transient stopover at Bergstrom AFB.

Jay Miller/Aerofax, Inc.

Bell Helicopter Textron's AH-1 "Cobra" has been popular with the U.S. Army as a ground support "gunship." Heavily armed and extremely maneuverable, it has been acquired by many foreign military services as well, including the now-defunct Imperial Iranian Air Force (shown).

Rockwell International's B-1B is the latest advanced technology aircraft to enter service on Texas soil. The first of these huge intercontinental bombers was delivered to Dyess AFB near Abilene in July, 1985. The type is now expected to become fully operational there during 1986.

123

Jay Miller/Aerofax, Inc.

Hot air ballooning has gained in popularity during the past decade primarily because it is enjoyable and marginally affordable. Additionally, ballooning licenses are relatively easy to obtain. A Piccard AX-6, capable of carrying two adults, is seen departing a small airport near Austin.

Goodyear maintains a blimp facility in Spring. The Goodyear GZ-20A blimp "America" is seen during a short visit to Austin in October, 1974. Blimp-supported television coverage of football and other sporting events has helped renew interest in these lighter-than-air giants.

Bell Helicopter Textron has developed the XV-15 tilt-rotor as a testbed vehicle to prove the concepts that will be utilized in its forthcoming V-22 "Osprey." The latter, being co-designed and co-produced with Boeing, will be a production tilt-rotor for use by the military services.

Aerospatiale, a French-based producer of conventional aircraft and helicopters, has set up a U.S. facility in Grand Prairie to assemble and sell its helicopter family. This sleek SA-365 "Dauphin II" is typical of the Aerospatiale line.

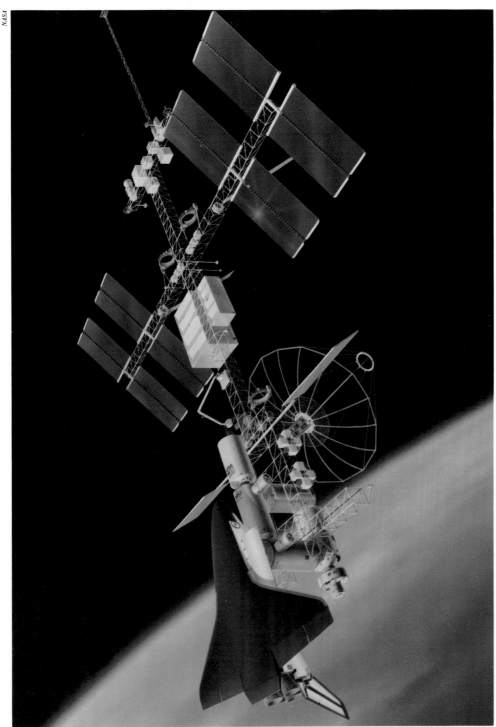

In mid-1984, Johnson Space Center released this "reference configuration" for its planned space station. The girder-like keel was to be 400 feet tall; the four pairs of solar panels were to provide electrical power; and the lab/living modules were to accommodate 4 to 6 astronauts.

A striking view of a USAF Thunderbirds General Dynamics F-16A "Fighting Falcon." This aircraft was chosen by the Thunderbirds based on its extraordinary maneuverability and its frontline use by the USAF. It is capable of speeds in excess of twice the speed of sound.

The USAF Thunderbirds aerial demonstration team uses the General Dynamics F-16A "Fighting Falcon." This aircraft is one of the most advanced fighter aircraft in the world and is in frontline service with the USAF and a large number of foreign air forces.

4. The Jet Age

Postwar Civil Trends

During the early postwar euphoria, many national aviation leaders predicted a boom in private flying. World War II had demonstrated the nation's capacity for mass production, which would lower the cost of personal airplanes. Millions of army, navy, and air force personnel had experienced flight as pilots, navigators, crew members, or passengers; they would all be potential customers. Moreover, the United States had become "air-minded," a popular phrase to denote awareness of the speed and flexibility of air travel. The market for thousands of airplanes seemed inevitable. Texas seemed to be an especially promising region.

The war years brought significant growth to all facets of Texas aeronautics, creating a strong momentum that carried into the postwar era. With over 2,000 planes and 4,000 pilots in the civil sector in 1942, Texas claimed that it was second in the nation; two years later, it was probably the leading state. By 1948, the legacy of the wartime boom could be seen in impressive new figures; 470 airports, 6,804 planes, and 20,700 pilots. In slightly more than a decade since 1936, the number of airports had more than trebled. The number of aircraft was 15 times greater, and pilots had increased some 28 times. Also, the Texas State Aviation Association was organized in Dallas in 1948 to promote flight and establish guidelines for development in the future. Aviation represented a major commercial force, involving aircraft maintenance and repair, the operation of airports, and the production of high-octane gasoline. Largely as a result of the wartime air force bases dotting the state and the production records for World War II aircraft, Texas had become unusually air-minded. Nearly every town with a population of 50,000 or more boasted an airport, and many of them had air service with local airlines.

During the early postwar era, numerous hopeful designers built light planes for the supposed boom in the general aviation market. Not everyone enjoyed success. Such ventures required considerable capital, a network of dealers, and a degree of luck. Four projects in Texas represented the trials and triumphs of the highly competitive market of light planes: the Anderson-Greenwood AG-14, the Globe *Swift*, the *Navion*, and Mooney Aircraft. The first two were smaller, two-place personal planes, while the latter two were high-performance four-place aircraft with retractable gear. There were also specialized developments that merit notice, including the advent of helicopters.

Anderson, Greenwood and Company (AGCO) began in Houston in 1940 as a partnership of several youthful engineers. Marvin Greenwood had an engineering degree from Rice Institute and an M.A. from the California Institute of Technology; Ben M. Anderson, who had a strong interest in aviation, represented the financial and business aspects; Loomis Slaughter, Jr., was also an engineer, with a degree from the University of Texas at Austin. Greenwood and Slaughter had been working on a military biplane trainer at the Southern Aircraft Company in Houston before they joined forces with Anderson. Unfortunately, their first design, the AG-11, never got past the drawing-board stage—military priorities made it impossible to obtain materials for construction. After a six-month partnership, the trio left for Seattle to work for the Boeing Airplane Company.

Not long after the end of World War II, the three men regrouped in Houston, where they began to work on another plane, the AG-12. Both of these preliminary designs were conventional low-wing planes with an engine in the "tractor" position, in the nose. During the war years, they discussed other configurations, including a pusher. Their conversations began to focus on the desirability of maximum vision, which led to the layout of a pusher design, placing the engine and propeller behind the passenger cabin. The tail, then, consisted of two tail booms equipped with twin vertical stabilizers with the elevator between them. Not many pushers of this type had ever been built, so the AG-14, as it was called, took a bit longer to design and build than its creators had anticipated. The plane emerged as a trim, two-place aircraft with a tricycle landing gear. During the first flights in 1947, it cruised at a very respectable 110 mph and proved to be virtually spinproof. Its comfort and exceptional visibility made it a promising personal plane.

Test flying and minor refinements took two years because of the small number of people available to work on the AG-14. During the summer of 1949, the design team made plans to produce an initial batch of five airplanes and purchased the necessary materials. The retail price was set at $4,500. But military priorities again intervened, this time in Korea, during the summer of 1950. The first five airplanes found buyers and got into the air, but shortages of aircraft construction materials forced AGCO into other lines of subcontracting. Three of the planes were still flying in the 1970s, a tribute to a sound design that never quite got the opportunity it deserved.

Consumers often seemed reluctant to risk money and ego on products of unique design. With its twin booms and unconventional appearance, the AG-14 perhaps had less appeal than more conventional aircraft with a snappy performance. In this respect, the Globe *Swift* found a comfortable niche. Like the AG-14, the *Swift*'s origins date to the pre–World War II era. In 1940, the Bennett Aircraft Corporation of Fort Worth completed a factory to build a twin-engine plane using the Duraloid process. This technique used plywood bonded with Bakelite and procedures that allowed large segments to be formed into aircraft components. The twin-engine plane never materialized, although the company got plenty of attention for its new design for a sporty new single-engine plane called the GC-1 *Swift*. The company was reorganized as Globe Aircraft, but World War II forced curtailment of civil designs. Globe Aircraft, with its experience in wooden airplane construction, spent the war years building the Beech AT-10, an all-wood twin used for multi-engine training by the air force, as well as subassemblies for the Lockheed P-38 and Boeing B-17.

When Globe turned to peacetime pursuits again, the company kept the appellation *Swift* for its trim, two-seat, single-engine model, but completely redesigned the aircraft, which was introduced in 1946 as the GC-1A. Although some 375 GC-1A models sold quickly, the plane's 85 hp engine made it a ho-hum performer. The GC-1B, dubbed the *Swift 125*, after its new 125 hp engine, was an exhilarating plane, with a cruise of 130 mph. Its popularity—due to its performance, retractable gear, and fighter-plane look—soon taxed Globe's ability to keep up with orders. The company gave a subcontract to Texas Engineering and Manufacturing Company (Temco), which built some 330 units. Despite the demand, Globe experienced financial problems, went bankrupt, and was taken over by Temco. Things went well for the Temco *Swift* until 1951, when military priorities during the Korean conflict brought an end to production. Never a docile plane in the air, the *Swift* was affectionately remembered as a challenging but stimulating airplane to fly. Its genuine leather seats and snappy looks gave it the adventurous aura of a sportscar. Loyal owners formed an active nationwide association that provided a constant source of maintenance and repair information, as well as a source of yarns about *Swift* planes and pilots.

Although the *Navion* had its origins outside the state, its evolution was strongly associated with Texas. The similarity of the *Navion*'s looks to the North American P-51 *Mustang* was no coincidence; *Navion* was a contraction of North American Aviation, located in Los Angeles, California. First flown in 1946, the *Navion* was North American's hedge on the future, as wartime manufacturers keyed the expected postwar boom in private flying. Within a year, about 800 planes had been delivered, with 300 more in various stages of production or on the inventory list—a remarkable record for a brand-new personal aircraft. But North American's price of about $7,000 was less than half of the recovery cost for the plane. The company halted production in the spring of 1947, but soon found a buyer in the form of Ryan Aeronautical of San Diego. Ryan delivered over 1,200 planes until suspending production in 1951; again, the Korean conflict forced a shift of priorities, and Ryan converted its assembly lines to military production.

But the *Navion* had developed the reputation of an unusually sturdy, stable airplane. As a four-place design with retractable gear, it possessed class and cruised at 160–170 mph, depending on the model, but it could also fly in and out of airstrips built for smaller, slower airplanes. In 1960, a firm called Tusco, located in Houston, made new plans to produce the *Navion* in facilities at Galveston's Scholes Field. Tusco had built several conversions of the *Navion*, and its success encouraged the company to put a new plane, model G, into regular production. By the spring of 1961, production reached five planes per month, and the Galveston Chamber of Commerce organized a "Navion Day" to celebrate *Navion*'s new success and the promise of enhanced employment for the city. Leo Childs, who had begun with States Aircraft in Center, supervised the redesign. The new version replaced the sliding canopy and created a roomy, five-passenger cabin by building up the rear fuselage and installing conventional cabin doors. Childs also redesigned the tail surfaces and added wing tip tanks, giving the *Rangemaster G*, as it was called, a range of over 1,800 miles. Production had reached twenty airplanes when Hurricane Carla blew in. Manufacturing and tooling facilities were severely damaged. The company finally decided to relocate in Harlingen, where buildings and jigs from air force surplus were immediately available. But time and financing ran out, bringing the Tusco chapter to a close in 1964. During the 1970s, subsequent efforts resulted in limited production of an H model in Seguin and in Wharton, totaling about sixty-four planes. For pilots like Leo Childs, surviving *Rangemasters* became prized possessions.

Although Mooney Aircraft has had a long history in Texas, it originated in Columbus, Ohio, and also operated in Wichita, Kansas, before settling in Kerrville. The Mooney brothers, Al and Art, worked for the Culver Aircraft Corporation in Columbus, where Al was vice-president and chief engineer, and Art supervised the factory operations. The brothers worked closely together and became known for a series of compact two-place planes, built with careful attention to aerodynamic refinements that made them outstanding performers in their class. The Culver *Cadet*, introduced early in 1940, was principally produced in Wichita, where the company moved late in the year. During the war years, Culver built over 8,000 of the diminutive planes for the Army Air Force, which designated them PG-8 and used them as radio-controlled target drones. In the postwar era, Culver offered an improved model of the side-by-side plane, but did better with a different design—a smaller, single-seat sport plane called the *Mite*. With a length of 17 feet 7 inches and a wingspan of only 26 feet 11 inches, the *Mite*'s 65 hp engine gave it a sprightly performance, as long as the pilot was of average height and weight and carried only 30 lbs. of baggage. The tail fin and rudder, angled sharply forward, gave the little plane a distinctive, rakish look that carried over into subsequent Mooney aircraft.

After the company was reorganized as Mooney Aircraft, nearly 300 *Mites* were built before moving to Kerrville in 1946 in search of a location with lower overhead and labor costs. About sixty-five *Mites* rolled off the assembly line after the move to Texas. Looking ahead, Al Mooney was soon at work on a new plane, built to carry four passengers and to compete with other high-performance retractables like the *Navion* and the Beechcraft *Bonanza*. Known as the M-20, it was a scaled-up *Mite*, complete with the forward-raked fin and rudder that had become a Mooney trademark. The M-20 first flew in 1953, only two years before the Mooney brothers sold the company and engaged in other aeronautical pursuits. Meanwhile, Mooney Aircraft prospered.

The *Mite* and the original M-20 were of wooden construction. In its next step, Mooney Aircraft introduced the all-metal *Mark 21* in 1961; this basic model became the best-selling four-seat retractable of its class in the United States. With a compact but comfortably designed cabin and careful attention to aerodynamic detail, the Mooneys could cruise at speeds as good or better than their higher-priced competitors with more horsepower—and their stingy fuel consumption was the envy of the industry.

Looking ahead to the next generation of high-performance single-engine planes, Mooney made a bold decision: it would build the world's first pressurized single. Pressurized twins, built by other general aviation manufacturers, had been successful, and the company felt confident in tackling this unique and advanced project. The prototype first flew in 1964, powered by a turbocharged Lycoming engine. Production models, christened the *Mustang*, appeared in 1967. With a 310 hp engine, the five-passenger *Mustang* could fly at 24,000 feet, cruising at 230 mph. For pilots who wanted to consort with airliners at high altitudes, the *Mustang* held a magnetic appeal. However, development costs were high, and the plane did not find the market the company had anticipated. Mooney Aircraft encountered financial difficulties during the late 1960s, but managed to stay in business. The 1970s and 1980s brought changes in the form of reorganization and merger, but the basic Mooney design survived; an important general aviation manufacturer remained in Kerrville.

In Fort Worth, R. S. "Pop" Johnson anticipated postwar success with a fast, two-place business plane called the *Rocket*. A long-time figure in Texas aviation, Johnson had three sons, all of whom became airline pilots. Pop Johnson himself flew Curtiss *Jennies* in the early 1920s and dreamed of building his own special airplane. In the summer of 1945, the first craft got airborne, and the production version, with a 185 hp Lycoming engine, gave the plane its official name—*Rocket 185*. During 1946, a reorganization of Johnson Aircraft Incorporated led to Rocket Aircraft, which eventually built about nineteen airplanes, including four demonstrators that received much attention on a nationwide tour. The *Rocket* had a retractable gear, and its unusually sleek appearance owed much to its construction, which utilized a plywood laminate covered by fabric. Many pilots ordered their planes finished in fire-engine red, a color intended to enhance the plane's reputation as a hot performer. Despite its maximum speed of 180 mph and cruise speed of 160 mph, a high-performance profile for its day, the *Rocket*'s small, two-place cockpit proved to be a severe drawback. A four-place Beechcraft *Bonanza* could fly nearly as fast, and its extra seats made more sense in a high-speed business aircraft. Neither the Johnson *Rocket* nor a successor, the *Bullet*, found commercial success, although they are fondly remembered, along with their builder, Pop Johnson.

One of the most unique planes built in Texas was the Windecker *Eagle*, using special construction techniques concocted by a dentist in Houston. After getting a D.D.S. from the University of Texas, Dr. Leo Windecker and his wife, also a dentist, set up a successful practice in Houston. During the mid-1950s, while consulting with a stockbroker, Windecker decided that the light plane industry might be an attractive investment area. Although he was not a pilot, he spent innumerable hours investigating various companies. He was struck by the strictly conventional construction approaches throughout the industry, especially the reluctance to incorporate new materials such as plastic. As a dentist, Windecker had a thorough knowledge of plastics and similar composites used in oral surgery. They had exceptional structural versatility, as well as high resistance to unusual stresses and structural fatigue. It hit Windecker that materials in dentistry had to meet many of the standards that were required in aircraft construction. The idea of an all-plastic airplane began to take shape in his mind.

At the University of Houston, he attended lectures on aerospace engineering and began experimenting with polyurethane, epoxy, polyester resin, fiberglass, and airplane wings in his garage. In 1959, he organized Windecker Engineering and won a research grant from Dow Chemical to build and, using a Monocoupe airplane, flight-test a full-sized wing made completely of plastics. Within two years, the plastic-winged Monocoupe had flown successfully, and Windecker moved to

Midland, where a group of investors had agreed to set up a manufacturing facility large enough to build a complete airplane. Dow Chemical was still involved, providing financial support in return for patent rights for the construction process. Over the next few years, the Windecker operation yielded some twenty patents for Dow.

A completed airplane, the *Eagle I*, finally took to the air in 1967. A four-place design with retractable gear and a 285 hp engine, the sleek plastic airplane cruised at over 200 mph. The plane's fuselage, wings, and tail surfaces were made of a patented material called Fibaloy, made from glass fiber impregnated with heat-set epoxy adhesives. Although a prototype crashed during spin trials, this was due to errors in loading the plane for a test, and the Windecker *Eagle I* received its FAA type certificate late in 1969. Five production planes rolled out of the Midland factory, but the company closed its doors late in 1971. Expenses had been very high; even though the *Eagle I* was a technical success, there were just not enough prospective buyers for plastic airplanes.

There was a curious footnote to the *Eagle* story. In 1973, one plane, the YE-5, was built under contract to the U.S. Air Force. The YE-5 was the basic *Eagle* airframe, packed with Department of Defense electronic test equipment. Plastics display virtually no radar signature, making the all-plastic YE-5 an ideal vehicle to test theories relating to so-called stealth aircraft, designed to evade enemy radar. The plane was so difficult to detect that pilots had to lower the landing gear many miles from an airport in order to make a radar-controlled approach. The tests were successful, but the only contracts that followed were for military RPVs (remotely piloted vehicles), small aircraft intended for aerial surveillance over hostile territory. This activity kept the Midland operation busy until the mid-1970s, when Windecker Engineering finally closed its books. The remaining five planes continued to fly, becoming stronger with each passing month. Epoxies and other materials used in the *Eagle* harden with age, making them 23 percent stronger than they were when removed from their molds. During the 1980s, the general aviation manufacturers began using more plastic-type composites in their products. Leo Windecker, D.D.S., was a decade or so ahead of his time.

Helicopters represented one of the most fascinating aviation technologies of the postwar era. For all the variety of aeronautical developments in Texas, there had been no manufacturing of rotary-wing aircraft. This situation changed suddenly in 1950, when Bell Aircraft decided to move to Hurst, on the outskirts of Fort Worth. Through the work of the brilliant Russian emigre, Igor Sikorsky, America had developed a strong lead in helicopter development. Sikorsky's VS-300, flown in 1939, set the pattern for modern helicopter design, with a large rotor blade atop the machine for lift and propulsion and a smaller tail rotor to counteract torque and help control the aircraft. But Lawrence Dale Bell, founder of Bell Aircraft, also developed a keen interest

in helicopters and began hiring a research and design team during World War II. In 1946, the simple and unadorned Bell Model 47 was licensed by the CAA, and the first commercial sale followed in the same year.

With a need to expand its new helicopter operations, Bell decided on a Texas location. The wartime work in the Dallas–Fort Worth region had created a pool of suppliers and engineers, the climate was agreeable, and the economic considerations in terms of land, labor, buildings, and taxes were all favorable. By the end of 1951, Bell occupied several existing facilities, but the company also built a new multi-million-dollar facility in Hurst. Much of the plant's early production went to Korea, where Bell helicopters evacuated 25,000 wounded from the battlefield to life-saving medical facilities. In the process, the ubiquitous little Bell Model 47 became a major component of MASH units and was immortalized as the incoming chopper on the remarkably successful television program *M*A*S*H**. But wartime service was only one aspect of Bell's helicopters. In civil applications, they herded cattle, sprayed crops, ferried city executives, served as broadcasting posts for radio traffic reports, scouted for ocean fish, carried news reporters, and patrolled high tension lines.

More sophisticated helicopters eventually complemented the original Model 47, although they never completely replaced it. The next major civil type produced by Bell was the Model 205, a turbine-powered (turboshaft) design based on the military UH-1 *Iroquois* of 1961. The Model 205 silhouette became a basic pattern for later and more successful helicopters like the Model 206 *Jetranger*. The *Jetranger* also originated as a military project for a light observation helicopter, with a prototype flying in 1962. Smaller than the 205, *Jetrangers* proved to be economical and practical aircraft, serving in a variety of executive, commercial, and utility versions, including crop sprayers. They undoubtedly helped establish a growing market for civilian helicopters from the mid-1960s onward.

Although not all Texas ventures in aircraft manufacturing proved successful, the general aviation sector rapidly developed throughout the state. As in the prewar years, the long distances between cities and industries prompted numerous individuals and corporations to purchase aircraft. Moreover, as Texas industry grew, many businesses saw the need for rapid air travel to business centers outside the state—far to the east, north, and west. Scheduled air transport was not always convenient; therefore, business and corporate flying rapidly increased. The long growing season and even terrain favored the spread of agricultural aviation. This factor also spurred the development of specialized ag aircraft (see chapter 5).

Within two decades of the war's end, there were over 11,000 aircraft registered in Texas. The remarkable vitality of the general aviation sector was reflected in the fact that only 141 planes were classed as commercial aircraft flying scheduled routes. All the rest were flown by corporations, business pilots, farmers, ranchers, crop dusters, students, pleasure pilots, and other people who found aircraft useful in one way or another. By 1965, this diverse population numbered 31,373 Texas pilots with access to 812 active airports. During 1964, itinerant aircraft traffic, most of it represented by general aviation pilots, made Love Field the nation's fifth busiest airport; over a quarter of a million planes used its facilities during the year.

As in the prewar decades, the types of aircraft visiting Love Field and other airports around the state ran the gamut, from comparatively simple planes like the two-place Piper J-3 *Cub* to luxurious twin-engine corporate aircraft, including business jets. In time, Piper offered four-place planes, suitable for pleasure and business flying, and developed a new family of low-wing types, which included high-performance, retractable-gear singles as well as twins. Cessna continued to improve on its line of high-wing singles, but began to carve out its own niche in the corporate market with its new family of low-wing, retractable-gear twins. Beechcraft brought out its phenomenally successful *Bonanza* in 1947, easily identified by its distinctive "V" tail. Beech also produced a succession of twin-engine corporate designs, including pressurized models. Aircraft dealers across the state successfully marketed these, as well as designs from Grumman, North American, Aero Commander, and others.

For clients who wanted customized interiors, elaborate avionics, different engines, unique paint combinations, and other changes, special companies could oblige them. Early examples were Dee Howard and Ed Swearingen, in San Antonio. Since a number of customers wanted corporate planes that were faster than available production models, several war surplus medium bombers were converted. Leo Childs, working for the Cameron Iron Company in Houston, presided over the conversion of a Martin B-26. But bomber conversions were expensive to fly and maintain, and they began to give way to improved corporate aircraft from the general aviation manufacturers. In any event, the early 1960s brought the first jets suitable for corporate travel—the Lockheed *JetStar*, North American *Sabreliner*, and Bill Lear's sleek *Learjet*. All these and more plied the airways.

The remarkable development of the general aviation sector was paralleled by the growth of airline travel. Love Field was also the state's busiest airport for scheduled airlines in 1964 and ranked tenth in the nation, with 146,447 arrivals and departures. But there were thirty-one other cities with regularly scheduled air service, provided by eleven different airlines. Braniff, based in Dallas, remained the largest operator and ranked as the sixth largest air passenger carrier in the country. Braniff's routes linked Texas and the Gulf Coast to the eastern and central regions of the United States, as well as to the Pacific Northwest. In the mid-1960s, a new class of feeder airlines, as well as international schedules, linked Texas communities to each other and to other continents.

Air service from Texas and the Gulf Coast to other urban areas in the United States rapidly expanded after 1945. Chicago and Southern Airlines, along with Eastern Airlines, had started new routes just before the war, only

to see them halted for the duration of the conflict. Eastern Airlines had a tradition of air service to the Southwest, adding San Antonio and Brownsville in 1939. In 1940, passengers between Houston and New York could reserve berths on Eastern's Douglas DST transports, whose sleeper accommodations represented the era's best in ultramodern travel. In the postwar era, these routes were reactivated, and additional airlines opened other routes to the Northeast and Southeast. With significant service already in place by way of American Airlines transcontinental flights through Dallas, the possibilities of air travel rapidly proliferated for Texans and for visitors to the state. Departing from Houston, residents of the Gulf Coast could fly to Chicago and Detroit in transports operated by Chicago and Southern. Mid-Continent also served Houston from Tulsa and Saint Louis. By the mid-1950s, these companies and their routes were absorbed by Delta and Braniff, respectively.

During the mid-1950s, the CAB held extensive hearings on route structures, giving special attention to some of the regional companies. As a result, the dominance of the "Big Four" (United, American, TWA, and Eastern) in major urban markets became less pervasive. Braniff won permission to begin flights from Dallas to New York, via Memphis, Nashville, and Washington. Another southern airline, Delta, also extended operations from its Atlanta headquarters into the Northeast and gave Gulf Coast residents additional airline choices through its service to Houston.

During this period, many cities attempted to win the blessing of the CAB to establish direct links to the East and West Coast, rather than making shorter flights to a major hub first. Passengers usually had to change airlines. Repeating the process on return frequently demanded many hours of waiting for appropriate flights. Direct routes could be significant time savers as well as being far more convenient. In Texas, the historic role of Dallas in the major southern transcontinental system meant that passengers from nearly every other city had to stop and change planes before continuing to coastal cities like Los Angeles or New York. In 1956, for example, Houston began a campaign to win direct routes to the West Coast. Over the next few years, the city filed numerous protests and counterpetitions with the CAB, which refused to grant the routes. Eventually, in the Southern Transcontinental case, a strong contingent from the Houston Chamber of Commerce won the argument, over protests from Dallas. Since Houston had already won service to Tampa and Miami, on the East Coast, the new routes to California in 1961 broke the Dallas monopoly on east-west traffic through the South and Southwest. Within a few years, direct service to other major cities in the North and Northwest emanated from San Antonio, as well as Houston and Dallas.

In the postwar era, events in Texas resulted in recognition of a new class of air transport—feeder airlines—which became one of the fastest-growing segments of the industry. The origins of feeder lines went back to the 1930s, when the growth of regular airline service made flying more and more popular. Smaller cities began to feel that their citizens could also benefit from the speed and efficiency of air service enjoyed by larger urban areas. The feeling seemed strongest in regions where distances were greatest and where highways and railroads frequently failed to provide direct point-to-point service. In his definitive study *Airlines of the United States since 1914*, R. E. G. Davies sums up the situation: "A new stratum of airline was needed to continue the development of service to the smaller communities on the airline map." These new carriers could "specialize in the shorter, sparser traffic routes between minor cities" and offer schedules to connect with major airlines. Not surprisingly, most of these new companies originated in the sprawling regions west of the Mississippi.

The first such airline was Essair, in Houston. In 1939, Essair planned passenger services to Amarillo, via Abilene. Braniff intervened through an appeal to the CAB, claiming that Essair would undermine the economic stability of Braniff's own operations in the area. But in 1943, the CAB gave Essair the go-ahead, recognizing that air transport had matured to the point where different levels of service were logical. The CAB also established a separate classification, "Feeder Airline." Essair finally began service in 1945, using a trio of Lockheed *Electras* seating twelve passengers. A year later, Essair changed its name to Pioneer Air Lines, an apt choice for the first feeder airline to spread its wings. Also, the *Electra* gave way to the ubiquitous DC-3.

By 1955, Pioneer had merged with Continental, but other airlines started up, and some ran as separate entities for many years. Trans-Texas Airways of Houston began service with DC-3 equipment in 1947 and made a success of its Houston/Dallas service, while reaching into Arkansas, Tennessee, and Louisiana. It retained its name for two decades before becoming Texas International. Central Airlines of Fort Worth operated primarily in north Texas and Oklahoma, as well as in nearby regions, starting in 1949 and merging with Frontier in 1967.

There was also Slick Airways, of San Antonio, founded in 1946 by a former pilot of the Air Transport Command, Earl Slick. Beginning with ten Curtiss C-46 twin-engine transports, Slick operated transcontinental routes and became the nation's largest commercial freight operator before merging with a rival, Airlift International, in 1966. The freight business had proved attractive to passenger airlines as well, and their increasing competition ultimately forced Slick to find a new partner. Airlift had the advantage of profitable international cargo contracts, enabling it to survive and swallow its competitor.

International passenger lines also reached outward. For a brief time, 1945–1946, Braniff had a Mexican subsidiary that ran from Mexico City to Nuevo Laredo, where it connected with Braniff's domestic routes. Pan American regarded Latin America as its special province; the Mexican government apparently took its cue from Pan Am when it suddenly suspended the certificate

for Braniff's subsidiary in 1946. The immediate cause of Pan Am's pique had been a Braniff coup, when President Truman overruled the CAB to give Braniff a major route from Houston to Buenos Aires. With intermediate stops in Havana, Panama, Bogota, Quito, Lima, La Paz, and Asuncion, including branches to Sao Paulo and Rio, the new Braniff award dramatically internationalized air travel for Texas. Protracted negotiations for landing rights followed, delaying operations for two years. Using Douglas DC-6 transports, Braniff finally inaugurated service to Lima in the spring of 1948. With a flourish, Braniff labeled the route *El Conquistador* and changed its name to Braniff International Airways at the same time. During 1949–1950, schedules included Rio de Janeiro and Buenos Aires, and Braniff continued to expand its South American routes throughout the decade.

At about the same time, Texas cities were attempting to get direct connections to additional international destinations. Direct flights from Texas to Latin American countries had begun right after World War II, but growing world trade and tourism led to a demand for European and Asian routes as well. Houston won a major concession in 1957, when KLM Royal Dutch Airlines ran its flights from Mexico City to Amsterdam through Houston with stops in Chicago and Newfoundland for refueling.

Hobby Airport in Houston, with feeder airlines, major national service, and international links, emerged as a major airfield. Nationally, however, Love Field held a commanding position. The early postwar emergence of Love Field as an airport of national prominence owed much to wartime activities, but Dallas' legendary rivalry with Fort Worth also played a strong role. After two decades as a civil airport between the wars, Love Field was reactivated as a military installation in 1942, bringing various additions and improvements to its facilities. Additional work occurred when it became headquarters for the First Army Airways Communication System in 1944. That same year, the Air Transport Command selected Love as its operational base. As a result, Dallas purchased additional land, and the air force spent nearly $6 million to rebuild and extend runways. Love Field entered the postwar era with unusually fine facilities, and Fort Worth's development of rival facilities triggered a new round of work at the Dallas airport. Over the next several years, several million dollars were allocated for various improvements at Love Field, intended to enhance it as a magnet for air traffic. A major step forward came when the city passed a $20 million bond in 1952. All of this activity added land, built more runways, and resulted in an opulent $7.7 million terminal, making Love Field the major airline hub in the Southwest by the mid-1960s. The airport handled 3 million passengers per year. Not everyone saw magic in the pyramiding numbers of passengers and planes. As early as 1961, several dozen activist residents of Dallas opposed further expansion, citing safety factors, but were unable to obtain injunctions to halt development.

Paralleling the development of Love Field in Dallas,

Fort Worth's municipal airport, Meacham Field, was considerably developed between the wars. From the original site, established in 1914 to serve the U.S. Army, the field was moved to a location about five miles northwest of Fort Worth. The City took over the lease in 1926, turned it into a municipal airport, and dedicated it in the name of the mayor, H. C. Meacham, the following year. Hangars were constructed over the next several years, and a new terminal building was finished early in 1937. Handling mail, express, and passengers, the airport had a steady business as the port of entry from Mexico for American Airlines and also had regularly scheduled service by Delta and Braniff. These and other operations kept Meacham busy in the postwar era.

With opposition to further expansion of Love Field in Dallas, and with Fort Worth's stubborn efforts to support a duplicate facility, the move to merge the air services of the two cities persisted. Eventually, more than two decades after the end of the war, government insistence finally triumphed over municipal obstinacy.

The Cold War Environment

Victory in Europe and Japan in 1945 brought holidays to war workers, although postwar celebrations were often tempered by the realities of unemployment. At the sprawling North American facilities, the break proved permanent, and only a few were recalled once the celebrating ended. North American eventually returned the Grand Prairie facility to the government, and the huge plant remained only partially occupied for a time.

Following North American's return to California, the Grand Prairie property was placed in the custody of the Reconstruction Finance Corporation (RFC), which immediately began the task of finding a tenant. Although numerous small companies examined the plant and found it to their liking, it was simply too big for most, and the postwar economy was not conducive to risky investments.

Two North American executives, Robert McCulloch and H. L. Howard, who had worked in the plant during the war years and who had stayed in Texas following North American's return to California, now decided to lease 550,000 square feet of the primary "A" plant (there were two facilities involved, one north of Fort Worth known as the "B" plant, and one next to Grand Prairie known as the "A" plant) and create a major subcontractor facility. To get the new venture started, two days after signing the lease, McCulloch signed a contract with the Fairchild Aircraft Corporation calling for the as-yet-unnamed new company to produce various subassemblies for the Maryland-based Fairchild Aircraft Company's C-82 *Packet*.

From this original decision to lease space, and the subsequent contract with Fairchild, came the Texas Engineering and Manufacturing Company, later known simply as Temco. By late 1946, the company employed no less than 2,500 and had acquired additional subcontracts, including one from Fairchild to manufacture 200 F-24 light aircraft. Globe Aircraft Corporation of Fort Worth also gave Temco a subcontract to manufacture its *Swift* all-metal light aircraft.

Following the war, Globe quickly discovered that the hoped-for postwar pilot boom was not to be. By 1947, Globe was in the throes of bankruptcy; major subcontractor Temco suffered with it.

Temco, in order to remain viable, now bought Globe's remaining assets and agreed to absorb many of its liabilities. The *Swift* was put back into production, and several advanced versions, primarily to meet military requirements, were initiated.

Among the latter were the T-35 and TE-1 trainers, and the TT-1 *Pinto*. The former two were tandem seating, militarized versions of the original *Swift*, and the latter was a lightweight jet-propelled trainer—the first jet built by the Temco operation. Demand for the trainers unfortunately proved limited; by the early 1950s, the company was again totally dependent on its subcontract work.

Subcontracting activity for Temco, along with the acquisition of the Luscombe light aircraft manufacturing company, kept the company viable throughout the mid- and late 1950s. Subassemblies for the Boeing B-47, the Lockheed P2V, the Martin P5M, the McDonnell F2H, and the Douglas A2D were included in the growing list of parts being manufactured for other companies. An air force contract calling for the conversion of a number of single-seat P-51s to two-seat TF-51s kept the company active in the full-scale aircraft business.

Temco, following a merger with James Ling in July, 1960, became the Temco Electronics and Missile Company. A contract to produce *Teal* and *Corvus* missiles gave the company prime-contractor status once again. Unfortunately, this was short-lived, as both missile programs were terminated following an abbreviated hardware and flight test program.

The Ling-Temco merger produced another merger, this time with the successful Chance Vought company. Chance Vought, interestingly enough, although larger than Temco, had been forced to sublease space from Temco following its move from Texas, due to McCulloch's and Howard's foresight in leasing the old North American plant from the RFC in 1946. Vought eventually reversed this situation, but not before the final merger of all three companies, as the LTV Corporation, in August, 1961.

Vought, the producer of no less than 13,000 aircraft for the navy during World War II, had begun searching for a new home base for its aircraft production facility in the late 1940s. Its Connecticut plant was old, outmoded, and terribly cramped, and there was little room for expansion or improvement. Vought directors and government representatives eventually consummated an agreement on April 8, 1948, whereby the company would sublease from Temco the partially occupied (and expanded to 3 million square feet) Hensley Field facility. The economic and climatic advantages of moving to Texas and the difficulties the company was facing in Connecticut gave Vought strong incentive to head south.

The logistical problems of uprooting nearly three decades of accumulated hardware and personnel from Connecticut proved extraordinary. By the time the relocation had been completed, more than 1,300 people and 27,077,078 lbs. of machinery had been transported by automobile, truck, train, and some 1,006 freight cars no less than 1,687 miles from Stratford to Grand Prairie. One item alone, an Erie metal press, weighed a staggering 245 tons.

It took over a year for the company to get completely organized and back into full aircraft production; but navy fighters and missiles were rolling out Vought plant doors once again by late 1949. Initial production centered around late models of the still-viable F4U *Corsair* piston-engine fighter and ground support aircraft, and initial preproduction batches of the company's first jet-propelled fighter, the F6U *Pirate*. These production runs were followed by the introduction of the radical, tailless F7U *Cutlass* into navy service and, later still, by the introduction of the F8U *Crusader*.

The *Crusader* became Vought's high-water mark in the navy fighter business and consequently became one of the great navy jet fighters of all time. Capable of Mach 2 speeds in level flight, yet docile enough to land and take off from an aircraft carrier, it was well liked by pilots and extremely competitive in almost any air-to-air combat situation. It entered navy service in the late 1950s and remains operational in its reconnaissance configuration.

After the war, Consolidated's activities continued at a much moderated pace. Though initiated during the early days of World War II, work on the awesome 200-ton B-36 intercontinental heavy bomber, with its six piston engines and (following later modifications) four jet engines, continued and in fact sustained the company until the birth of the supersonic B-58 bomber nearly a decade later.

In a somewhat premature attempt to bring the company gracefully into the jet age, the B-36 program was punctuated with a modified version called the B-60. Basically a stock B-36 fuselage with swept wings, swept vertical and horizontal tail surfaces, and power provided by eight jet engines, the B-60 was a direct attempt by Convair (as the company was beginning to call itself) to compete directly with the powerful Boeing Company of Seattle, Washington, for a major bomber contract. Boeing, with the success of its six-jet-engine B-47 and the strong support of the air force for the newly completed B-52, had started from scratch while designing a new heavy jet bomber. Convair had simply modified an older design. In the end, Boeing won hands down and, in so doing, forced Convair into pursuing its rapidly

developing supersonic bomber project.

Convair's B-58, known as the *Hustler*, was in fact the first supersonic bomber ever. It was capable of cruising at over twice the speed of sound. Graced with a delta wing and four General Electric–built turbojet engines, it was a technologically advanced, politically controversial nuclear weapons delivery vehicle that, for a ten-year period from 1960 to 1970, served to complement the capabilities of the lumbering, subsonic Boeing B-52. All 116 B-58s eventually completed were produced by Convair's Plant 4 facility from 1956 through 1961.

The B-58 was eventually followed by the extremely versatile but no less controversial Tactical Fighter Experimental (TFX) program. Later designated the F-111, it stretched the state-of-the-art in design to its limits, like many other Convair products, suffering through numerous political and technological assaults in the process.

As an aeronautical pioneer, the F-111 became the first production aircraft ever to employ a totally encapsulated ejection system; the first to utilize afterburning turbofan engines; the first to incorporate high-flotation/rough terrain landing gear; the first to be equipped with terrain-following radar; and, perhaps most importantly, the first to utilize the distinct performance advantages provided by a variable-sweep wing. Problems with each of these systems eventually marred what initially promised to be a bright operation and production career. As a result of the F-111's difficulties, contracts for several thousand were eventually cut back to a total of 562 after a merciless, though not entirely unmerited, attack by the media and congressional and Department of Defense opponents.

On March 1, 1954, Convair officially became a division of the immense General Dynamics Corporation conglomerate. This event did not, at the time, lead to any major changes in the Fort Worth Convair operation; but, over a period of years, the General Dynamics name slowly obscured the long-standing Convair title. Beginning with the F-111 program and continuing to the present day, the company refers to itself officially as the Fort Worth Division of General Dynamics Corporation.

Like many large aerospace manufacturers, General Dynamics has surrounded itself with a veil of secrecy to protect the company's proprietary interests and also to permit the company—and its primary customer, the Department of Defense—to develop technological advances that permit tactical and strategic advantages over the "enemy."

In order to accomplish these objectives without intrusion, many aerospace companies, such as General Dynamics, have created advanced technology departments that are sometimes referred to colloquially as "skunk works" (a title first coined for the advanced design department at Lockheed-California's Burbank plant). Here the most advanced design configurations and technologies are woven together to create aircraft that represent absolute state-of-the-art performance and capability. Several such machines have come from General Dynamics' Fort Worth Division "skunk works" facility, not the least of which was the RB-57F sensor system platform.

The twenty-one RB-57Fs built by General Dynamics, with an altitude capability of nearly 70,000 feet, proved to be exceptional sensor system transports during their many years of service with the air force, the Central Intelligence Agency, the Department of Energy (Atomic Energy Commission), and NASA (which is still operating one aircraft at Houston's Ellington Field). Heavy, high-resolution cameras, nuclear particulate samplers, and other electromagnetic energy sensors were all part of its payload during its operational career.

In 1950, Bell Aircraft Corporation, a relatively small but respected and innovative manufacturer of fighter and research aircraft, made a decision to move its rapidly growing helicopter division from its main Buffalo, New York, plant to a 55-acre site near Hurst, Texas, just east of Fort Worth. The land, originally a small farm, had been purchased from Mrs. W. E. Duskey at a price of about $165,000. Bell, the first company to have a helicopter licensed by the Civil Aeronautics Administration (the Bell Model 47, licensed on March 8, 1946), had become enamored with the helicopter following a series of demonstrations and tests conducted in 1942 by Arthur Young, a mathematician at Princeton University. Lawrence Bell, founder of the company, had been impressed by Young's work and eventually financed the construction of the prototype Model 30—which effectively became the first of over 25,000 helicopters built by Bell to date.

Climate and the possibility of a strong commercial and military helicopter market brought Bell to Texas in 1950. By January, 1951, the first Bell personnel had begun to transfer south; by the end of the year, the world's first dedicated helicopter production facility, at a cost of some $13 million, stood completed on Mrs. Duskey's retired farm land. During the following five years, some 1,200 helicopters were completed, most of them to fill a burgeoning military requirement.

The first flight of Bell's first turbine-powered production helicopter, the Model 204 (military designation at that time, XH-40), on October 22, 1956, marked a major change of pace for Bell's production facility. This helicopter, perhaps the most significant production type in the history of vertical takeoff and landing–capable aircraft, was a turning point in helicopter technology. Not only did it integrate the technological advances inherent in turbine engines; it also provided, for the first time ever, a helicopter that was truly dependable, practical, and utilitarian.

The 1960s, with the help of the Vietnam War, proved particularly lucrative for Bell's Hurst, Texas, operation, as the air force, navy, marines, and army placed extraordinarily large orders for various versions of the Model 204 (as the UH-1) and its numerous improved and updated configurations. The company also developed and produced lightweight observation helicopters such as the OH-58 and a uniquely successful dedicated attack helicopter known as the AH-1.

All told, Bell produced well over 10,000 helicopters during the course of the Vietnam conflict, not to mention a similar number of helicopters for civil operations, which today make up a sizable percentage of Bell's total production output. The versatility of the helicopter—coupled with its unique capabilities—makes it ideal for oilfield and offshore drilling support, certain types of crop dusting, executive transportation, and commercial transport operations.

The various military installations in Texas were quick to feel the impact of a heavily constrained postwar military economy. With the sudden deemphasis on training and the rapid deactivation of operational combat units, the need for the seemingly innumerable military airfields in the state no longer existed.

Initially, the cutbacks were not considered catastrophic, as the aircraft industry and its peripheral elements expected that postwar interest in civil aviation would take up most of the slack created by the military's departure. Accordingly, plans were made to convert many of the military airfields in Texas to civilian fields and to readdress instruction and training procedures in order to adapt them to civilian requirements.

Unfortunately, this early optimism quickly soured, as many military aviators did not pursue flying following their military tours. The end result was a terrific slump in the postwar aircraft industry and a severe cutback in flying activity throughout the country.

The worst aircraft accident in the history of the Corpus Christi NAS occurred at this time. On the night of November 8, 1945, two Martin PBMs collided in midair about 200 feet over Corpus Christi Bay. As one aircraft was landing following a lengthy training mission, another was taking off. By mistake, both were operating in the same sea lane. Twenty-two crew members were killed, with five surviving.

Immediate postwar activities at Corpus Christi included the modification of twenty-eight Consolidated PB4Y-2Ns into weather reconnaissance aircraft. Their missions, which included hurricane research and the study of nuclear explosion effects under the auspices of *Operation Crossroads*, conducted at Bikini Atoll, Marshall Island, in August, 1946, dictated strengthened structures and the addition of dedicated research equipment.

Corpus Christi NAS, for a short while, also served as a German prisoner of war camp. After four and a half months of operation, this facility was ordered closed on March 18, 1946. After that date, all army personnel and prisoners were returned to Fort Sam Houston in San Antonio, where the prisoners were processed and prepared for their return trip to Germany. Following the deactivation of the POW camp, a decision was also made to deactivate the surviving major auxiliary airfields surrounding the Corpus Christi complex. Included in this list were Beeville, Waldron, and Kingsville. By the end of 1947, almost all of Corpus Christi's peripheral training facilities had been either decommissioned or turned over to the affected communities.

In August, 1947, the navy announced that the Basic Air Training Command then located at Corpus Christi would be moved to Pensacola, Florida. The main station operation, the Acceptance and Repair Department, and the Naval Air Transport Group remained functional. The Advanced Training Command stationed at Corpus Christi officially opened on December 1, 1948, and became the Headquarters for the Naval Air Advanced Training Command.

With the move of the Command to Corpus Christi came the U.S. Navy's Blue Angels aerobatic team. At that time flying piston-engine Grumman F8F *Bearcat* fighters, the Blue Angels consisted of six pilots and ten enlisted crewmen commanded by Lt. Comdr. R. E. "Dusty" Rhodes. The unit had been formed at the Jacksonville, Florida, Naval Air Station on April 1, 1946, with the express purpose of promoting naval aviation and serving as U.S. Navy goodwill ambassadors. By performing team aerobatics at airshows around the country, they helped inform the public of naval aviation's capabilities, the prowess of the navy's pilots, and the performance of the navy's most modern combat aircraft. The Blue Angels' initial stay in Corpus Christi was relatively short, about nine months, and they would not return again for almost two years. In September, 1949, they moved to their new home base at the Naval Auxiliary Air Station, Whiting Field, Milton, Florida.

The Naval Air Station received its first helicopter, a Sikorsky S-51 modified for navy use, from the navy's Lakehurst, New Jersey, facility on March 22, 1949. The helicopter had been assigned to the station as an aid in air/sea rescue missions. Within thirty minutes after its arrival, the helicopter was dispatched on its first rescue mission (to Padre Island) to pick up a Cabaniss Field flight student who was forced down on the island when the engine of his Vought *Corsair* fighter failed in flight. The student was picked up and returned to Corpus Christi without incident.

In early 1949, the air force gave the go-ahead to the Strategic Air Command to attempt the world's first nonstop round-the-world flight. There were several reasons for this, but perhaps the most important, yet least heralded, was to bolster the air force's claims that its bomber force was truly intercontinental in range. Opponents of the large fleet of heavy bombers the air force had amassed both during and after World War II had claimed that, because of the airplanes' relatively limited range, it was unlikely they would be of much use in any post–World War II conflict. By proving unequivocally that bombers such as the Convair B-36 and Boeing B-50 could fly nonstop to any spot on the globe and return, this argument, it was assumed, would be permanently laid to rest.

Because of its central location, Texas' Carswell AFB was chosen as the takeoff and landing spot for the record attempt. A Boeing B-50A was picked for the mission and modified to accept an in-flight refueling system (not a standard item on the B-50 at that time). The flight's unequivocal success proved a great morale booster for the air force. The B-50A, nicknamed *Lucky Lady II* and manned by fourteen crew members, completed its 23,452-mile flight in 94 hours and 1 minute at an average

speed of 239 mph. Four in-flight refuelings and over 56,000 gallons of avgas were required.

In 1949, another air force bomber, the immense Fort Worth–built Convair B-36, flew a mission from Carswell AFB to Muroc AB (now Edwards AFB), California, while carrying a total bomb load of 84,000 lbs. Two 42,000-lb. *Grand Slam* non-nuclear bombs were mounted inside the B-36's cavernous bomb bay in a successful attempt to prove that the B-36 had the weight-lifting ability guaranteed in its original contract. The flight proved the point beyond any doubt; interestingly, the 84,000-lb. bomb load remains the heaviest ever carried by any aircraft.

Records continued to fall to the B-36's awesome capabilities throughout the early 1950s. On March 15, a Convair B-36B flew a nonstop, nonrefueled 43 hour and 37 minute mission from Carswell that covered 9,600 miles, setting yet another bomber mark. This record was shattered when an RB-36D, on January 17, 1951, flew a 51 hour and 20 minute mission without stopping or being refueled.

On June 10, 1949, the navy announced that it would again start using the runways at the Chase Field facility at Beeville due to the congestion and increased activity at Corpus Christi. The City of Beeville signed a leasing agreement with the navy shortly thereafter, receiving in exchange crash and fire-fighting equipment, runway improvements, and ambulance services for the field. On October 5, 1953, the chief of Naval Air Advanced Training announced the permanent reopening of the field. This was followed, on July 1, 1954, with a recommissioning by the navy.

The decision about the Beeville facility was followed, on January 15, 1951, by similar information about the Kingsville Auxiliary Air Station. Kingsville was scheduled to be used as a jet transitional-training facility. The base was physically recommissioned on April 1, 1951; some two years later, in May, 1953, the construction of the first permanent buildings was authorized.

On October 1, 1951, it was announced that the Blue Angels, temporarily disbanded during the first few months of the Korean War, would be reformed and again stationed at Corpus Christi NAS. The aerobatic team's new purpose was not only to promote naval aviation, but also to test combat equipment under rugged conditions. When reformed, the team was assigned six Grumman F9Fs, two Vought F7Us, and one Grumman F8F—the former two representing state-of-the-art U.S. naval fighters. The Blue Angels left Corpus Christi on July 6, 1955, and immediately headed for their new permanent home at Forrest Sherman Field near Pensacola, Florida, which remains their primary base of operations.

Perhaps the most interesting, yet least known, military activity ever to take place in Texas began during the summer of 1957. On June 11, a mysterious and rather strange-looking aircraft entered the landing pattern at Laughlin AFB near Del Rio. The pilot, Col. Jack Cole, was delivering—from the Central Intelligence Agency's secret Groom Lake flight test facility in Nevada—the first Lockheed U-2A to be assigned to the air force.

Under the auspices of the air force's secretive 4080th Strategic Reconnaissance Wing, the 4028th Strategic Reconnaissance Squadron had been assigned to fly U-2s from Laughlin on missions that had both sensitive and unsensitive objectives. Eventually, some fifteen aircraft and about thirty pilots would make up the U-2 element at the remote Laughlin facility, flying a wide variety of missions spanning everything from particulate sampling to surreptitious overflights of unfriendly countries.

The U-2, a refined gliderlike design with a cruise-altitude capability approaching 80,000 feet, had originally been designed to meet a Central Intelligence Agency requirement released to selected airframe manufacturers in 1954. From 1956 to 1960, these aircraft and their civilian pilots conducted some thirty flights over the Soviet Union. On May 1, 1960, Francis Gary Powers was shot down by Soviet antiaircraft missiles deep in the Russian heartland; the political repercussions that followed ended U-2 Iron Curtain overflight missions, at least temporarily.

Powers' ill-fated flight heralded the beginning of the end for Central Intelligence Agency use of the U-2, but marked an upsurge in U-2 activity by the air force. Missions from Laughlin eventually played key roles in the discovery of strategic missile emplacements in Cuba, documentation of radioactive materials in the upper atmosphere (and the subsequent decision to end atmospheric nuclear tests), and various studies pertaining to sensors, the environment, and human physiology in high-altitude flight.

U-2 operations continued at Laughlin until 1963. On July 12, however, following a Strategic Air Command decision to move the operation to a more accessible facility, the last U-2 left Laughlin for the 4080th's new home at Davis-Monthan AFB, outside Tucson, Arizona.

The fifties and sixties were halcyon years for the military air services in Texas. Once again, because of the state's climate, terrain, and scattered population centers, the services made extensive use of available facilities in order to train new pilots and to develop and test new aircraft. Strategic Air Command, Air Defense Command (later, Aerospace Defense Command), Tactical Air Command (which would later absorb the Aerospace Defense Command), and, perhaps most importantly, Air Training Command facilities were located at numerous bases all around the state.

Brown Flying Service located at San Antonio Municipal Airport, as it was then called, was one of the early post-WWII authorized Piper aircraft dealerships. A Piper J-3 "Cub" equipped for crop spraying is seen being loaded with chemicals. The windsock provided visual indication of wind direction.

This Sikorsky S-43 amphibian was owned for many years by Howard Hughes. Hughes, an expert pilot, was almost killed in this aircraft in the late 1930s when he misjudged a water landing. Restored, the aircraft later was kept on constant call for Hughes at Houston's Hobby Airport.

The Johnson "Rocket" was a post-WWII attempt to produce a high-speed single-engine light aircraft for the civilian market. Designed by Texan R. S. "Pop" Johnson, the "Rocket" proved only modestly popular due to the limitations of its two-seat configuration.

The Texas "Bullet," also developed by "Pop" Johnson, was a significantly different aircraft. Though of modern design and capable of exceptionally good performance, it too suffered the fate of its tricycle-geared predecessor for exactly the same reasons.

Jay Miller/Aerofax, Inc. collection

A solid and dependable aircraft, the Ryan/North American "Navion" was produced on occasion in Galveston under the product name of "Rangemaster." Though performance was only average for aircraft in its class, the "Navion's" roomy cockpit and extraordinary ruggedness sustained its popularity.

Roger Bilstein collection

The Aeronca C-3 is considered one of the classic light aircraft designs of the 1930s. Many of these two-seat fabric monoplanes were found throughout the state being used as sport and recreation transportation. Today only a few survive. This pristine example is based at Justin Time Airport near Justin.

The size and range of the Fairchild 24 made it attractive to many Texas pilots. A very popular aircraft after WWII, it could be bought with either an air-cooled inline or conventional air-cooled radial engine. The Fairchild 24 could accommodate four adults and modest baggage in reasonable comfort at a cruising speed of 125 mph.

The Globe "Swift," a high-performance all-metal single-engine light aircraft built in Fort Worth, proved to be modestly popular after WWII. This was not an airplane for the novice pilot, as its stalling characteristics and low-speed handling demanded a pilot's full attention.

Surviving "Swifts" often are seen at airshows and fly-ins. Many, such as this example at Kerrville, have been modified and given more powerful engines. Because of its rugged airframe, the "Swift" can be flown aerobatically within limits, adding to its long-standing popularity.

The famous Link trainer, used for ground pilot instruction, acquired a modern look in the post-WWII era. Many pilots acquired basic piloting skills while "flying" these simulated aircraft. The Link trainer was eventually replaced by today's super-sophisticated flight simulators.

Joe Nieto collection via Jay Miller/Aerofax, Inc.

The Luscombe 8E "Silvaire," produced for a short while in Texas, was a two-place all-metal light aircraft. Popular during the late 1940s and early 1950s, it was similar in many respects to the Cessna 120/140 family. Many Luscombes can still be seen at Texas airports today.

Joe Nieto via Jay Miller/Aerofax, Inc.

For a short while a state distributorship for the rare Stearman-Hammond Y-1S all-metal monoplane was maintained in Midland. Though the success of this distributorship remains unrecorded, the production life of the Y-1S was extremely short.

Rugged, dependable, easy to fly, inexpensive to maintain, and modestly priced, the Piper "Cub" remains one of the most popular light aircraft of all time. Many "Cubs," such as this one seen at Kerrville, are flown in Texas for both business and pleasure.

The versatile Lake amphibian was manufactured near Houston in the late 1970s and early 1980s. It made up for its minor performance deficiencies by being able to operate from a variety of surfaces, thus making it useful for both business and pleasure.

The Anderson-Greenwood AG-14 was a compact all-metal two-seat pusher. Developed at Anderson-Greenwood's facility near Houston it was a promising design when first unveiled in the late 1940s. The Korean War and shortages of materials eventually terminated its production.

A rather eye-catching publicity photo released by Mooney Aircraft Corporation to promote its diminutive M-18 "Mite," illustrated well the pleasing lines of the all-wood single-seat aircraft. The "Mite's" performance and low price made it popular for sport flying.

Institute of Texan Cultures

Jay Miller/Aerofax, Inc. collection

Many Mooney "Mites" can still be seen flying at private airports and airshows around the state. A restored "Mite" is seen during an airshow at Kerrville.

The Texas Department of Public Safety found air transportation particularly suitable to its needs. In 1954, a Cessna 195 was acquired for use by the department as a "scout" aircraft.

Mooney Aircraft

The basic design of Mooney's single-engine light aircraft line has not changed significantly since the basic design was first unveiled in the mid-1950s. One of the most recent Mooney products is the Mooney 201, which is capable of cruising at 195 mph. Mooney's production facility is located at Kerrville, where the company is a major employer.

The Bronze Eagles, as the Texas Chapter of Negro Airmen International calls itself, is a group of dedicated black pilots whose primary objective is to promote aviation within the black community. The organization sponsors several important programs for young people. Many members are ex-military pilots and several own aircraft.

This early 1970s line up of the Mooney Aircraft family illustrates well the diversity of the company's product line. Everything from the small two-seat Mooney "Cadet" trainer to the sophisticated pressurized Mk.22 "Mustang" was available. The prices of these aircraft ranged from a low of about $8,000 to a maximum of nearly $50,000.

In 1984, Mooney reentered the market for pressurized singles with the unveiling of the Mooney 301. This six-place aircraft of advanced design and performance is now scheduled for first customer deliveries in 1987. Flight testing has been ongoing at Mooney since the prototype's first flight in 1984.

Texas has for years been home base for a large number of companies whose sole purpose is the modification and update of readily available production aircraft types. In the 1950s one of the companies best known for such modification work was Temco, whose D-16 "Twin Navion" was a modestly successful product of the period.

Jay Miller/Aerofax, Inc. collection

The San Antonio "Palomino" was an abortive two-seat all-metal light aircraft project from the mid-1960s. Though it was an aesthetically pleasing design, a modest promotional effort eliminated it from serious contention in the light aircraft market.

The Texas civil aircraft register harbors many unusual planes. Examples include WWII aircraft such as this Douglas A-26, which is purported to have been used during the Bay of Pigs debacle. At the time the photo was taken it had become part of the Confederate Air Force fleet.

*Quiet San Antonio genius Edward Swearingen gave birth in the early 1960s to Swearingen
Aircraft Corporation. His aircraft design philosophies led to several innovative corporate
and commercial aircraft and numerous aircraft modification programs.*

Swearingen's production facility is located at San Antonio International Airport. Current production is centered around various commuter airline and corporate types including advanced versions of the company's "Merlin" and "Metro" aircraft.

Swearingen's "Merlin III" is a turboprop-powered corporate aircraft designed to accommodate up to eight passengers and cruise at speeds in excess of 300 mph. It is a relatively economical aircraft to operate and its performance capabilities are on par with any comparable turboprop aircraft in the world.

Fairchild Industries

Swearingen's "Merlin IV" is an executive transport based on the design of the company's "Metro" commuter airliner. Both types are capable of seating up to twenty passengers while cruising at speeds in excess of 300 mph. The "Metro" has proven popular in the commuter airline industry and has sold well for Swearingen.

Fairchild Industries

Swearingen's ability to accommodate customer requirements are underscored by their in-house interior design and fabrication shops and their in-house custom paint shop. Many aircraft such as this "Merlin III" are outfitted strictly to customer specifications.

In 1983, following a takeover by Fairchild Industries, the name Swearingen was dropped from the designations of all Swearingen aircraft then in production. Fairchild then renamed the entire extant Swearingen line in its own name. This Fairchild 300 is basically an updated "Merlin III" incorporating more powerful engines and winglets.

In a unique program for an American manufacturer Fairchild Industries joined with Sweden's Saab-Scania to develop and produce the new Saab-Fairchild 340 light transport. This advanced technology twin-turboprop has been optimized for commuter airline use.

On March 28, 1984, the second Saab-Fairchild 340 twin-turboprop regional airliner and corporate aircraft was rolled out of the new Saab-Scania civil aircraft plant in Sweden. The aircraft was painted in company colors and bore the Saab-Fairchild 340 logo on its fuselage.

Mitsubishi Aircraft

Japan's Mitsubishi Aircraft following a short-term agreement with an indigenous U.S. aircraft manufacturer, opened its own production facilities at San Angelo's Municipal Airport in the early 1970s. Two of its recent products include the "Marquise" and the "Solitaire" turboprops.

Mitsubishi Aircraft

The twin-turboprop "Solitaire" is somewhat smaller than the "Marquise" and seats only six passengers. Modestly priced at a little over $1,750,000, it has few competitors in the marketplace while offering exceptional comfort and excellent performance.

Mitsubishi Aircraft

In 1981, Mitsubishi received certification for the first of three versions of its "Diamond" executive jet series. Capable of cruising at over 500 mph, it represents Mitsubishi's first major attempt to penetrate the lucrative pure jet corporate market. A "Diamond" was recently acquired by the State of Texas for use by the governor and other state officials.

The Texas arm of the Civil Air Patrol did duty during WWII by patrolling the Gulf coastline and Mexican border areas. Several of the CAP's aircraft are seen at Biggs Field in January of 1943 prior to embarking on their daily sorties. Included in this line up are (from right to left) a Beechcraft Model 17 "Staggerwing," a Waco cabin biplane, and a pair of Bellanca "Cruiseairs."

The attributes of the Civil Air Patrol were extolled by cartoonist Milton Caniff in these 1950s-vintage illustrations. CAP membership was sustained by such unsolicited support.

Seen in magazines across the nation, promotions such as Milton Caniff's cartoons helped recruit new Civil Air Patrol members when they were needed most.

In wet weather like this seen in the Valley area of Texas, even crop dusters remained in their hangars. Though rare, flooding such as this could easily destroy an entire season's income.

A pair of aging Travel Air biplanes are seen at the end of their Valley dusting days with one serving as a parts supply aircraft for the other.

Ken Medders is seen standing beside his modified "Stearman" biplane at Sun Valley Dusting Company in 1949. The clean uniform and airplane were not typical of ag-aviation operations.

The early 1960s brought major technological improvements to the ag-aviation industry. The Piper "Pawnee" shown here represented one of the first dedicated ag-aircraft designs.

Many attempts to develop efficient, dedicated ag-aircraft were made during the 1950s and 1960s. Most, such as the obscure Texan A-7T shown with its unusual cockpit offset to the left side of the fuselage, failed. These were, however, the first aircraft that did not use standard production types, such as the "Stearman," as their airframe basis.

Another little-known dedicated ag-aircraft design indigenous to Texas was the Clark 1000. This aircraft, unlike many ag-aircraft contenders, based its design parameters on the proven "Stearman" configuration. Powered by a 220 hp radial engine, it improved upon the "Stearman's" design by replacing the "Stearman's" fabric surfaces with metal skin.

One of the more successful contemporary ag-aircraft designs has been Cessna's "Ag Truck." Powered by a horizontally-opposed air-cooled engine and capable of carrying a sizable chemical payload, it has proven to be a profitable production aircraft for its manufacturer.

The versatile "Ag Truck's" success is due in part to its relatively low acquisition price of $100,000. This, coupled with the scarcity of radial engines used to power many of the older ag-aircraft, has led to a renewed interest in newer, dedicated ag-aircraft designs. Many of the latter are now powered by turboprop engines.

THE N-M TOUCH: HIS AND HER AIRPLANES

Have you a husband or wife who's utterly impossible to buy for? Here's the one great (but however-believe-it,
Christmas gift you've searched the world to find! His is the incomparable, big 7-place Beechcraft Super G18.

Hers is the 4-place Beechcraft Bonanza. Both speed along the skyways at more than
three-miles-a-minute, both can be bought in your choice of color, style, cabin arrangement, and any number
of combinations of individual navigational equipment. 2 A His, 27,000.00. 2 B His, 149,000.00. Both are
"Fly Away Factory" prices. 2 C Her jacket with the right dash is Russian white ermine
with a Blétched white fox Saddle; (A) 2,975.00 incl. Federal tax. Fur Salon.

In 1960, trendy Neiman-Marcus launched its famous "His-and-Her" holiday gift packages with the twin-engine
Beechcraft G-18 (for him) and the trim "Bonanza" (for her), noting that "both can be bought in your choice of
color, style, cabin arrangement, and any number of combinations of individual navigational equipment."

The classic Douglas DC-3, which first flew on December 17, 1935, became the backbone of the United States air transport system and faithfully continued to serve the industry into the 1960s. One of the last major state airlines to utilize the DC-3 was Texas International.

With the advent of large four-engine transports like the Douglas DC-6, air cargo became a major source of airline revenue. Many airlines named their aircraft after the major cities they served; the American Airlines DC-6 shown receiving containerized cargo was the "Dallas."

Larger airliners, like the pressurized Douglas DC-6, were the first post-WWII aircraft designed specifically to replace the venerable Douglas DC-3. These new airliners provided speed and comfort advantages that could never be realized with the older Douglas transport.

For many years, the epitome of piston-engine elegance was the graceful, triple-tail Lockheed "Constellation." This aircraft, often seen at Texas airports during the 1950s and 1960s, was initially developed for use by Pan American Airways and the U.S. Air Corps.

After beginning with cast-off Douglas DC-3s, commuter airlines, such as the now-defunct Texas-based Emerald Airlines, eventually replaced them with more modern types such as the Netherlands-manufactured Fokker F-27 twin-engine turboprop.

Many major Texas corporations utilize small turboprops and turbine-powered transports, like these Conoco-operated Grumman "Gulfstream Is," to make regularly scheduled runs to offices across the state and around the nation. These aircraft constitute a sizable investment for the many companies that operate them.

Commuter airlines, such as Metro, have made a successful business operating de Havilland "Twin Otters" between Houston Intercontinental Airport and outlying population centers like Clear Lake, on the city's south side. The "Twin Otter," because of its short takeoff and landing capabilities, is ideal for this type of operation.

The Texas Aeronautics Commission, established in 1945, played a significant role in promoting intrastate air transportation like that provided by Chaparral Airlines and others. Chaparral, which operates modified Grumman "Gulfstream Is", serves the needs of larger airlines by delivering passengers to DFW airport from outlying areas.

Austin's Bruce Hallock, considered by many to be a master aircraft designer and homebuilder, has devoted his life to the pursuit of efficient tailless aircraft designs. His first full-scale effort was the "Road King," which first flew successfully in the mid-1950s. Several subsequent tailless aircraft designs have since rolled from the Hallock construction shop.

Odessan Tommy Dempsey, a jeweler by profession, modeled his twin-engine "Beta-Lightning" homebuilt after the famous WWII Lockheed P-38 "Lightning" fighter.

The "Beta Lightning" besides being an innovative design was also extraordinarily difficult to fly. After a short career, its engines were removed and its airframe was discarded.

Jay Miller/Aerofax, Inc.

The doyen of Texas homebuilders, Austin's Tony Bingelis has built at least a half-dozen aircraft, such as this French Piel "Emeraude," in numerous garages across the country.

Jay Miller/Aerofax, Inc.

Texan Leeon Davis' DA-2, an innovative all-metal homebuilt, has been successful enough in terms of plans sales to permit Davis the luxury of making his hobby into his vocation.

Jay Miller/Aerofax, Inc.

Possibly the most successful high-performance aerobatic homebuilt ever is the Pitts "Special." Many of these dimunitive, rugged biplanes, such as this colorful S-2A variant owned by Jan Colmer of Dallas, have been acquired by Texas aerobatic pilots for use in both sport and competition flying. Pitts' prices vary greatly, but new fully-equipped models usually cost in excess of $50,000.

The rapidly escalating costs of owning and operating conventional aircraft have given birth to ultra-light sport aircraft which permit flying enthusiasts the fun of flying without having to bear the expense. This Eipper "Quicksilver" seen at Stinson Field is one of several hundred different ultra-light aircraft available in today's market.

Ultra-lights, such as this biplane configuration seen at a Kerrville airshow, are priced from less than $1,000 to over $5,000. For single-seat configurations a conventional pilot's license is not required. Flight training and skill levels are primarily acquired through instruction by other ultra-light pilots.

Only the most rudimentary accommodations are provided pilots in ultra-light aircraft such as this Maxair "Hummer" seen at a Kerrville airshow. With maximum speeds of less than 50 mph and ranges of less than 200 miles, these minimal aircraft have serious practical limitations. Both single- and two-seat versions are available.

Warbirds, though an expensive hobby, have grown increasingly popular among well-heeled Texans. Alan Preston of Dallas, the owner of several warbirds kept at Addison Airport, includes in his stable this immaculate North American T-28 "Trojan." The "Trojan" was used as a trainer by both the air force and navy.

One of the more popular warbirds due to its nostalgic value and its relatively low price is the Stearman PT-13/-17 biplane trainer of WWII-vintage. Though many of these aircraft were destroyed while being used as crop dusters many of the survivors have been given a second life as sport aircraft.

Air racing, which during the 1930s was a national pastime, has only recently made a resurgence as a popular sport. Only a few races, such as those in San Marcos in 1980, have taken place in Texas.

Aircraft designer Jim Miller of Marble Falls is one of the most ardent proponents of air racing. His unconventional JM-2, capable of speeds in excess of 200 mph, has been a modestly successful contestant in air races around the country and remains active on the air racing circuit.

Jay Miller/Aerofax, Inc.

Jay Miller/Aerofax, Inc.

Airline pilot Jerry Mullens of Dallas, after acquiring Jim Bede's exotic BD-2 powered sailplane, set a world's absolute distance record in 1981 in excess of 10,000 miles.

Oilman Buzz Hurt of Odessa, long an avid aerobatics enthusiast, has owned and operated a variety of aerobatic aircraft types including this highly modified Taylorcraft.

Jay Miller/Aerofax, Inc. collection

Summertime airshows and fly-ins are extremely popular, drawing thousands of enthusiasts and sightseers from around the state every year. Many of the shows, such as this fly-in at Georgetown Municipal Airport, tend to revolve around particular themes. In this instance the objective was to bring together vintage light aircraft and homebuilts.

Parachuting is also proving popular in Texas. Sport parachutists often make many jumps in a single day, and many parachuting clubs own their own jump planes and parachute packing and rigging equipment. Though appearing otherwise, sport parachuting is a decidedly safe sport.

West Texas is considered by soaring enthusiasts to be the best soaring country in the world. Many major soaring competitions take place near Odessa, Marfa, and other west Texas towns, where high-performance sailplanes such as this Elan DG-100 can often be seen taking advantage of the lift-sustaining thermal activity found there.

The success of Bell Helicopter's precedent-setting Model 47, in 1949, led to a corporate decision to build a large production facility in Hurst.

Several thousand Model 47s rolled from the Bell's Hurst production facility during the 1950s and 1960s. This design eventually gave way to the more advanced Model 204 series.

One of Bell Helicopter's most successful products has been its "Jetranger" family. Used by both the military and civilian sectors, it has become the standard by which most other helicopters in its class are judged. The "Jetranger" is available in several models ranging in price from $360,000 to nearly $1,000,000.

The "Jetranger" is capable of accommodating a large number of options including an agricultural spray rig. Crop dusting and spraying using helicopters, though not well known, can trace its origins back to early helicopter development in the mid-1940s.

The helicopter has proven ideal for offshore oil rig logistical support. Its vertical takeoff and landing characteristics make it ideal for the delivery and retrieval of both personnel and equipment. A Bell "Jetranger" is seen during a delivery to an offshore rig in the Gulf of Mexico.

One of Bell's most recent products for the corporate market is the Model 222. Like most of its more recent predecessors it is turbine-powered and capable of above-average performance. With a list price in excess of $1,000,000 it is not an inexpensive means of transportation.

The Model 214ST is currently the largest member of Bell's helicopter family. Its ability to carry large payloads has made it popular both in the U.S. and abroad. A Chinese registered Model 214ST is seen during a test flight from Bell's Hurst facility.

Aerospatiale Helicopters of Grand Prairie offers a rather extensive family of corporate and military models including the turbine-powered "Ecureuil." Aerospatiale's line up competes directly with the better-known Bell Helicopter family.

U.S. Coast Guard facilities dot the Texas coastline. Rescue teams are highly dependent on the skills of their helicopter pilots, who fly rescue missions in both Sikorsky HSS-2s and the newer Aerospatiale SA-365s. The latter, effectively Texas products, will eventually replace the older Sikorsky helicopters completely.

At the end of WWII the military services found themselves with significantly more aircraft than they could possibly utilize in a peacetime environment. Accordingly, aircraft were scrapped and their metal was smelted at places like Pyote Air Base in west Texas.

Vought Aerospace has manufactured several aerospace products outside of its normal product line. Among these are the "Airtrans" people-movers in daily use at DFW International Airport. Seen on the production line in the background is an incomplete Vought A-7 attack aircraft.

After departing Carswell on February 26, 1949, the world's first nonstop around-the-world flight was completed on March 2 by a Boeing B-50 bomber nicknamed "Lucky Lady II." The crew was welcomed by top air force officials including air force secretary Stuart Symington.

Brooks AFB has a deserved reputation as one of the world's foremost aerospace physiological research centers. It also serves the air force by providing training facilities for flight crews. This altitude chamber is used to introduce pilots to the dangers of high altitude flight.

In the Brooks AFB altitude chambers trainees are exposed to high altitude flight by the controlled elimination of oxygen. Inside the chambers, altitudes equivalent to near space are possible. Oxygen masks are removed so that phenomena such as hypoxia can be experienced.

Perhaps the most common military trainer in use at the various Texas air force bases is the Cessna T-37. Hundreds of these small, twin-jet aircraft have been acquired to provide basic training for neophyte air force pilots. Two Randolph AFB T-37s are seen preparing to land.

Because of Randolph AFB's heavy training bias, many unusual training aircraft have passed across its ramps. Among them was this German RFB "Fantrainer," which was an unusual, and unsuccessful, contender for a rather large air force contract.

In yet another attempt by a foreign government to sell a training aircraft to the U.S. military, a French and German consortium proposed that the U.S. military buy the versatile "Alpha Jet." This aircraft was demonstrated at Randolph AFB to both the air force and the navy.

The most important advanced trainer in the air force inventory is Northrop's supersonic-capable T-38 "Talon." This two-seat aircraft, capable of speeds in excess of 800 mph, has control characteristics very similar in many respects to most high-performance fighters. Most of the air force's fleet of T-38s is stationed at various training bases in Texas.

A McDonnell TA-4F, one of several advanced trainers utilized by the various navy training facilities that dot the Texas coast, is seen on final approach to Dallas Naval Air Station.

Navy transport requirements are accommodated using a variety of aircraft, including the Douglas VC-9B. Comparable to the commercial DC-9, it is the largest Texas-based navy aircraft.

Much of the long-standing secrecy surrounding the Lockheed U-2 high-altitude surveillance and reconnaissance aircraft was lifted following the loss of a Central Intelligence Agency–operated version over the Soviet Union in 1960. This at one time highly classified aircraft was flown from Laughlin AFB outside Del Rio for a period lasting through the Cuban missile crisis.

General Dynamics' massive production plant west of Fort Worth is one of the largest facilities of its kind in the world. The main building, which contains the main production line, makes up the bulk of the plant, stretching continuously for nearly a mile from one end to the other.

The FICON (Fighter Conveyor) was an unconventional mid-1950s Convair effort permitting a parasite fighter to be carried over long distances. Utilizing a trapeze assembly mounted in the B-36's bomb bay, the F-84F could be launched and retrieved while both aircraft were in flight.

Convair's FICON program actually reached operational status with the air force as a long-range reconnaissance system. Specially modified RF-84Fs, with nose-mounted cameras, were utilized for sensitive overflights of unfriendly territory during a one-year period from 1954 through 1955.

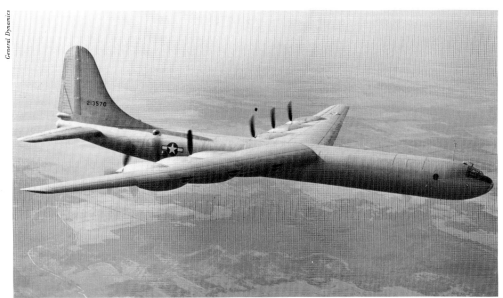

Convair's XB-36 was, at its unveiling in the fall of 1945, the world's largest aircraft. Powered by six twenty-eight cylinder radial engines and having a gross takeoff weight of over 160 tons, it was capable of flying nearly half-way around the world, non-stop and unrefueled.

The B-36 presented an awesome sight from almost any angle. Sobriquets such as "aluminum overcast" and "big stick" were often used to describe it. On one occasion, a single B-36 became airborne with a 42-ton bomb load—a record that remains unbroken to this very day.

Most B-36s were eventually equipped with four turbojet engines in wing tip pods in addition to the six conventional radial engines. The additional power provided by these engines permitted "feather weight" B-36 configurations, as some special reconnaissance versions were called, to reach altitudes in excess of 55,000 feet.

Logistical support for the B-36 was provided by the San Antonio Air Material Area facility at Kelly AFB. The B-36's massive size dictated a highly specialized support system capable of assimilating and maintaining many thousands of parts. Each of its six R4360 radial engines, for instance, required no less than 56 spark plugs.

In a highly classified program to develop a nuclear-powered bomber for the air force, Convair, during the mid-1960s, built and flight tested the NB-36H nuclear reactor testbed. Some fifty flights with a functioning nuclear reactor onboard were completed over Texas before the program was terminated due to lack of funding.

The NB-36H carried its nuclear reactor in its aft bomb bay. A special lead-lined pressurized crew cabin was provided, and all missions were flown with special radiation monitoring chase aircraft in tow. One chase aircraft carried a contingent of parachute-equipped marines who were to keep civilians away from the aircraft if it crashed.

Two typical air crews pose on the wing of Convair's huge XC-99 transport while, below, 400 airmen from Lackland AFB pose to show its capacity. The XC-99, built from the basic components of the B-36, served out most of its operational career at Kelly AFB. At the time, it was the largest operational cargo aircraft in the world.

The size of the XC-99 was comparable to that of contemporary Lockheed C-5A and Boeing 747 jumbo transport aircraft. It had upper and lower decks for accommodating freight loads and could load palletized cargo using a series of internal cargo hoists. Though in dilapidated condition, it can still be seen next to Kelly AFB.

Hoping to keep the B-36 alive until its B-58 project reached the hardware stage in the mid-1950s, Convair built two YB-60 jet-powered versions to compete against Boeing's B-52. Underpowered and marginally acceptable as bombing platforms, their lives were short.

Convair's bomber designs leaped from the piston to the jet age with the unveiling of its stunningly beautiful delta wing B-58 "Hustler." Capable of speeds in excess of 1,300 mph, it was the world's fastest operational bomber during the ten years it served with the air force.

Though plagued with problems that were the end product of the quantum leap forward it represented in technology, the B-58 was an effective weapon and greatly admired by all who flew it. Only 116 were completed by Convair before political elements finally eliminated its funding.

Two variants of the "Hustler" were manufactured: the standard bomber and a special trainer (shown). Both carried only three crew members. The B-58's payload, which consisted of nuclear weapons or reconnaissance equipment, was carried in a separate pod.

General Dynamics

Convair's "Skunk Works" served not only as a design and fabrication facility for advanced company projects, but also as a modification shop for special military aircraft. Among the many were Martin RB-57D high-altitude reconnaissance aircraft, stepping stones to the Lockheed U-2.

NASA

In a successful attempt to develop a high-altitude sensor platform that could fill various military and government agency requirements, General Dynamics manufactured twenty-one RB-57Fs. With a wingspan of 122 feet, they were capable of cruising at altitudes in excess of 68,000 feet.

The variable-sweep-wing General Dynamics F-111 wood and cardboard mock-up, which served as a detailed full-scale model of the real aircraft, was completed in early 1962, immediately prior to the beginning of fabrication of the first real aircraft.

The Tactical Fighter Experimental (TFX) program (which was the brainchild of then-Secretary of Defense Robert McNamara), after giving birth to the General Dynamics F-111, became the most controversial military program of its day.

George Cockle

The F-111 was plagued with myriad problems during the early stages of its career, none of which were easily or inexpensively overcome. Compounding these problems were rapidly escalating production costs that eventually made the F-111 the most expensive fighter aircraft of its day. An FB-111A bomber version is illustrated here.

General Dynamics

F-111s have been updated periodically by General Dynamics under contract to the air force. Some of the early updates involved modifications that corrected design deficiencies discovered after the aircraft entered operational service. Particularly serious problems concerned wing failures and inefficient engine operation.

Now producing A-7 attack aircraft and subassemblies for other manufacturers, Vought Aero Products Division of LTV Aerospace occupies the Grand Prairie plant that was originally built to accommodate the North American Aviation Company during WWII. Visible (at top) are Hensley Field and Dallas Naval Air Station.

Vought's V-173, a pancake-shaped testbed designed to prove the aerodynamics of the stillborn post-WWII XF5U-1 fighter, was one of the most radical configurations of its day. It was damaged during an emergency landing with Charles Lindbergh at its controls.

The tailless, aircraft carrier–borne F7U "Cutlass" was one of Vought's less successful fighter designs. It proved to be marginally underpowered and somewhat difficult to land. It was not popular with the navy and soon recorded a relatively short operational career.

Because of its unusual wing design, the "Cutlass" was forced to have an exceptionally tall nose landing gear assembly. Just over 300 F7Us were built by Vought before the type was replaced on the company's production line by the significantly more successful F8U "Crusader."

The Vought F8U "Crusader" was the navy's first aircraft capable of flying at speeds in excess of twice the speed of sound. An aggressive and extraordinarily capable fighter, it was exceptionally popular with the navy and a fearsome weapon in the hands of an experienced pilot.

LTV Aerospace

Vought's "Crusader" was eventually blooded in combat in the skies over Vietnam. A number of air-to-air victories were claimed, and the type also proved effective in the reconnaissance and ground support roles. Both reconnaissance and fighter configurations were built.

LTV Aerospace

Philippine technicians make a last-minute check of a "Crusader," the first of an initial batch of 25 which Vought refurbished for the Philippine Air Force in 1978. The reconditioning program utilized ex–U.S. Navy F-8s that had been stored in the Arizona desert following navy service.

Vought's unsuccessful contender for the "Crusader's" successor was the Russell Clark–designed F8U-3 "Super Crusader." Though resembling its predecessor, it was in fact a totally new aircraft with a maximum speed of nearly two and one-half times the speed of sound.

The F8U-3 was the most advanced fighter of its day, but it suffered from two major failings: it had room for only one crew member—and the navy wanted two; and it was powered by only one engine—and the navy thought two engines would be safer. These shortcomings, though questionable, killed it as a production program.

Another one of Vought's many innovative designs was the mid-1960s-vintage vertical takeoff and landing XC-142A cargo aircraft. Designed for operation into and out of small fields and onto and off surface ships, the XC-142A derived its unique capabilities from its hinged wings and powerful engines.

The tilt-wing XC-142A was designed to accommodate the needs of the army, air force, navy, and marines. Five prototypes were built by Vought for testing by these services, though flight tests proved the concept viable, no production contract was forthcoming.

Though maintaining a relatively low profile, E-Systems, with its headquarters in Dallas, is one of Texas' major aerospace companies. It specializes in exotic modifications to little-known air force reconnaissance and surveillance aircraft such as this highly classified Boeing RC-135S.

Both the Boeing E-4A (background) and the Boeing RC-135W have electronics systems that were modified, updated, and/or installed by E-Systems' Greenville division. Most of these systems are technologically sensitive and therefore highly classified.

Bell Helicopter Textron's Hurst plant, one of the largest helicopter production facilities in the U.S., is the most important of several facilities operated by the company. Many thousands of military and civil helicopters have been produced here, with deliveries going to virtually every noncommunist country in the world.

Bell's most famous product is the "Huie". Deriving its name from its UH-1 military designator, this helicopter family was perhaps the most important of the Vietnam War. Several thousand "Huies" served in a large variety of roles in Vietnam, both delivering troops to the front and removing the dead and wounded from battle zones.

The appropriately named "Cobra" was a successful attempt by Bell to develop an armed helicopter for use as a ground support and escort vehicle. Having only two crew members and mounting a formidable collection of rockets and machine guns, it was maneuverable, fast, and terribly effective.

Bell Helicopter Textron

The AH-1 "Cobra" remains in operational service with the U.S. Army and the armed forces of numerous foreign countries. Advanced versions remain in production at Bell, and further design improvements are continuing.

Bell Helicopter Textron

Military versions of Bell's "Jetranger" family include the OH-58, which has been ordered in sizable quantities by both foreign and indigenous military services. An advanced "AHIP" (Army Helicopter Improvement Program) OH-58 is seen with a mast-mounted sight.

Aerospatiale Helicopters of Grand Prairie has recently begun deliveries of its HH-65A search and rescue helicopter to the Coast Guard. Specially equipped for their oftentimes difficult mission, they are a much needed replacement for the now outdated Sikorsky HSS-2 helicopter, which is rapidly approaching its second decade of service.

Texas Air National Guard

Hensley Field has served as home base for a number of air force reserve aircraft, including the Boeing KC-97L inflight refueling tanker. This piston-engine aircraft was made superfluous by the development of jet-powered tankers and the speed requirements of the aircraft being refueled.

The Ellington AFB contingent of the Texas Air National Guard has recently made a transition to the McDonnell F-4 "Phantom II." This fighter, capable of flying at twice the speed of sound, is one of the most common in the air force. It was used extensively during the Vietnam War.

Inflight refueling, here being performed with a Texas Air National Guard F-4C from Ellington AFB and a Boeing KC-135A tanker from the Maine Air National Guard, is the primary means for extending the range of combat aircraft beyond their normal capability.

Kelly AFB's "Super Hangar," one of the largest enclosed facilities of its kind in the world, is operated on an around-the-clock basis, serving to accommodate the maintenance requirements of the air force on select aircraft types such as these Boeing B-47s seen during the early 1960s.

Special service docks were built at Kelly AFB's San Antonio Air Material Area facility during the early 1950s to accommodate the maintenance requirements of the immense Convair B-36. The roof and aft doors were electrically operated and are here seen in their fully open position.

USAF/Kelly AFB History Office

Douglas C-124 cargo aircraft were among the many 1950s-vintage air force types maintained under the auspices of the San Antonio Air Material operation at Kelly AFB. These large troop and cargo haulers were powered by the same engine type used in the B-36 heavy bomber.

USAF/Kelly AFB History Office

The Convair F-102A, a delta wing fighter developed during the early 1950s, was one of the small types also maintained and supported by the San Antonio Air Material Area facility. The F-102A was phased out of air guard service during the early 1970s and today is used as a target drone.

The Space Shuttle "Discovery" heads for its third mission in space, attached to two solid fuel rocket boosters and an external fuel tank. The crew consisted of Thomas Mattingly II, Loren Shriver, James Buchli, Ellison Onizuka, and Gary Payton.

5. The Space Age
The Military Presence

The persistence of cold war tensions brought new contracts to military aerospace firms in north Texas. Vought produced various prototypes during the postwar years, but the company's main production program centered around the unquestionably successful A-7 *Corsair II*. This stubby attack aircraft (first flown in late 1965), superficially resembling its namesake but otherwise having little in common, proved its worth during thousands of sorties in Southeast Asia during the Vietnam War. Capable of carrying extraordinary payloads over long ranges in all kinds of weather, it was eventually ordered by the air force, navy, and several foreign air forces.

The A-7's effectiveness during the Vietnam War caused it to remain in production for the following decade. Word of its combat successes and other attributes eventually spread beyond U.S. borders and production orders from such countries as Portugal and Greece followed with some regularity. Enough orders were received to keep the production line viable into the late 1980s. Interest in the A-7 remains strong as of this writing and there appears to be renewed hope with the revelation of several advanced configuration studies that the U.S. military may again require it for service.

During the past two decades, Vought has diversified into areas outside the airframe production field and now specializes in subcontracting work in electronics, materials, and flight simulation. Additionally, it serves as the prime contractor on the army's MLRS (Multiple Launch Rocket System), the air force's ASAT (Anti-SATellite) aircraft-launched missile, and NASA's *Scout* space launch vehicle. It is also a major parts subcontractor for Boeing on the 747, 767, and 757 airliners, and it provides similar services for McDonnell Douglas with the KC-10A, Lockheed with the C-130, Rockwell International with the B-1B, and Northrop with the ATB (Advanced Technology Bomber). Current annual sales run about $2 billion, with the company employing about 17,000 people at its various plants.

In yet another somewhat bitter struggle to maintain its rightful position as one of the big five primary contractors in the U.S. aerospace industry, General Dynamics succeeded, in 1972, in winning what was then a small air force contract calling for the design and prototyping of two YF-16 lightweight fighters (LWFs). Controversy within the air force concerning the LWF's capabilities versus those of larger fighters raged unabated for over a year; when the dust finally settled, a major production contract had been garnered for General Dynamics' Fort Worth Division.

Today, the F-16 is considered by most authorities to be the best combat aircraft in the world. Small, light, fast, versatile, and extremely maneuverable, it is in production for the U.S. Air Force, the U.S. Navy, and numerous foreign air forces. Total orders stand at over 3,000, with long-term production prospects at almost twice that figure. Some 1,300 have been delivered to date.

Advanced F-16 configurations are the primary concern of the company at this time. One of the few to have reached the full-scale hardware stage to date, the F-16XL, is an extremely advanced ogival-delta configuration that promises improved payload, increased range, and internal space for equipment not applicable to the conventional F-16 configuration. The Fort Worth Division of General Dynamics currently employs about 17,000 people. Annual sales are approximately $2 billion.

Bell continues to remain at the forefront of advanced helicopter technology with various design innovations. Perhaps the most graphic example of the company's future aspirations is the Model 301/XV-15 tiltrotor testbed. A technology proof-of-concept aircraft that takes off and lands like a helicopter but operates in horizontal flight like a conventional aircraft, the XV-15 provides high cruising speeds as well as VTOL (Vertical Take Off and Landing) capability. Military requirements are presently being evolved based on this new Bell development; under a co-sponsored program known as the JVX, a production program (as the V-22 *Osprey*) is expected to develop in the late 1980s. Bell Helicopter today is a division of the Textron Corporation and employs some 6,500. Annual sales are a healthy $672 million and are expected to improve significantly as the need for military and commercial helicopters continues to increase.

Not surprisingly, there are literally hundreds of additional primary contractors and subcontractors in Texas whose renown is not necessarily on a par with that of General Dynamics, Vought, or Bell, but whose contributions to national defense are substantial. The most important of these include the Dallas-based Texas Instruments Corporation, which employs 85,000 and has annual sales of $5.7 billion, and E-Systems, which employs 12,000 and has annual sales of $820 million. Texas Instruments, a high-technology company with heavy involvement in computers, missiles, avionics, and myriad other military-related systems, is now considered an aerospace industry giant and a prime contractor for the various military services. E-Systems, at one time a division of today's Vought Corporation, is a company similar in many respects to Texas Instruments, but somewhat more heavily involved in "black box" technology and the modification of aircraft and related systems. The company is well known for its work in the field of electromagnetic sensors, electronic countermeasures, and remotely piloted vehicles.

The Vietnam War, like the major conflicts that had preceded it, invigorated an already active military aviation community in Texas. Renewed emphasis on pilot training, large infusions of capital into the Texas aerospace industry (which already had a hefty military bent), and the fact that the reigning president throughout many of the more trying days of the Vietnam campaign was a Texan all contributed to a burgeoning military aviation economy. Though much of the rest of the country was torn over the philosophical soundness of U.S. involvement in Vietnam, the Texas antiwar community remained only a muffled voice in a rather pro-war crowd.

Operational military activity in Texas continues at a rapid pace. In 1985, Rockwell International's controversial B-1B strategic heavy bomber entered the operational air force inventory for the first time, and Dyess AFB, just west of Abilene, Texas, was scheduled to become the first unit to operate the strategic bomber as samples were delivered from the production line in California in June or July.

Costing nearly $400 million per copy, the B-1B is the most expensive *mass-produced* aircraft in the history of world military air services. Though it is considered extraordinarily capable and a significant improvement over its predecessors by its proponents, those who oppose it argue with more than a little justification that it is an anachronism in a world of high technology and dwindling support for strategic nuclear systems.

Military aviation's future in the Lone Star state, regardless of the B-1B's prognosis, is unquestionably bright. The state's strong economy, generally excellent weather, and national political status ensure primary involvement in U.S. Army, Air Force, Navy, and Marine Corps planning for the forseeable future.

The "military presence" in contemporary Texas is represented not only by major aerospace contractors, but also by the number of bases dotting the state map. Appendix 1, which lists these installations, is evidence of their significance in terms of employment and payrolls—major factors in the economics of the areas where they are located. The units that are housed on these bases occasionally change, but Appendix 8 summarizes the situation as of 1985.

Texas and Space Exploration

Texas was not only a major center for aeronautics. In the 1960s, the drama of space flight propelled Houston into headlines around the globe. At the historic moment when astronauts first touched down on the surface of the moon in 1969, the first word proclaimed the role of Texas in NASA's space program: "Houston, Tranquility Base here; the *Eagle* has landed." If the city lacked a worldwide identity prior to the space program, the situation changed radically during the 1960s. Similarly, the caricature of Texas as the feudal domain of cattle kings and oil barons necessarily changed to acknowledge the impact of futuristic space technology and astronautical engineers. Like a rocket taking off, the space age hit Texas suddenly and spectacularly.

The origins of modern American space technology date to 1926, when Dr. Robert Goddard successfully launched the world's first chemical rocket from an apple orchard in Massachusetts. World War II brought many significant advances in propulsion systems and guidance mechanisms. In 1944, Texas shared in this growth when the U.S. Army established an Air Defense Center for guided missiles at Fort Bliss, near El Paso. The presence of the missile center and its test range, which sprawled northward into the desert of New Mexico, made it a logical spot to test German rockets captured at the end of the war. The German hardware consisted primarily of the awesome V-2 missiles, capable of carrying a 2,000-lb. payload to a height of 60 miles, then hurtling down on targets at ranges up to 200 miles.

In terms of space technology, the event destined to have the biggest influence in Texas occurred on October 4, 1957, when the Soviet Union launched *Sputnik I*, the world's first artificial satellite. The United States, presumably the world's leader in aerospace technology, had been upstaged. A confused and concerned public followed congressional debates dealing with strategies to regain that leadership. In July, 1958, legislation reorganized the old National Advisory Committee for Aeronautics and created a new organization, the National Aeronautics and Space Administration (NASA).

The space agency moved quickly to set up *Project Mercury*, to put a human into orbit. In 1961, following Alan B. Shepard's suborbital mission, President John F. Kennedy delivered his famous speech setting a national goal of a manned lunar landing by the end of the decade.

It was a monumental task, dramatized by the apparent Soviet lead in space flight. Yuri Gagarin had already made the first manned space flight on April 12, 1961, and the Soviets beat the United States again with the first three-man mission in 1964. In the meantime, the United States began putting together a network of centers to achieve success in the "space race." Cape Canaveral (later Cape Kennedy) in Florida handled rocket launches. Marshall Space Flight Center, in Huntsville, Alabama, had primary responsibility for booster vehicles, like the big *Saturn* rockets. The Space Task Group, at NASA's Langley Research Center in Virginia, took over interim responsibility for astronaut selection, crew training, and mission planning until a new site was selected. The new location would also include the mission control center, and site selection became a major topic of speculation and political pressure.

The site selection team itself worked with specific criteria. Requirements for a temperate climate focused attention on twenty potential locations in southern states from Florida to California. The NASA team looked for an urban area with academic institutions and research facilities; adequate supplies of water and utilities; housing; recreational and cultural attractions; and transportation by water, land, and air. Late in the summer of 1961, the site selection team completed its visits and prepared a recommendation. On September 19, 1961, NASA administrator James Webb made it official: the new Manned Spacecraft Center would be built near Houston, along the shoreline of Clear Lake, one of Galveston Bay's major inlets. Located about twenty-five miles from downtown Houston, the land for the center came from the transfer of 1,000 acres from Rice University to the government.

Indignant protests came from the leaders of losing cities and from congressional representatives of losing states. The decision for Texas, they argued, smacked of pork-barrel politics. NASA's Webb firmly denied such attacks, noting how well Houston fitted the desired profile. No city met all the requirements; certainly Houston filled the bill as well as other frontrunners. But it was no drawback that Albert Thomas of Texas held a key post on the House Appropriations Committee or that Vice-President Lyndon B. Johnson was chair of the National Aeronautics and Space Council.

In any case, the U.S. Army Corps of Engineers went to work on the future Manned Spacecraft Center; the Space Task Group assumed the same title, even though it remained at Langley for several more months. By the fall of 1962, about 1,100 personnel had transferred to Houston, working in temporary offices scattered around the city. Early in 1964, NASA employees began moving into the Manned Spacecraft Center's modernistic complex near Clear Lake, where NASA Road One became a principal thoroughfare. Within two years,

5,000 personnel worked on-site, with several thousand contractor personnel housed in new office buildings around the perimeter.

The Manned Spacecraft Center had an immediate impact on Houston, with secondary effects felt throughout the state. The news of the site selection for MSC triggered a wave of optimism and expectation. The Houston Chamber of Commerce hailed it as "the most significant single event" in the city's economic history. Other cities across the state noted Houston's euphoria. The *Dallas Morning News* remarked that "NASA has put Houston in orbit." In the summer of 1962, when MSC completed its move to Houston, the city acknowledged as much with a rambunctious new slogan, "Space City, U.S.A." Even President Kennedy endorsed futuristic hopes during a visit on September 11, 1962. Addressing a crowd of 50,000 at Rice Stadium, he commented that Houston would become the center of a comprehensive research and development complex.

Kennedy's visit, and his vision of space exploration to come, intensified public fascination with the space program. MSC rapidly mounted a community awareness program for Houston and neighboring communities, dispatching dozens of personnel to PTA groups, business meetings, college campuses, and press briefings. When the Gulf Coast seemed saturated with NASA appearances, the agency expanded across the state, including space forums from the Rio Grande Valley to the Texas Panhandle. MSC also hosted official tours for educational groups and established a permanent display for foreign visitors at the Houston World Trade Center. Grade school children around the state were captivated by visits from a "spacemobile," with rocket paraphernalia and informative demonstrations. Through all these various contacts, citizens and students in the state began to see the world in the bold new dimensions of the Space Age.

The influence of NASA was much more than public relations and transmitting information to civic groups. MSC established special contacts with public schools, including training programs that brought teachers to MSC laboratories on a weekly basis. Similarly, university professors did work in NASA labs, while NASA scientists became visiting lecturers on local campuses. NASA also made thousands of dollars available for graduate student fellowships. A number of cooperative research programs were instituted with Baylor University College of Medicine, the Texas Medical Center, Rice, the University of Houston, and Texas A&M. Colleges realigned curricula to offer space-relevant courses and upgraded graduate programs, including a new department of space science at Rice, the first in the nation.

The economic impact was immense. By 1963, NASA had spent some $150 million for permanent facilities at Clear Lake, with most of the money going to businesses in the Houston area. Monthly expenditures to over 500 local firms for paper clips, typewriters, electronics, and so on amounted to $1 million. Another $80 million in contracts was held by firms from Houston to

San Antonio and El Paso. MSC employees received salaries of about $3 million per month, money that poured into the local economy for housing, groceries, entertainment, and the accoutrements of suburban life. It was an economic cornucopia of awesome proportions, and it was only the beginning. Billions of dollars were to be committed for prime contracts relating to advanced crew capsules, control systems, a lunar lander, and a host of other hardware items. Although much was to be spent by aerospace firms on the West Coast and elsewhere, the prime contractors set up district offices in Houston, and dozens of subcontractors did the same. Flights at Houston Intercontinental Airport rose 7 percent, largely due to the more than 300 business people per month who were attracted by Houston's aerospace boom. Traditional Houston firms like Hughes Tool, Cameron Iron, Brown and Root, and others created electronics or aerospace subsidiaries, diversifying their normal business interests.

Space Age themes quickly appeared across the state, but nowhere was the astronautical motif as pervasive as in Houston. The city's professional basketball team inevitably became the Rockets. When the first covered sports stadium made its appearance, cagey promoters christened it the Astrodome. The baseball team fielded in the stadium became, naturally, the Astros. And, because the huge domed structure doomed the growth of real grass on the playing field, an artificial greensward was required, resulting in the birth of AstroTurf. A huge entertainment complex near the Astrodome emerged as Astroworld; nearby facilities included Astrohall and Astroarena. There were other variations on words related to space, but the prefix *Astro* remained the favorite and embellished numerous commercial establishments, from a fashion shop (Astrotique) to purveyors of transmissions, concrete, insurance, child care (Astro-tots), bail bonds, and insect extermination (Astropest Control).

In addition to the economic impact of civil and military aviation in the state, the aerospace sector continued to have economic, social, and cultural effects. The Manned Spacecraft Center in Houston played a central role in the *Mercury* program, as well as the *Gemini* and *Apollo* programs. Additional missions to the moon followed the first lunar landings in 1969. From Houston, the terse introductory words "This is Mission Control" reminded television and radio audiences around the world of Texas' basic participation in space missions following launches at Cape Kennedy in Florida. Moreover, the NASA operation in Houston was the "lead center" in all of these missions, with major responsibilities for industrial contracts as well as mission operations.

As the primary location for astronaut selection, training, and mission operations, Johnson Space Center, or JSC (the name was changed in 1973), assumed principal leadership in the *Apollo-Soyuz* Test Project, linking American and Soviet spacecraft in orbit in 1975, and in the *Skylab* program from 1973 to 1974. As a space station in orbit, *Skylab* housed a three-man crew, changed three times during the lifetime of the program. It produced significant results in space medicine, manufacturing techniques in space, scientific experiments, and astronomy.

The *Space Shuttle* was another manned program for which JSC had principal responsibility in terms of crew training, vehicle design, and contracting. Beginning in 1981, the reusable *Shuttle* opened a new era in space exploration. JSC also began studies for America's first space station, scheduled for operation in the early 1990s. Collectively, all of these activities funneled millions of dollars into a broad region of the Gulf Coast around Houston. In 1985, JSC employed 3,400 civil service personnel; approximately 5,600 contractor personnel either worked on-site at JSC itself or in one of the dozens of office buildings in the vicinity. The budget at JSC amounted to $2 million per workday for the local economy. Even though Houston's petrochemical industry represented the city's primary employer, the aerospace business contributed an impressive economic total for Houston and for the state of Texas, as well as increasing international recognition of both city and state.

Airlines and Airways

As the major airlines rapidly acquired jet transports in the 1960s, passengers enjoyed a new era of faster, quieter travel. At the same time, improved engine efficiency and the decreasing cost of jet fuel made jet airliners highly economical to operate. The Boeing 707, which had entered service in 1958, was soon joined by transports of similar appearance and performance, like the Douglas DC-8 and the Convair 880/990 series. In addition, the Boeing 727 began flying in 1964. A trijet, with two engines on the aft fuselage and a third mounted in the tail, the 727 also featured an array of flaps and wing slots for enhanced lift at lower speeds. It proved to be an unusually versatile airliner with performance that enabled it to operate from many airports incapable of handling the larger jet transports. Since the major airlines flew the same Boeing, Douglas, and Convair jet transports, marketing efforts were bolder, in an effort to win customer interest. By the mid-1960s, Braniff's fleet was almost entirely comprised of jet equipment. To attract attention, Braniff commissioned the internationally acclaimed artist Alexander Calder to repaint its DC-8 transports in multicolored abstract designs characteristic of his style. Braniff's planes, painted in various shades of blue, green, red, and other hues, were easy to spot at any airport. During the early 1980s, when Braniff operated a big 747 on intercontinental flights to London, the plane was quickly and appropriately dubbed "The Big Orange."

Brightly painted or not, the jets of Delta, American, Eastern, Continental, United, TWA, and many foreign carriers soon took thousands of Texans on business or pleasure throughout the United States and around the world.

Following KLM's Houston/Montreal/Amsterdam service in 1957, Air France opened Houston/New York/Paris service in 1962, using Boeing 707 transports; British Caledonian introduced long-range 707 airliners for nonstop Houston/London service in 1977 and later used the Douglas DC-10 on these flights. By the 1970s, completion of both Houston Intercontinental and DFW meant that the big new Boeing 747 transports could mount additional nonstop service to European cities. For DFW, the goal was reached in 1978, with direct flights to London and Frankfurt. Two years later, DFW won single-plane service to the Orient, when Thai International launched service to Tokyo and Bangkok. Along with Latin American connections, trans-Atlantic and trans-Pacific routes are now taken for granted by passengers using airports at Houston and DFW, which offer nonstop flights, and from San Antonio, which offers direct flights via several airlines.

In the early postwar years, most of the local or feeder lines had used piston-engine equipment. Beginning with DC-3 transports, often acquired as war surplus, they moved on to twin-engine *Convairs*, followed by *Convairs* re-engined with turboprops. This progression characterized the growth of Trans-Texas in the mid-1960s. Since the major trunk lines flew faster, quieter jet transports, business travelers and other patrons aboard the propeller-driven airplanes of the feeder lines complained about old-fashioned coffee-grinders. New smaller jets like the Douglas DC-9 and Boeing 737 held the promise of operating from the airports of smaller cities, while offering the speed and comfort of bigger jets. Between 1965 and 1969, these jets rapidly appeared on domestic feeder routes; Trans-Texas began DC-9 service in the fall of 1966. Although the jets carried many more passengers than the piston-engine transports they replaced, the jets' popularity kept seats full and brought increased profits. Their speed and range also gave the local airlines regional status. Trans-Texas reflected this trend with a long new interstate route in 1968, all the way from Houston to Los Angeles via Albuquerque. The airline also adopted a more grandiose title, Texas International Airlines.

The new equipment, additional routes, and success now took them into many of the same markets flown by the major airlines. It was an era of excitement for travelers, who enjoyed the reductions in fares, especially as the locals moved into larger geographic patterns. By the 1980s, Texas International was not only flying west, to Los Angeles and other cities, but east to Washington, D.C., and to New York. The intense competition generated extensive and colorful advertising campaigns, like the Texas International promotion of "peanuts fares," including illustrations of peanut-shaped airliners wing-ing toward a variety of new destinations.

The rapid expansion of Texas International and its cousins came as a result of the Airline Deregulation Act of 1978, permitting the marketplace to sort out airline routes and schedules. By this time, the CAB, scheduled to self-destruct in 1984, had also recast its nomenclature for different levels of airlines. An annual revenue of $1 billion or more qualified an airline as "major"; $75 million to $1 billion was the "national" category; the remainder were "regional" carriers, with further gradations for large and medium regionals.

In the meantime, another kind of specialized passenger service began to emerge, an intrastate carrier specializing only in service between metropolitan areas within the state. Few states were large enough to have two or more such centers. Airlines in California were the first to offer such service, followed by Texas. In 1967, Southwest Airlines applied for a certificate from the Texas Aeronautics Commission. Braniff, Continental, and Texas International argued against the service, which did not clear all of its legal hurdles until 1971. Southwest began in the Dallas/Houston and Dallas/San Antonio markets, scheduling twelve daily round trips on the former and six on the latter. Southwest's *Love Bird* service, with Boeing 737 equipment, began in the spring. At $40 for a round trip, the upstart company undercut the competition by $14 to $16. As it rolled up impressive profits with its low-frills, low-cost fares, Southwest became known as one of the most innovative carriers in the industry. Regular travelers could save considerable time by advance purchase of prepunched IBM-card packets of tickets. Stewardesses and counter personnel appeared in eye-catching outfits of bright red hotpants and short orange vinyl skirts. Many feminists sniffed at the overtly sexy hype, but male travelers kept the Southwest jets flying at full capacity. The airline eventually clothed its female personnel in more sedate uniforms, but innovations continued, including automatic ticket dispensers. One simply inserted one's credit card into the machine, punched in the destination, removed the credit card along with a ticket, and headed for the boarding area. In order to keep up with Southwest, competitors likewise reduced fares, offered additional flights, and generally improved service. As airline historian R. E. G. Davies succinctly notes, "Texan air commuters were delighted on all counts."

Deregulation brought unbridled competition to the industry. Those in favor of the move approved the decline in fares and the increase in services to many cities. Critics noted that such advantages accrued primarily to larger cities in attractive market areas; smaller cities and markets off the beaten track suffered decreases in service and increases in prices. Many airlines used deregulation to expand into high-volume markets, including major intercontinental routes. These were the steps taken by Braniff, which bit off more than it could chew. One of the oldest airlines in the country, Braniff declared bankruptcy in May, 1982, stranding hundreds of travelers and throwing thousands out of work.

To be sure, there were many factors in Braniff's demise. Oil embargoes imposed in the Middle East drove fuel costs to unprecedented levels; there was a stiff recession; the 1981 strike by air traffic controllers meant the reduction of many revenue-generating flights. But Braniff had also flung itself into an inordinate expansion program and various costly experiments, including a short-lived interchange service from Dallas to London/Paris by the Anglo-French *Concorde* supersonic transport. The costly service lasted eighteen months and required the high-speed, high-altitude *Concorde* to cruise at subsonic speed and unfavorable altitudes over the continental United States. Beginning in 1979, Braniff also added dozens of new domestic segments, offered discount fares, and launched new services to the Far East and Europe. Some longtime observers of air transport felt that a sensible CAB might have kept destructive fare wars and grandiose, but impractical, route expansion under control. Braniff finally reorganized in 1984 under the financial control of the Hyatt Hotel chain. As a lean, born-again operation, Braniff nonetheless found it difficult to recapture the success of its earlier years.

In contrast to Braniff, brash Texas International seemed to thrive in the deregulated environment. Flush with profits, TI, as it became known, decided to become a national force through the acquisition of an existing carrier with established routes and clientele. The target was, appropriately, National Airlines, which also had routes to London and to the Caribbean. Caught in the pressures of the exceedingly competitive East Coast environment, it was in trouble in the late 1970s. After a spirited bidding war for control of the airline waged by TI and Pan Am, which wanted access to National's domestic markets, Pan Am won. Texas Air Corporation, the holding company for TI, lost the battle but won the profits when Pan Am bought up the shares that TI controlled. The chief of TI, Frank Lorenzo, now had an even larger war chest with which to pursue another takeover target. His sights settled on Continental Airlines, a company with an extensive national route system that also extended west across the Pacific to Hawaii. Texas Air Corporation successfully won control of Continental in 1982 and moved Continental's headquarters to Houston. Although Texas Air Corporation retained its name, the airline's identity as Texas International gave way to the designation Continental Airlines.

Lorenzo incurred the ire of passengers, personnel, and pilots by declaring a Chapter 11 bankruptcy in 1983. In statements to the press, Texas Air Corporation officials explained their action by citing operational costs, high interest rates, fuel prices, and other factors. Cynics saw the bankruptcy move as a tactic to break up union wage agreements. In any case, courts cleared the way for Continental to resume flying operations, although on a reduced scale. In addition, pilots and other personnel who went back to work did so at lower salaries than before. Continental Airlines remained aloft with a line of continuity dating back to 1934, when Varney Speed Lines, a Continental predecessor, operated Lock-

heed *Vegas* from El Paso into Colorado and New Mexico.

During the mid-1960s, yet another type of airline emerged, generically known as commuters. Using light, twin-engine aircraft, they provided service from small, outlying communities to larger airports. One operation, Metro Airlines of Houston, offered service to Houston Intercontinental Airport, on the city's northern edge, from the Clear Lake City area, about fifty miles away on the city's southern edge. As home of the Johnson Space Flight Center, its aerospace contractors, and several large petrochemical companies, the Clear Lake area generated enough business to make up to fifty flights daily at the height of the space program. The Short Take Off and Landing characteristics (STOL) of the de Havilland DHC-6 *Twin Otter* allowed it to operate from a single short strip in the middle of a growing urban and residential area.

Elsewhere in Texas many other commuters took to the air. In 1978, the Texas Aeronautic Commission issued certificates to no less than twelve such operators, located in several different sections of the state. Equipment varied, including models of Beech, Cessna, and Piper aircraft, primarily twin-engine designs. During the 1980s, major metropolitan areas like Dallas–Fort Worth and Houston also had several helicopter airlines that carried passengers to airports from congested areas downtown.

Houston Intercontinental was among the first new airports built expressly for the jet era. For years, the city had relied on Hobby Airport, which could handle planes as big as the Boeing 707, but its runways were not adequate for some of the big new jets being designed. Since the city had grown around it, there was no further opportunity to build newer, longer runways. The city needed a brand-new field. With costs projected at $100 million, work on Houston Intercontinental Airport began in 1962. The original concept called for a terminal flanked by two major runways. To eliminate endless walking between ticket counters, gates, and baggage areas, the terminal was designed as a series of vertically stacked levels, connected by escalators, ramps, and elevators. A series of "fingers" branched off the main terminal, leading to boarding areas. By the time the field opened in 1969, its initial outlines had changed somewhat. Runways no longer straddled a single terminal; rather, a pair of terminals and a hotel sat in a line to one side of the major runways. The vertical concept was still evident: arriving passengers entered at a middle level of each terminal, to reach ticket counters and departure lounges; departing passengers left from the lower level, where baggage areas were located. There was a parking area on the third level atop each terminal, and additional parking on the street level.

Since the distance between terminals was considerable, especially for passengers arriving or departing from the hotel at the end of the line of buildings, a novel passenger-moving system was incorporated into the design. This was the "people-mover," an automated series of passenger cars that ran on a continuous track looping underground beneath the three structures. The cars made automatic stops at specified points every few minutes to accommodate people from parking lots as well as terminals. The final system, designed by engineers from Disney World, proved to be admirably trouble-free and efficient and became an important model for similar systems. Houston Intercontinental soon became a major airport in the United States, consistently ranked in the top fifteen in terms of passengers and ranked seventh for numbers of international arrivals and departures. In the 1980s, the airport offered service by some two dozen major airlines and several commuters. In addition to foreign service offered by American flag lines, a dozen foreign airlines also used the airport, offering service to thirty cities around the world. Several other airlines offered freight services on domestic as well as international routes, making Houston a leading city in this category.

One of the nation's liveliest aviation stories of the 1960s centered on a sprawling new airport built between Dallas and Fort Worth. Its size, unique arrangement, and sudden role as one of the world's premier airports brought worldwide recognition to a facility universally referred to by its initials—DFW.

With two major fields located in cities so close together, sharing many commercial ties, proposals for a joint facility inevitably succeeded. But the legendary rivalry of Dallas and Fort Worth disrupted progress for nearly a quarter of a century. The eventual development of Dallas/Fort Worth Airport had much to do with Fort Worth's drive for aeronautical parity with Dallas. Fort Worth's stubborn persistence underscored the growing perception that airliners had indeed replaced passenger trains in long-distance travel. Furthermore, any city with an eye to the future required an impressive airport as a symbol of its growth and progress. Airports had replaced train terminals as the gateway to a city; an eye-catching airport was a monument both to civic pride and to public relations. The splendor of Love Field threatened Fort Worth in more ways than one.

Early in the 1940s, when the DFW area began to boom as a center for aircraft production and business travel mushroomed, the Civil Aeronautics Administration recommended a regional airport somewhere in the neighborhood of Arlington, about midway between Dallas and Fort Worth. Bulldozers went to work on the site in 1942, even though details were still under negotiation by the CAA and the cities involved. Planners sketched out a site, taking into account the existing access roads and the airport's layout relative to prevailing winds. When drawings crossed the desk of Dallas mayor Woodall Rogers, the first major snag occurred. The terminal's entrance faced the wrong way, Rogers growled. His administration simply would not accept a plan in which the terminal's back side confronted Dallas.

Meanwhile, builders completed work on the airport to the point where it served as a training field during World War II. Bucking opposition from its rival in the postwar years, Fort Worth annexed the site in 1948, renamed it Amon G. Carter Field, and upgraded facilities. During the 1950s, Fort Worth made several overtures to Dallas for joint ownership, changing the name again to a more neutral title—Greater Southwest International Airport. Dallas responded with more improvements to Love Field. In the meantime, traffic at Fort Worth's airport fell sharply. During the early 1960s, the Civil Aeronautics Board began to tire of the bickering and refused to allocate any more federal funds to two airports so close together. In September, 1964, the CAB told the cities to agree on a single site or the CAB would do it for them. The next year, a joint organization, the Interim Airport Board, agreed on an area near Grapevine. The Dallas/Fort Worth Airport was finally under way.

True to the Texas heritage of having lots of space and thinking bigger than anyone else, DFW sprawled over 17,800 acres, making it the largest airport in the world. Presiding over this city-sized piece of real estate was the Dallas/Fort Worth Regional Airport Board, set up in 1968. The board's eleven members were divided to reflect population ratios of the two cities, giving Fort Worth four positions and Dallas seven. Given the cities' past record of municipal infighting, the board has been remarkably effective. One especially successful decision was the hiring of Tom Sullivan to oversee the design and construction of the new airport. Sullivan arrived on the job with over thirty years of aviation experience, including highly regarded projects at airports such as Newark, La Guardia, and John F. Kennedy. He played a major role in rethinking the traditional design with one central terminal, choosing instead to adopt a futuristic concept of several terminals looped along a central spine. This approach permitted travelers to drive directly to airline gates. Passengers who had to change airlines moved between distant terminals via an automated transportation link called Airtrans. After early troubles, Airtrans ran at nearly 100 percent efficiency, pleasing passengers; pilots appreciated the generous space between the terminals that gave them plenty of room to maneuver big airliners.

Costs for the airport included $65 million in land and $810 million in construction. To cover construction costs, eight air carriers agreed to underwrite revenue bonds; by 1984, additional outlays brought the total investment to $1.6 billion. As a self-supporting operation, DFW retired the bonds from income generated by landing fees, parking fees, terminal rent, and other sources.

A ceremonial opening took place during a four-day celebration in September, 1973. Over 150,000 visitors came out for airshows and other events, proving that modern-day airport openings had as much drawing power as Brownsville's, some forty-four years earlier. Brownsville heralded the 120 mph Ford Tri-Motors; DFW welcomed the supersonic *Concorde*, which made its first landing on the North American continent during the ceremonies. The official opening occurred on January 13, 1974, when American Airlines Flight 341 winged in from Little Rock. All told, the airport listed 9 major carriers and 3 commuters, offering service to

110 American cities and 2 foreign destinations.

Ten years later, DFW Airport offered service by 37 American carriers and 5 foreign flag lines. These companies served over 150 cities in the United States, plus 24 foreign cities on 3 continents. The airport became the headquarters of American Airlines in 1979 and its primary hub in 1981. In 1983, DFW ranked fifth in the nation for passenger traffic and sixth in the world. For the state of Texas, 50 percent of all air passengers and 60 percent of domestic cargo passed through DFW.

The impact of DFW in north Texas has been immense. During the 1970s, the population in the Dallas–Fort Worth region rose by 25 percent, its labor force by 40 percent, and retail sales by an astonishing 260 percent. It is true that many forces were responsible for this growth, but the impact of DFW Airport was probably the most significant. The airport itself represented a major industry, employing 22,000 persons and generating about $4 billion per year. The airport was also a key factor in attracting corporations. Between 1974 and 1984, over 2,300 businesses, new or relocated, moved into the area, making the DFW Metroplex third in the nation (behind New York and Chicago) as a center for corporate headquarters. Although many considerations—such as low taxes, climate, and so on—obviously influenced corporate decisions, DFW Airport represented a major attraction. "In repeated studies over the last 10 years," one planning official noted, "DFW Airport is the most often mentioned reason for a company move to the Metroplex." Corporate moves broadened the airport's economic impact. Analysts calculated that when a corporation brought 100 people into the area, another $4 million annually found its way into the regional economy. As the Dallas–Fort Worth area grew, it created a ripple effect, stimulating economic activity throughout the state.

The sudden emergence of Southwest, TI, and others—like Muse Air, started in 1980—renewed the importance of smaller, older fields like Love in Dallas and Hobby in Houston. For years, they operated in the shadow of bigger newer complexes like DFW and Houston Intercontinental. Their principal traffic took the form of charter operators, corporate aircraft, and itinerant general aviation pilots. But the rationale of Southwest was fast, convenient service for business travelers between the central areas of the two cities, where the principal banks, corporate centers, and business offices were located. This meant flying between airports that were closer in, which eliminated tedious walks through cavernous terminals and interminable drives downtown on congested highways. In this context, direct flights between Love and Hobby fields, a scheme pioneered by Southwest Airlines, became very appealing. Other carriers began to take note; soon, regional carriers like Ozark, U.S. Air, Republic, and others winged into Hobby, although Southwest continued to dominate Love. The rising traffic at Hobby and Love required a new round of improvements to both airports to cope with dramatically increased passenger traffic.

Although the ripple effect at Love and Hobby was less pronounced in comparison to DFW and Houston Intercontinental, the appearance of new motels, restaurants, office buildings, and other construction in the immediate vicinity of these airports gave testimony to the tangible impact of their activities. In the 1980s, San Antonio launched a major airport improvement program, and Austin also upgraded its airfield. The subsequent appearance of other commercial construction around these fields again reinforced the significance of aviation's ripple effect in these cities and elsewhere throughout the state.

Although not creating the headlines of space flight and airline travel, general aviation activities continued at a lively pace throughout the state. Few Texas projects have had as much impact on aircraft design for one type as a product from Texas A&M called the Ag-1. The project also helped serve as the springboard for the career of Leland Snow, a native of Brownsville. If most of the agricultural airplanes in the world look very much like Snow's *Air Tractor* and its forebears, it is no accident. Conceived from firsthand experience as a crop duster and crafted with the insights of an aeronautical engineer, Snow's burly ag planes are already legendary.

Growing up in Brownsville, Snow was drawn to the airport where Pan Am's transports winged southward toward the mythical jungles and mountains of Latin America. As a teenager, he did odd jobs for various flight service operators and finally attained his cherished goal, becoming a licensed pilot. When he enrolled at Texas A&M, he knew his major would be in aeronautical engineering. Before he graduated, in 1952, Snow became involved in a special project to design and build a new agricultural aircraft, one that would have increased payload and performance, but would eliminate the vices that attended so many gallant Stearman biplanes, the standard crop-dusting planes built for training in the 1930s. The air force ordered thousands of Stearmans during World War II. As postwar surplus, dozens of them were converted for agricultural work by removing the forward cockpit and creating additional space for a compartment to hold a variety of chemicals. The Stearman was a rugged old bird, but not designed for climbing turns on hot summer days while dusting crops from an altitude of fifteen feet. Many planes stalled, and many pilots died.

The project at A&M got started when Cessna, Piper, and Beechcraft decided to offer support for the design of a new ag plane, dubbed the Ag-1, that would take advantage of postwar advances in aerodynamics, construction, and materials. George Haddaway, publisher of an aviation magazine in Texas, had pushed the idea; the principal professor who guided the structural design was Prof. Ben Hamner. The project also benefited from the contributions of Fred Weick, a veteran NASA designer and engineer working as a Piper consultant. As a result of the collaborative project, Piper Aircraft and Cessna evolved designs of their own. Piper took the lead in mass-producing a new plane, called the *Pawnee*, largely at the insistence of Bill Piper's son, Howard "Pug" Piper. Piper's *Pawnee* thriftily used the tail group of the *Super Cub* and the wings of the J-3 *Cub*, although the new plane was a low-wing design. Cessna eventually brought out its own series, beginning with the *Agwagon* in 1966.

The original A&M plane, the Piper, and the Cessna were all very similar in design concept, emphasizing pilot safety and operational reliability. The cockpit area was heavily reinforced and featured an arched, tubular framework to protect the pilot in a crash. Details of aircraft construction and of spraying and dusting equipment were carefully considered from the standpoint of practical operations. But Leland Snow developed other ideas, based on personal experience, that resulted in the Snow S-1 and S-2, planes that preceded Piper and Cessna and established significant patterns for ag plane production.

Snow built the S-1 and became a barnstorming crop duster during the mid-1950s, working fields from Texas to Nicaragua. Many pilots saw the plane do its job and signed up to buy one, provided Snow could get a loan to go into production. Banks refused the loans because Snow did not want to incorporate, believing that he would risk losing control of the design and construction of the production version, the S-2. Meanwhile, he saved what he could from his dusting jobs and took deposits from forty-one operators who put money down for a design they instinctively admired. In 1958, a group of businessmen from Olney, in north central Texas, backed an $18,500 loan and agreed to build a small manufacturing facility at the Olney Municipal Airport. Leland Snow, age twenty-seven, became president of the Snow Aeronautical Company.

Using temporary facilities at the airport, Snow and a handful of local co-workers built the precedent-setting S-2, which took to the air early in 1958 and received its CAA certification in July. Its cockpit was situated closer to the tail, behind the cargo compartment, so that more of the airplane's structure would absorb the impact of the crash. It featured other safety and operational features based on Snow's experience in dusting and spraying work in a wide range of climates and topographies. A big radial engine simplified maintenance and gave the plane an unusually large load capacity, which meant that operators could treat more acres before landing to load up again. One of the first buyers, from Colorado, pointed out that the S-2 took only two trips to deliver the same payload that his other planes had to make in three. The plane developed an international reputation. In 1965, Snow completed his 300th airplane; 100 of them had gone to customers in Latin America, Africa, and other countries, including New Zealand.

Snow's success attracted wide attention in the aviation industry, as well as keen interest from some corporations looking for promising investments. Rockwell-Standard, one of the world's largest producers of car and truck components, also built the twin-engine *Aero Commander* and broadened its aviation interests in 1965. When Rockwell-Standard acquired Snow Aeronautical, Snow became a vice-president of the Aero Commander Division and general manager of the Olney

operation, a position he kept through a corporate merger with North American Aviation in 1967, which created the North American Rockwell Corporation.

Production was expanded, new models were added, and improvements were made, but Snow's old fear of losing control to corporate interests was realized in 1970, when North American decided to move ag plane production to a plant in Albany, Georgia. The corporation attributed the move to a sales slump for ag planes, coupled with unused plant capacity in Albany that permitted it to consolidate manufacturing efforts. Snow was disappointed, since Olney had taken a chance on his dream in 1958 and had shared his pride in the success of the planes built there. Snow stuck it out with North American for less than two years, then resigned and came back to Olney to start again, working with only a handful of people to design and build a new plane, once more backed by a group of local business people.

The new concern was called Air Tractor Incorporated, and the first plane, the AT-300, made its first flight, with Snow at the controls, in the autumn of 1973. Within two months, a record time, the plane was certified, and Snow was airborne again with a remarkably successful aircraft.

Some people are just never satisfied with a plane's performance. The plane itself may do quite well, but there are pilots and engineers who constantly see ways to improve its comfort, convenience, range, cruising speed, and so on. Ed Swearingen of San Antonio was one such inveterate tinkerer. During the 1960s, his repair and maintenance shop made a specialty of making changes to the Beech *Twin Bonanza* and the Beech Model 65 *Queen Air*, by installing bigger engines and making a number of exterior and interior refinements. Irresistibly, the Swearingen operation was drawn to an even more radical conversion—one so comprehensive that the resulting aircraft was certificated as a totally different airplane, the Swearingen *Merlin II*.

The new plane began as the *Merlin I*, with modified landing gear from a Beech Twin *Bonanza*, modified wings and tail group from a Beech *Queen Air*, and a completely new pressurized and streamlined fuselage produced by Swearingen. During flight tests, the *Merlin I* seemed an ideal candidate for turboprop engines, so it was shelved in favor of the *Merlin II*. Powered by turboprops built by Pratt & Whitney of Canada, the *Merlin II* first flew in 1965, with FAA certification the next year. Over the next five years, the fast, eight- to ten-place corporate plane sold so well that the *Merlin III* resulted. This larger version carried heftier engines in redesigned nacelles, a new landing gear, and a redesigned tail group. Like its predecessor, the *Merlin III* succeeded as a high-performance corporate turboprop, with subsequent models offering a range of options in passenger seating and performance.

With growing experience in twin-engine aircraft, a Swearingen design team came up with a brand-new pressurized turboprop transport, the *Metro*. With a capacity for twenty passengers, the *Metro* represented the first such plane built in Texas. Deliveries began in

1973, and the *Metro* proved popular with numerous airlines in the United States, as well as several countries abroad. It was followed by *Metro II* and *Metro III*, firmly establishing Swearingen in the market for commuter airliners. In addition to an integral airstair/door forward, the *Metro* series was designed for quick conversion to cargo space and included a large door aft, a feature that enhanced the plane's utility for many operators, especially those in overseas areas, where cargo often represented a significant source of revenue.

The growing success of Swearingen corporate planes and transports attracted the attention of several larger aerospace firms. Fairchild Industries acquired the San Antonio company in 1972 and operated it as a subsidiary. With an eye on the expanding market for turboprop commuter transports, the company planned a larger plane than the *Metro* series, designed to utilize many new fabrication technologies, instrumentation, and fuel-efficient engines of the 1980s. As Fairchild Aircraft Corporation (the name was changed in 1983), it also followed another new pattern of the 1980s, choosing to make the development of a joint international effort. In this instance, an agreement was reached with Saab-Scania of Sweden, an experienced manufacturer of light planes, transports, and high-performance military aircraft. By linking, the two companies shared the high development costs and dispersed the possible losses if the project proved unsuccessful. But the project seemed promising, given the strong reputation for quality and performance enjoyed by both companies. Moreover, the Swedish firm could share in the plane's potential American market, already represented by American operators of the *Metro* series, while the American firm improved its chances in the highly competitive European market. Final assembly was done in Sweden, and the plane began reaching its first customers in 1984. The Saab-Fairchild 340 *Commuter* symbolized the sophisticated, complex, multinational character of many aerospace projects of the 1980s.

The helicopter industry in Texas continued to play a significant role. In the late 1960s, Bell began development of a new helicopter that had a familiar outline but featured a revolutionary change in its twin turboshaft engines. The airframe was taken from the Model 205/-UH-1 type, but the twin turboshaft engine was developed by Pratt & Whitney Aircraft of Canada. In fact, development of the Model 212, as it was called, was distinctly international from the start. In addition to Pratt & Whitney of Canada, the Canadian government itself assisted in financing the project as a joint venture. The twin turboshaft engines were mounted side by side, but a gearbox transferred all the power to a single shaft. The whole machinery package was designed to run the engines at reduced power; in the event of one engine's failure, sensors signaled the remaining engine to take over at full power, giving the 212 a true engine-out capability. The military services of both the United States and Canada began to take deliveries by 1971, when the FAA gave certification to the civil version. The *Twin Two-Twelve*, as it was known, became widely used for offshore operations and other tasks around the world.

Although other models followed, they were principally derivatives of various military designs. When the company announced a purely civil design in 1974, the announcement caught the attention of the international aviation press. The Bell Model 222 was the first commercial twin-engine helicopter in the United States. The first prototypes flew two years later, and certification came in 1979. The new chopper incorporated new technologies developed earlier for both military and civil machines, including an advanced main rotor hub design and glass fiber/stainless steel rotor blades. A basic version carried a pilot and seven passengers; models for offshore operations were IFR (instrument flight rules)–equipped for a crew of two; the executive version, also IFR-equipped, had luxury appointments for five to six passengers. With the advent of craft designed and built solely for the civilian market, the helicopter seemed to have come to full maturity.

International development programs also appeared in the helicopter business. One of the earliest was Bell Helicopter's joint venture with Canada in the late 1960s. However, a Japanese firm, Mitsubishi, inaugurated the state's first true international aviation program in 1965. While the Mitsubishi work did not involve joint venture activities in R&D, the manufacture of a Japanese plane in the Texas Hill Country marked the first time that a foreign design in the general aviation field was actually built in America. Mitsubishi was no stranger to aircraft design and production. By the end of World War II, the Japanese company had built some 80,000 aircraft over its twenty-five-year history. In the postwar era, Mitsubishi performed overhaul and maintenance work for the U.S. Air Force and, in 1956, began building the first of 300 North American F-86 *Sabres* under license.

At about the same time, Mitsubishi started the design of a light utility transport powered by two turboprop engines. Designated the MU-2, the first prototype was flown in 1963. It differed from most American corporate twins of similar size and performance. The MU-2 had a high wing, giving the propellers plenty of ground clearance. This meant that the fuselage sat low to the runway, so that entry and exit for passengers was simple and convenient; cargo handling was also enhanced. The main gear retracted into fairings which were externally attached to the lower portion of the pressurized fuselage. The wings were thus unencumbered by retracting main gear and had a very favorable airfoil for high-speed flight. Although the MU-2 looked somewhat stubby, it was a very clean airplane in aerodynamic terms, and its impressive cruise speed of 370 mph was a strong selling point.

The principal market for corporate planes was North America, so that is where Mitsubishi decided to build its airplane. In practice, basic airframe components went to San Angelo for final assembly. This procedure also facilitated installation of the numerous American components on the two models marketed worldwide—the *Solitaire* and the slightly longer *Marquise*, which could seat up to eleven passengers. American components included avionics, engines, propellers, interiors, and other equipment. The San Angelo production line turned out planes not only for the North American market, but also for the international market.

In 1979, Mitsubishi entered the highly competitive executive jet market with the *Diamond*, built and finished at San Angelo by the same procedures established for the MU-2 turboprop series. With several hundred Mitsubishi turboprops and jets in worldwide service, this unique Japanese-Texas partnership has been remarkably fruitful.

The skies of Texas are plied by a bewildering variety of aircraft on an equally bewildering variety of tasks. Southwest Conference football games may be covered by aerial TV operated from a distinctive Goodyear blimp, based in Houston. Along the Gulf Coast, dozens of helicopters make their runs to offshore oil rigs, carrying relief crews, mail, groceries, repairs, and many other cargoes in their shuttle operations. In west central Texas, hang gliders fill the sky with bright, multicolored wings. Elsewhere around the state, weekend pleasure fliers take to the air in equally colorful ultralights. There are sport balloonists and several firms that offer balloon flights to romantic citizens; the touchdown is traditionally followed by an elegant champagne picnic. Special charter airlines fly passengers, packages, and other priority mail. Flying fast business jets, several companies run overnight aerial delivery services to banks in other parts of the United States.

And Texans still take to the air in search of records. Using a Bell *Long Ranger II* helicopter, the *Spirit of Texas*, Ross Perot, Jr., and Jay Coburn hopscotched around the globe from September 1 to September 30, 1982, setting a new record for circumnavigating the world in a rotary-winged aircraft.

The uses for aircraft have been as varied as the human imagination. Helicopters have played a dramatic role in emergency medical service. *Life Flight*, supported by Hermann Hospital in Houston, Texas, offers convincing evidence of such emergency work and is frequently cited as a model for other cities. Begun in 1976, *Life Flight* expanded from one to three helicopters in as many years and averaged over 1,000 runs per year. Later, the service added a *Learjet*, enabling patients to reach specialized facilities in the world-famous Texas Medical Center from all over the United States, as well as most of Canada and Central America. Similarly, aircraft can speed the shipment of human organs for transplants; transfer by scheduled airlines simply may not be fast enough. In Houston, an emergency transportation service called *OIL* (Oil Industry Lifesaving) *Flights* solved the time problem. The organization is a group of fifty-nine oil-related firms that have agreed to donate the use of their corporate aircraft to carry surgical teams to obtain an organ and deliver it to waiting patients. Within two years of its organization in 1983, Oil Flight could call on over forty-five corporate planes in twelve different states. If no volunteer plane is available, the group has pledged to charter a jet to do the job.

Another unique aeronautical medical service, Project Orbis, combats blindness on a global scale. The idea came from Dr. David Paton, chair of the Department of Ophthalmology at the Baylor College of Medicine in Houston. Paton had spent years flying around the world, demonstrating surgical procedures, but the unavailability of certain specialized equipment in many countries frustrated the transfer of advanced techniques. Project Orbis is a flying eye hospital, uniquely equipped for state-of-the-art surgery and for teaching. Worldwide, more than 42 million people are blind, and another 500 million suffer from eye diseases that could lead to blindness. According to a Project Orbis document, "nearly two-thirds of these cases could be prevented or cured if only current medical knowledge were as widespread throughout the world as the tragedy of sight loss." Organized in 1982, Project Orbis is physically represented by a DC-8, donated by United Airlines. The four-engine jet was modified to include an ultramodern operating suite studded with TV cameras; an eighteen-seat classroom with TV monitors to observe operations in progress; an examination/treatment area equipped for laser work; a library; a patient recovery area; and several other compartments. Retired pilots volunteered to fly the plane; rotating teams of surgeons and assistants donate their time during the length of a mission, which usually reaches a dozen or more countries. Thousands of patients and doctors have benefited from Project Orbis, and a surprising amount of information on surgical techniques from other countries has been acquired by the American teams who went out to teach. In its primary mission, transmitting advanced surgical knowledge, Project Orbis has had outstanding success.

Aviation has become an integral part of government activities, affecting Texas at the local, state, and federal levels. At the local level, many Texas cities rely on one or more helicopters for a variety of tasks, including traffic control, crime prevention, and general law enforcement. After getting three helicopters in 1970, the Houston Police Department eventually acquired a fleet of sixteen. Many county jurisdictions also bought helicopters. At the state level, the Texas Rangers and the Department of Public Safety use a number of rotary and fixed-wing aircraft. In fact, the State of Texas operates a fleet of thirty-three airplanes and nine helicopters. All aircraft are under the jurisdiction of the Aircraft Pooling Board, which has responsibility for their custody, control, operation, and maintenance. At Robert Mueller Airport in Austin, the Pooling Board maintains hangars and offices for its activities, although about one-half of the aircraft are stationed at cities elsewhere in the state. Many planes are twin-engine turboprops, intended to carry several officials on state business at one time, although the range of types runs from a Mitsubishi *Diamond 1A* executive jet to a single-engine Cessna 182 allocated to the Parks and Wildlife Department. For state agencies without a plane, or in case of special need, the Aircraft Pooling Board arranges for temporary assignment of a plane from a different agency.

A number of aircraft owned by federal agencies also

operate in Texas. Less well known are the activities of the Immigration and Naturalization Service, which flies regular patrols along the border with Mexico, scouting for illicit drug activity and for illegal aliens. The operations of the Coast Guard have been more publicized. With major points of operation at Corpus Christi and at Houston, the Coast Guard covers the length of the Texas Gulf Coast. Coast Guard helicopters make rescues day and night in all kinds of weather. Until 1984–1985, the Coast Guard also flew twin-engine C-131 transports, navy versions of the *Convair* airliner. After that time, Guard pilots began flying *Falcon 20* jets, produced in France by Dassault and outfitted in the United States. Designated the HU-25 *Guardian*, it included modifications such as sophisticated radar and arrangements to jettison specially equipped rescue boats through a hatch in the underside. The Coast Guard counted on the jet's ability to reach accident scenes at high speeds, before storms and high seas overwhelmed victims.

In the 1980s, the pace of aviation activity in Texas showed few signs of slowing down. Historically, Texans used commercial air service in numbers well above the national average. In 1970, just over 10 million passengers boarded airliners in the state. That figure easily doubled by 1980; in 1982, state officials reported 30,662,441 enplanements, just over 10 percent of all scheduled passengers in the United States. By the year 2000, state aviation officials predict that Texas airports will handle 96 million passengers, representing 15 percent of the national total. Within the state, nearly one-half of the passenger traffic involved Dallas–Fort Worth; over 25 percent was linked to Houston; about 15 percent was shared by San Antonio, Austin, and El Paso. With these five metropolitan areas accounting for approximately 90 percent of the market, the remaining traffic was spread among twenty-five other cities in the state.

Although these thirty airports are the principal fields with scheduled airline service, they by no means represent the total. The Texas Aeronautics Commission uses a functional classification for airports. Of those designated "commercial service" for the year 1982, twenty are primary fields, supporting scheduled service by large and medium transports and enplaning 31,500 or more passengers. Ten nonprimary fields enplaned at least 2,500 passengers and were served by smaller transports. Both categories of airports were equipped to the standards necessary for precision instrument approaches.

But the Texas Aeronautics Commission recognizes 278 other airports which are functionally classed as general aviation fields and are divided into three categories: business, community, and basic. The first two have nonprecision instrument approaches, while the third offers visual approach only. There are 89 business service fields that can handle all aircraft up to large business jets. Next in line are the community service fields that can handle light twin-engine turboprops and piston aircraft on shorter runways. Finally, there are 65 basic service fields, built primarily for single-engine aircraft operations.

The general aviation and commercial services combined support a network of planes and pilots that is one of the busiest in the nation. In 1982, there were some 60,000 pilots in Texas and a general aviation fleet of over 22,000 aircraft—about 10 percent of the 247,000 planes in the United States. The Texas Aeronautics Commission neatly summarizes the reasons for the high level of activity: "Over the past decade general aviation has become an increasingly important means of transportation for business and industry, especially in Texas. Centralized management, dispersed plants, tax advantages, and changes in airline routes have made general aviation a highly competitive mode of transportation." As the state's industry grew, the demand for corporate flying increased the fleet of business aircraft. In the early 1980s, one of every six business jets in the nation was registered in Texas, operating from over 100 airports that provided access to 92 percent of the state's population.

Conclusion

The role of Texans in contributing to aerospace development within the state, within the nation, and around the world has had many facets. For example, aviation/aerospace journalism transmits news about products, services, federal regulation, and other topics. George Williams, of Temple, published such a magazine in the late 1920s, although his untimely death made it a short-lived venture. A more long-lasting effort was launched by George Haddaway in 1934, when he began publication of *Southern Flight*. Haddaway's magazine endured for forty-three years and was widely read and respected—not only throughout the Southwest, its major market, but around the United States as well. Over the years, the personable and energetic publisher be-

came an elder statesman of American aviation. Haddaway also played a significant role in many notable aviation ventures, like the agricultural plane at Texas A&M, *Wings of Hope* (a medical and missionary operation in remote parts of the world), and more. Haddaway's vast collection of books, photos, and memorabilia formed the core of the Aviation Collection of the University of Texas at Dallas, making it one of the most significant aerospace history research centers in the United States. Another example of journalistic impact is the influential scholarly quarterly *Journal of Air Law and Commerce*, published by Southern Methodist University.

Texas can also point to special aerospace legacies in terms of popular culture. Among aviation artists with international reputations, Keith Ferris and Robert Carlin come to mind, and a younger generation of aviation artists are also at work. Roy Crane, of Sweetwater, was the creator of the comic strip *Buzz Sawyer*, about a U.S. Navy flier. And Gene Roddenberry, creator of the famous *Star Trek* television series, hailed from El Paso and received his World War II flight training in San Antonio.

The process of aerospace evolution from biplanes to air travel to space flight has been remarkably consistent in Texas. From the earliest days of aviation, Texas enjoyed a special vantage point in aeronautical development, with the opportunity to share in several aerial events. Even if they were not always direct participants, citizens across the state were fascinated spectators, and this consistent exposure made them much more "airminded" than many contemporaries elsewhere. Moreover, the state's broad plains, temperate climate, and economic characteristics gave special advantages in the implementation of military aviation, air transport, and aerospace industries.

Historically, major airports in Texas represent an important factor in the commercial growth of the Southwest, and the concentration of business and corporate aircraft in the state has been one of the nation's largest. The manufacture of civil and military aircraft involves international arrangements representing billions of dollars. Operational air bases and training fields dot the state. The spirit of innovation continued with Houston's Space Services Incorporated which was developing a family of privately funded rocket launchers, and which carried out a test launch from Matagorda Island in 1982. Through NASA's Johnson Space Center, Texas played a central role in space exploration that continues in the missions of the *Space Shuttle* and plans for a permanent space station to orbit earth. These trends have enriched Texas economically and also have knit the state together, linked the state to the nation and the world, and widened the cultural perspectives of the state's citizens. The leap into space opens new horizons whose effect on our imaginations is just beginning.

Along with sensible management and the integration of high-technology automated equipment, the eye-catching uniforms of Southwest Airlines personnel helped build the company into the successful intrastate carrier it is today.

The Southwest Airlines fleet is made up almost totally of Boeing 737s. This twin-jet transport normally carries approximately 115 passengers and is capable of cruising at speeds in excess of 500 mph. Because of its size and cost, it is ideal for the Southwest Airlines route system.

Most of Southwest Airlines routes are relatively short, thus creating a need for an aircraft that is optimized for high utilization rates and a large number of landing and takeoff cycles. The 737 fills that requirement nicely, having been conceived by Boeing with such parameters in mind.

Texas International Airlines, which has now been merged under the Texas Air banner to become part of Continental Airlines, was a regional carrier with a limited interstate network. Its primary aircraft type was the twin-engine Douglas DC-9 (shown), though some Convair 600 turboprops were still on inventory when the airline merged with Continental in the early 1980s.

Braniff International Airlines, with roots that can be traced back to the early 1930s, is one of the best-known Texas-based regional carriers. The airline's aircraft, such as this red, white, blue, and gold Boeing 727 seen during final approach to DFW International Airport, are also particularly well known due to their unusually colorful, high-visibility markings.

Braniff's aircraft, such as this Boeing 727 seen departing Austin's Mueller Airport, have gone through a variety of color scheme changes during the past decade, all in order to catch the attention of the flying public. Among those consulted during Braniff's well-known color scheme campaigns was Alexander Calder, one of the most famous and notable contemporary American artists.

Nicknamed "Big Orange" and regularly seen departing DFW International Airport during Braniff's heyday in the early 1980s, this Boeing 747 was the largest aircraft in the Braniff fleet until it was sold to another airline. Braniff normally used it on its Dallas-to-Hawaii route.

In a public relations scheme that never reached fruition, Braniff at one time seriously considered leasing several BAC/Aerospatiale "Concorde" supersonic airliners to serve international routes between the U.S. and Europe. Because these supersonic aircraft would have been forced by noise regulations to fly subsonically once they were over U.S. soil, the scheme was never consummated.

The wide-body, three-engine American Airlines' McDonnell Douglas DC-10 is one of the three largest airliner types currently serving DFW International Airport.

The McDonnell Douglas "Dash 80" series, evolved from the original McDonnell Douglas DC-9 family, is one of the newest types to enter the American Airlines fleet.

The Boeing 727 family has been a workhorse for American (and other) airlines and has been used on many American routes between Texas and other parts of the U.S.

The most recent addition to the ever-expanding American Airlines fleet is the state-of-the-art Boeing 767. This large twin-jet is one of the most efficient airliners in the world.

The Boeing 747, operated by American Airlines and others, is the world's largest commercial air transport. Flown regularly from DFW International and Houston Intercontinental airports, it is capable of carrying over 500 passengers over distances in excess of 4,000 miles.

Scheduled airline service began at DFW International Airport in early 1974. At that time, it was the world's largest airport with physical dimensions quite similar to those of Manhattan Island. Later, it was discovered to have attracted many corporations to the Dallas/Fort Worth area and to have become a significant economic factor in the state.

Project Orbis, originated by a Houston ophthalmologist, used a highly-modified Douglas DC-8 transport to demonstrate advanced eye surgery techniques all over the world. The objective of the project was to teach Third World ophthalmologists state-of-the-art technique that was otherwise inaccessible to them because of their location.

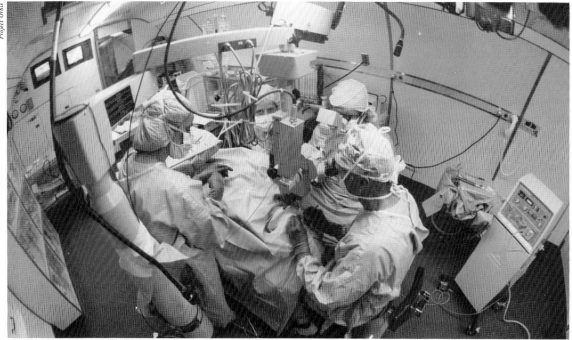

The Project Orbis DC-8 was equipped with a sophisticated sterile operating room and a full complement of surgery equipment. As medical teams performed surgery, a TV-system displayed the procedure to students in a classroom located near the front of the airplane. This work was always done with the airplane parked statically.

Jay Miller/Aerofax, Inc.

Bell Helicopter Textron's XV-15 tilt-rotor demonstrator represents the state-of-the-art in vertical takeoff and landing aircraft. Two were built to accommodate an extensive flight test program that was undertaken by Bell, NASA, and the various military services. A follow-on program is presently in the development stage.

Bell Helicopter Textron

In an interesting contrast in technology, a WWI-vintage SE-5 pursuit is seen next to one of the two XV-15s at NASA's Ames, California, facility. The XV-15 acquires its unique capabilities by rotating its helicopter-like prop-rotors to a vertical position. Once in flight, the prop-rotors and their engine nacelles rotate forward.

General Dynamics' innovative lightweight fighter design, which reached the hardware stage in the form of the YF-16 prototype, defeated several contenders in a contest that led to one of the largest aerospace procurement contracts ever. Additional F-16s have since been ordered and the total buy is expected to be over 5,000 aircraft.

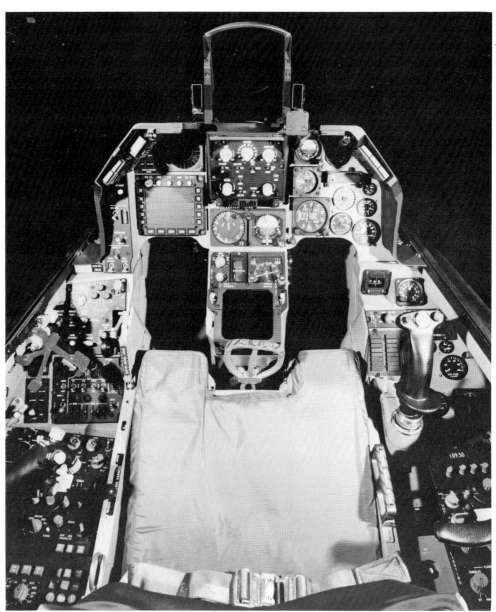

The F-16's cockpit is typical of contemporary fighter aircraft. Though appearing extraordinarily complex, it is relatively easy for pilots to master. The avionics complement is all solid-state, and the control stick is mounted unconventionally on the right side.

The mile-long General Dynamics production line is filled with F-16s in the process of completion. Some 3,000 F-16s are presently on order, which should be sufficient to keep General Dynamics busy until at least the early 1990s. Additionally, F-16s are being produced in total, or in part, in a number of countries other than the U.S.

Two Texas products, some forty years apart in vintage, are seen overflying Colorado Springs, Colorado. The North American P-51D in the foreground is an interesting contrast to the General Dynamics F-16A. The F-16's cruising speed is almost twice as fast as that of the P-51, and its maximum speed is over three times greater.

In an attempt to build a cheaper F-16 and make it available to more countries, General Dynamics developed the F-16/79. This version, powered by an older technology engine, did not have quite the same performance as the standard model and thus proved somewhat less appealing. To date, no sales have been consummated.

An advanced F-16, known as the F-16XL, has been successfully flight tested. Incorporating a "cranked arrow" delta wing in place of the more conventional planform found on the standard production aircraft, it is one of the most advanced fighter aircraft presently flying. The air force has not yet made a firm commitment to buy.

The F-16XL has been designed to carry most of the aircraft-borne weapons presently in the air force inventory, including the forthcoming AMRAAM (Advanced Medium Range Air-to-Air Missile). Though lacking some of the maneuverability of the standard F-16, the F-16XL offers increased range and greater weapons payload.

Vought's rugged and versatile A-7 "Corsair II," sometimes referred to by crew members as the "SLUF" ("Short Little Ugly Fellah"), is in use by the air force (shown), navy, marines, and several foreign air forces. A new requirement may again see it in production for the U.S.

Because of its size and impressive capabilities, the navy has found the A-7 to be particularly suitable to its needs. The air force aircraft, in fact, was actually developed from the navy version, after the type had been developed to a navy requirement.

Vought's MLRS (Multiple Launch Rocket System) is a highly mobile tank-mounted unit designed for a quick and accurate response to ground troop combat requirements. Up to twelve rockets can be fired before reloading is required.

The 1,000th production rocket built for the army's MLRS (Multiple Launch Rocket System) is seen coming off the production line of Vought's highly automated plant at East Camden, Arkansas. The army plans to buy more than 300 MLRS launchers and some 400,000 rockets.

Bell Helicopter Textron's XV-15 is serving as a tilt-rotor research aircraft for the forthcoming V-22 "Osprey." The latter is a co-production tilt-rotor project involving both Bell and Boeing, that is now expected to reach fruition in the form of a production contract in the early 1990s.

The BAT (Bell Advanced Tiltrotor) was a design study for a small two-seat vertical takeoff and landing aircraft optimized for specialized military missions. Though the BAT will never reach the hardware stage, evolutionary studies stemming from it will provide Bell design engineers with a full-scale model on which to test new ideas.

Lockheed-Austin Company

Lockheed's "Aquila" drone system, manufactured in Austin, is an unmanned radio-controlled surveillance aircraft designed to provide field commanders with real-time information about enemy activity. It is equipped with an extensive array of sensors, including a television camera.

David Morgan

Rockwell International's B-1B is the newest bomber to enter the air force inventory. The first operational B-1B was delivered to Dyess AFB on June 29, 1985, and is now being utilized as a service introduction trainer and operational test and evaluation vehicle.

NASA's Johnson Space Center, near Houston, is a sprawling complex of laboratories and office buildings created for the sole purpose of supporting the U.S. manned space program. Astronauts and engineers work here in a coordinated effort to explore space for the benefit of all mankind.

This view of the Mission Operations Control Room in the Mission Control Center, Building 30, of the Johnson Space Center, was taken during the lunar surface extravehicular activity of "Apollo 11" astronauts Neil Armstrong and Edwin Aldrin, Jr. This was man's first lunar visit.

Powered by a small jet engine and controlled in pitch and roll axes by several small rocket motors, NASA's LLTV (Lunar Landing Training Vehicle) was used at Ellington AFB to train "Apollo" crews in lunar landing techniques.

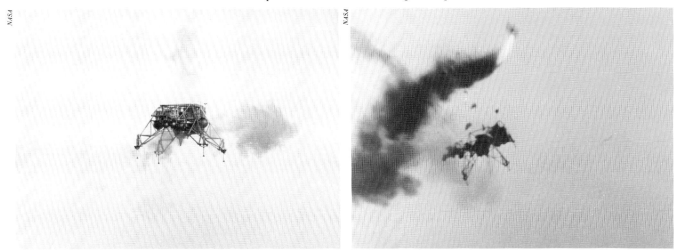

At left, NASA pilot Joseph Algranti flies the Bell Aerospace Textron–manufactured LLTV during a test at Ellington AFB. Moments later, severe oscillations caused Algranti to eject at an altitude of only 200 feet (right). Fortunately, Algranti's ejection was successful and his parachute lowered him safely to the ground; the LLTV crashed and was totally destroyed.

Led by renowned rocket pioneer Wernher von Braun, a German rocket team assembled after WWII at Fort Bliss, near El Paso, helped launch captured German V-2 rockets on test missions that laid the foundation on which America's later space program was created.

Roger Bilstein collection

262

NASA

Perhaps the single most impressive engineering feat ever, the "Apollo" moon rocket stood over 360 feet tall and weighed over 3,000 tons. Some seventeen Apollo missions were flown, though not all were manned. "Apollo" communications were handled by the Johnson Space Center.

Two Grumman "Gulfstream IIs" have been heavily modified by NASA to provide realistic "Space Shuttle" pilot trainers. These aircraft, equipped with special control systems that cause them to handle like the real "Space Shuttle" during landing, are used at Ellington AFB by Shuttle astronauts to hone landing techniques.

NASA, like the air force and navy, has found that Northrop's small, supersonic T-38 is an excellent training aircraft for the maintenance of pilot proficiency. A number of T-38s are assigned to NASA's Ellington AFB facility and are used not only for pilot proficiency maintenance, but also for cross-country business transportation.

The bulbous Aero Space Lines "Super Guppy" was created to carry oversize spacecraft components to and from the manufacturing facilities and the Kennedy and Johnson Space Centers. The "Super Guppy" was eventually bought by NASA from its owners and is now based at Ellington AFB, where it is used to transport Space Shuttle payloads and miscellaneous components.

The enormous internal volume of the "Super Guppy's" payload bay is readily apparent in this late-1960s-vintage photo of a "Saturn" rocket instrument unit being on-loaded.

The "Super Guppy" and NASA's Boeing C-135A (humorously referred to as the "Vomit Comet" in consideration of its use as a weightlessness trainer) are seen at Ellington AFB.

Moving serenely in orbit, the "Skylab" space station, launched on May 14, 1973, is photographed from the "Skylab 4" Command and Service Module during a fly-around before its final three-man crew, consisting of Gerald Carr, Edward Gibson, and William Pogue, heads for home.

In the late 1970s, Johnson Space Center proposed a permanent space station known as the Space Operations Center. This artist's concept showed a "Shuttle" preparing to dock with previous "Shuttle" flights having already delivered modules for living quarters and a laboratory.

Appendices

Appendix 1. Currently Active USAF and Naval Aviation Facilities in Texas

BERGSTROM AFB—located seven miles southeast of downtown Austin. Activated on September 22, 1942; named for Capt. John A. E. Bergstrom, the first Austin serviceman killed in World War II, on December 8, 1941, at Clark Field, Philippines. The base has a total area of 3,998 acres and a mean altitude of 541 feet above sea level. It is currently a Tactical Air Command base with a total military employment of 5,252, a total civilian employment of 924, a payroll of $89.57 million, and housing for 78 officers and 1,268 enlisted men and women. It is headquarters for the 12th Air Force; headquarters for the 10th Air Force (Air Force Reserve); host to the 67th Tactical Reconnaissance Wing with McDonnell RF-4C aircraft, the 924th Tactical Fighter Group (Air Force Reserve) with McDonnell F-4D aircraft, and the Tactical Air Command Non-Commissioned Officer Academy West (ph. 512/479-4100).

BROOKS AFB—located seven miles southeast of San Antonio. Activated on December 8, 1917; named for Cadet Sidney J. Brooks, Jr., who was killed on November 13, 1917, on his final solo flight before commissioning. The base has a total area of 1,310 acres and a mean altitude of 600 feet above sea level. It is currently an Air Force Systems Command base with a total military employment of 1,500, a total civilian employment of 1,100, a payroll of $45.3 million, and housing for 70 officers and 100 noncommissioned officers. It is the home of the Aerospace Medical Division of the USAF School of Aerospace Medicine; the USAF Occupational and Environment Lab; USAF Human Resources Lab; Air Force Systems Command Systems Acquisition School; and tenant units that include the USAF Medical Service Center, a security squadron, and a communications group (ph. 512/536-1110).

CARSWELL AFB—located seven miles west-northwest of downtown Fort Worth. Activated in August of 1942; named on January 30, 1948, for Maj. Horace S. Carswell, Jr., a native of Fort Worth who was a B-24 pilot during World War II and was posthumously awarded the Medal of Honor. The base has a total area of 2,750 acres and a mean altitude of 650 feet above sea level. It is currently a Strategic Air Command base with a total military employment of 5,050, a total civilian employment of 961, a payroll of $79 million, and housing for 92 officers and 790 noncommissioned officers. It is the home for the 19th Air Division, the 7th Bomb Wing with Boeing B-52H aircraft, and the 301st Tactical Fighter Wing (Air Force Reserve) with McDonnell F-4D aircraft. Additionally, on the west side of the field is the main Fort Worth production facility for the General Dynamics Corporation, with some 17,000 employees (ph. 817/735-5000).

DYESS AFB—located about five miles west-southwest of downtown Abilene. Activated in April, 1942; deactivated in December, 1945; reactivated as Abilene Air Base in September, 1955; in March, 1956, renamed for Lt. Col. William E. Dyess, a World War II fighter pilot known for his escape from a Japanese prison camp. Dyess was later killed in the crash of a Lockheed P-38 at Burbank, California, in December, 1943. The base has a total area of 6,058 acres and a mean altitude of 1,789 feet above sea level. It is currently a Strategic Air Command base with a total military employment of 6,097, a total civilian employment of 442, a payroll of $78.2 million, and housing for 150 officers and 848 noncommissioned officers. It is home base for the 12th Air Division and 96th Bomb Wing with Boeing B-52G/H aircraft; the 463rd Tactical Airlift Wing (Military Airlift Command) with Lockheed C-130 aircraft; the 1993rd Communications Squadron (Air Force Communications Command); and the 417th Field Training Detachment (Air Training Command). It has been selected as the first base for the Rockwell B-1B and the 4018th B-1 Combat Training School (ph. 915/696-0212).

ELLINGTON AFB—located approximately seventeen miles southeast of Houston. Activated in 1917; named for Lt. Eric L. Ellington, a pilot killed in the early days of Signal Corps operations in November, 1913. The base has a total area of 2,283 acres and a mean altitude of 40 feet above sea level. It is currently an inactive AF base with a total military employment of 971, a total civilian employment of 155, and an additional 103 government technicians, and a payroll of $16.3 million. It serves the needs of the 147th Fighter Interceptor Group with McDonnell F-4C aircraft; NASA operations with a variety of aircraft (including Northrop T-38As, a Lockheed C-130, a Lockheed P-3, Grumman *Gulfstream Is* and *IIs*, a Boeing C-135A, and miscellaneous other types); the U.S. Coast Guard (currently initiating operations with Aerospatiale HH-65A helicopters); the Army National Guard; the Federal Aviation Administration; the Military Sealift Command; and the Air National Guard Transition Caretaker Force. Ellington is now owned by the City of Houston. (ph. 713/481-1400).

FORT HOOD—located several miles northeast of Killeen. Activated in 1942 as a tank destroyer center; named after John Bell Hood, a Confederate general. The facility has a total area of 216,915 acres and two aviation facilities consisting of Robert Gray Army Air Field, with a mean altitude of 1,015 feet above sea level, and Hood Army Air Field, with a mean altitude of 930 feet above sea level. It is currently an army training facility with a total military employment of 38,888, a total civilian employment of 9,065, a payroll of $208,554,208, and housing for 896 officers and 4,341 noncommissioned officers. It is home base for a larger number of army aircraft units (ph. 817/287-1110).

GOODFELLOW AFB—located two miles southeast of San Angelo. Activated in January, 1941; named for Lt. John J. Goodfellow, Jr., a World War II pilot killed in combat on September 14, 1918. The base has a total area of 1,127 acres and a mean altitude of 1,877 feet above sea level. It is currently an Air Training Command base with a total military employment of 2,406, a total civilian employment of 484, a payroll of $41.47 million, and housing for 3 officers and 96 enlisted men. It is home base for the 3480th Technical Training Wing and the USAF Cryptologic Training Center. Present plans call for Goodfellow to serve as one of the primary sites for a new over-the-horizon radar system code-named "Pave Paws" (ph. 915/653-3217).

HENSLEY FIELD—located northeast of Grand Prairie. Activated in 1929; named for Maj. William N. Hensley, who participated in the first trans-Atlantic dirigible crossing by the R-34 in 1919. The base has a total area of 49 acres and a mean altitude of 495 feet above sea level. It is currently part of a large complex made up of Dallas Naval Air Station and Hensley Field. The main Hensley Field tenant is the 136th Tactical Airlift Wing of the Texas Air National Guard with Lockheed C-130 aircraft. Additionally, Vought Corporation, a major aerospace manufacturer, has its primary production facility on the west side of the field. Total military employment for Hensley Field is 959, and total civilian and other technician employment is 245, with a payroll of $11.3 million (ph. 214/266-6111).

KELLY AFB—located five miles southwest of San Antonio. Activated on May 7, 1917; named for Lt. George E. M. Kelly, who became the first army pilot to be killed in an operational military aircraft on May 10, 1911. The base has a total area of 3,992 acres and a mean altitude of 689 feet above sea level. It is currently an Air Force Logistics Command base with a total military employment of 4,837, a total civilian employment of 18,216, a payroll of $527.9 million, and housing for 46 officers and 368 noncommissioned officers. It is the headquarters for the San Antonio Air Logistics Center; headquarters for the Electronic Security Command; and home for the AF Electronic Warfare Center; the AF Cryptologic Support Center; the Joint Electronic Warfare Center; the AF Service Information and News Center; the AF Commissary Service; the 433rd Tactical Airlift Wing (Air Force Reserve) with Lockheed C-130 aircraft; and the 149th Tactical Fighter Group (Air National Guard) with McDonnell F-4C aircraft (ph. 512/925-1110).

LACKLAND AFB—located eight miles west-southwest of San Antonio. Activated in 1941; named for Brig. Gen. Frank D. Lackland, an early commandant of Kelly Field flying school, who died in 1943. The base has a total area of 6,783 acres, which includes 3,972 acres at the Lackland Training Annex, and a mean altitude of 787 feet above sea level. It is currently an Air Training Command base with a total military employment of 19,314, a total civilian employment of 4,700, a payroll of $415.7 million, and housing for 106 officers and 619 noncommissioned officers. It is a basic military training facility for aviators; a technical training facility for teaching advanced security police/law enforcement personnel; a school for patrol dog handlers and animals; a training center for instructors, recruiters, and social actions/drug abuse counselors; a USAF marksmanship training center; home base for the USAF Officer Training School; home for the Defense Language Institute–English Language Center; and the location of the world-famous Wilford Hall USAF Medical Center (ph. 512/671-1110).

LAUGHLIN AFB—located six miles east of Del Rio. Activated in October, 1942; named for 1st Lt. Jack T. Laughlin, a B-17 pilot killed over Java on January 29, 1942. The base has a total area of 4,008 acres and a mean altitude of 1,080 feet above sea level. It is currently an Air Training Command base with a total military employment of 2,977, a total civilian employment of 872, a payroll of $62.6 million, and housing for 255 officers and 348 noncommissioned officers. It is the home of the 47th Flying Training Wing with Cessna T-41, Cessna T-37, and Northrop T-38 aircraft (ph. 512/298-3511).

MAJORS FIELD—located southwest of Greenville. Training facility during World War II. Now civil airport and location of E-Systems mod facility.

RANDOLPH AFB—located twenty miles east-northeast of San Antonio. Activated in June, 1930; named for Capt. William M. Randolph, who was killed on February 17, 1928, when his Curtiss AT-4 crashed on takeoff at Gorman, Texas. The base has a total area of 2,901 acres and a mean altitude of 761 feet above sea level. It is currently an Air Training Command base with a total military employment of 5,617, a total civilian employment of 2,708, a payroll of $248 million, and housing for 209 officers and 810 noncommissioned officers. It is home base for the 12th Flying Training Wing and the primary school for T-37 and T-38 pilot instructor training. Major tenants include the headquarters for the Air Training Command; the Air Force Manpower and Personnel Center; the Occupational Measurement Center; the Foreign Military Training Affairs Group; the Office of Civilian Personnel Operations; and the headquarters for the USAF Recruiting Service (ph. 512/652-1110).

REESE AFB—located six miles west of Lubbock. Activated in 1942; later named for 1st Lt. Augustus F. Reese, Jr., a P-38 fighter pilot killed in Sardinia on May 14, 1943. The base has a total area of 2,467 acres and a mean altitude of 3,338 feet above sea level. It is currently an Air Training Command base with a total military employment of 2,588, a total civilian employment of 570, a payroll of $71.6 million, and housing for 112 officers and 295 noncommissioned officers. It is home to the 64th Flying Training Wing and serves as a primary facility for undergraduate pilot training (ph. 806/885-4511).

SHEPPARD AFB—located four miles north of Wichita Falls. Activated on June 14, 1941; named for Morris E. Sheppard, a U.S. senator from Texas who died in 1941. The base has a total area of 5,000 acres and a mean altitude of 1,015 feet above sea level. It is currently an Air Training Command base with a total military employment of 7,952, a total civilian employment of 1,607, an annual payroll of $180 million, and housing for 200 officers and 1,087 noncommissioned officers. It provides resident courses in aircraft maintenance, civil engineering, communications, and missile, comptroller, transportation, and instructor training. The 3785th Field Training Group provides specialized and advanced training at seventy-two field training detachments and eighteen operating locations worldwide. The School of Health Care Sciences provides training in medicine, dentistry, nursing, biomedical sciences, and health service administration. The 80th Flying Training Wing conducts undergraduate pilot training and instructor training for the Euro-NATO Joint Jet Pilot Training Program. The wing trains fighter pilots for twelve NATO countries (ph. 817/851-2511).

Appendix 2. Miscellaneous Government and Military Aerospace-Related Facilities

LYNDON BAINES JOHNSON SPACE CENTER—located south of Houston, Texas. The LBJSC designs, tests, and develops manned spacecraft, selects and trains astronauts, and directs the *Space Shuttle* program. Mission Control for manned space flight is located at the Center, and responsibilities include operational planning, crew selection and training, flight control, and experiment/payload flight control for the Space Transportation System. Definition and development of in-flight biomedical experiments are included in the life sciences research responsibilities of the Center, named for President Lyndon Baines Johnson.

AIR FORCE COMMUNICATIONS COMMAND—though it has headquarters at Scott AFB, Illinois, the AFCC provides data services to the air force through the San Antonio Data Services Center located at Kelly AFB, San Antonio. Additionally, the Air Force Central NOTAM facility, falling under the jurisdiction of the AFCC, is located at Carswell AFB.

SAN ANTONIO AIR LOGISTICS CENTER (AIR FORCE LOGISTICS COMMAND)—located at Kelly AFB, this is one of the most important and largest of the five major Air Logistics Centers in the United States. As part of the AFLC, whose mission is to supply the fuels, air munitions, spare parts, and maintenance support for the combat elements of the air force, the San Antonio facility is responsible for all major maintenance and support of such aircraft as the Boeing B-52 and the Lockheed C-5.

ELECTRONIC SECURITY COMMAND—located in San Antonio, this facility is responsible for all USAF communications security worldwide and also for all electronic warfare activities. Direct reporting units include the Air Force Electronic Warfare Center and the Air Force Cryptologic Support Center. A peripheral unit is located at Bergstrom AFB.

Appendix 3. Name Evolution of the U.S. Air Force

Aviation Division of the U.S. Signal Corps from August 1, 1907, to July 18, 1914; Aviation Section of the U.S. Signal Corps from July 18, 1914, to May 24, 1918; Army Air Service (AAS) from May 24, 1918, to July 2, 1926; Army Air Corps (AAC) from July 2, 1926, to June 20, 1941; Army Air Forces (AAF) from June 20, 1941, to September 18, 1947; United States Air Force (USAF) from September 18, 1947, to present.

Appendix 4. U.S. Military Aces (Army, Navy, Air Force, Marines) Born in Texas

An ace must have five or more kills (i.e., five or more enemy aircraft destroyed—fractions represent probable kills). This list is not complete; there are almost certainly a number of Texas-born aces not listed.

World War I:
Baucom, B. V., Milford, 6 victories
Clay, Henry R., Jr., Fort Worth, 8 victories
Tobin, Edgar G., San Antonio, 6 victories

World War II:
Adams, Louis W., Kingsville, 6 victories
Anderson, Woodrow W., Stockdale, 13½ victories
Andrew, Stephen W., Dallas, 14½ victories
Barnaby, Harold T., Waco, 5 victories
Bearden, Aaron L., Houston, 5 victories
Bennett, James H., Morton, 5½ victories
Bennett, Joseph H., Morton, 6½ victories
Bond, Charles R., Dallas, 9 victories
Bonebreak, Robert R., Taylor, 7 victories
Bradley, Jack T., Brownwood, 15 victories
Bradley, John L., Dallas, 5 victories
Carter, Joseph D., Sherman, 5½ victories
Chandler, Van E., Waxahachie, 9 victories
Collins, Frank J., Breckenridge, 8 victories
Collinsworth, J. D., Berger, 8 victories
Compton, Gordon B., Dallas, 21½ victories
Cranfill, Niven K., Temple, 5 victories
Crombie, William F., El Paso, 9 victories
Cunnick, John W., Waco, 9 victories
Dillard, William J., Grand Saline, 6 victories
Duncan, Glenn E., Houston, 26⅘ victories
Dunning, John A., San Antonio, 5 victories
Evans, Andrew J., San Antonio, 8 victories
Fiedler, Clemens A., Fredericksburg, 5⅓ victories
Freeman, William, Bonham, 6 victories
Gallup, Kenneth W., Clint, 11 victories
Griffith, Robert C., Austin, 5 victories
Haworth, Russell C., Cedar Hill, 5 victories
Hill, David L. "Tex," Hunt, 12¼ victories
Jenkins, Otto D., Kermit, 10½ victories
Johnson, Martin H., Jr., Fort Worth, 10 victories
Joiner, Joe H., Corpus Christi, 8½ victories
Jones, Lynn F., Mercedes, 5 victories
Julian, William H., Dallas, 8 victories

Jure, James M., Dallas, 5 victories
Lamb, Huie H., Abilene, 5½ victories
Landers, John D., Joshua, 28½ victories
Lee, Louis W., Houston, 6 victories
Lynch, William J., Kenedy, 5 victories
Marshall, Bert W., Greenville, 7 victories
McArthur, T. H., Caradan, 5 victories
McCasland, Darwin D., Morton, 5 victories
McMahan, Bruce D., Houston, 6 victories
McMullen, Joseph D., Victoria, 10 victories
Miller, John, El Paso, 5 victories
Montgomery, Gerald E., Littlefield, 17½ victories
Murphy, Randel L., Houston, 12 victories
Prescott, R. W., Fort Worth, 5 victories
Priest, Royce W., San Antonio, 5 victories
Randolph, John P., Schertz, 5 victories
Reeves, Leonard R., Lancaster, 10 victories
Richardson, Elmer W., San Antonio, 11 victories
Righetti, Elwyn G., San Antonio, 34½ victories
Sears, Alexander F., Abilene, 6 victories
Shoup, Robert L., Port Arthur, 6 victories
Smith, Virgil H., McAllen, 5 victories
Spann, Bobby J., San Antonio, 5 victories
Stanley, Morris A., Alvin, 6½ victories
Stewart, David, Dallas, 15 victories
Sublett, John L., Odessa, 9 victories
Turner, William L., Idalon, 10½ victories
Tyler, Gerald E., Houston, 7 victories
Vincent, Clinton D., San Antonio, 6 victories
Weatherford, Sydney W., San Marcos, 5 victories
Webb, Roy A., Pampa, 9 victories
Williams, James M., Huntsville, 8 victories

Korea:
Baker, Royal N., McKinney, 13 victories
Davis, George A., Jr., Lubbock, 14 victories
Foster, Cecil G., San Antonio, 9 victories
Latshaw, Robert T., Jr., Amarillo, 5 victories
Moore, Robert H., Houston, 5 victories

Appendix 5. Air Force Medal of Honor Winners Born in Texas

World War II:
Maj. Horace S. Carswell, Jr., Fort Worth
Col. John R. Kane, McGregor
Col. Neel E. Kearby, Wichita Falls
1st Lt. Raymond L. Knight, Houston
1st Lt. Jack W. Mathis, San Angelo
2nd Lt. John C. Morgan, Vernon

Korea:
Maj. George A. Davis, Jr., Hale Center

Vietnam:
Capt. Steven L. Bennett, Palestine

Appendix 6. Aviation Museums and Collections Located in Texas

ADMIRAL NIMITZ CENTER, P.O. Box 777, Fredericksburg, 78624; director, Douglas Hubbard. An excellent, though small, collection of primarily World War II–related items with heavy emphasis on memorabilia pertaining to Admiral Chester Nimitz's illustrious naval career. Only a few aircraft are on display, though they are all virtually unique, including: Aichi D3A-1 *Val*—WWII Japanese dive bomber; Douglas RA-24B (SBD-5) *Dauntless*—WWII American dive bomber; Kawanishi N1K-1 *Rex*—WWII Japanese floatplane fighter; Radioplane *BAT*—WWII American antiship missile.

CONFEDERATE AIR FORCE, P.O. Box CAF, Rebel Field, Harlingen, 78550. An excellent and very large collection of World War II aircraft of all combating nations. Most CAF aircraft are flyable and are utilized for airshow displays and promotional services. A small museum building also permits display of World War II aviation-related memorabilia such as flying suits, paraphernalia, and powerplants. During nonairshow periods, aircraft are statically displayed for viewing. The Harlingen location is considered the CAF's home base, though CAF "Wings" exist throughout the world. Aircraft officially considered part of the CAF collection include Beechcraft C-45H/J *Expeditor*—WWII cargo and VIP transport; Bell P-39Q *Airacobra*—WWII pursuit; Bell P-63 *Kingcobra*—WWII pursuit; Boeing (Stearman) PT-17 *Kaydet*—WWII primary trainer; Boeing B-17G (PB-1W) *Flying Fortress*—WWII medium bomber; Boeing B-29A *Superfortress*—WWII heavy bomber; Cessna T-50 (UC-78) *Bobcat*—WWII advanced trainer; Consolidated PBY-5A *Catalina*—WWII patrol and rescue amphibian; Consolidated B-24 (LB-30) *Liberator*—WWII medium bomber; Curtiss P-40N *Warhawk*—WWII pursuit; Curtiss C-46 *Commando*—WWII transport; Curtiss SB2C-5 (A-25) *Helldiver*—WWII dive bomber; de Havilland DH 82 *Tiger Moth*—WWII primary trainer; de Havilland DH 94 *Moth Minor*—WWII basic trainer; Douglas C-47 (DC-3) *Skytrain*—WWII transport; Douglas C-54 (DC-4) *Skymaster*—WWII transport; Douglas SBD-5 (A-24) *Dauntless*—WWII dive bomber; Douglas A-1E (AD-5) *Skyraider*—post-WWII attack/dive bomber; Douglas A-20G *Havoc*—WWII light bomber; Douglas A-26 (B-26) *Invader*—WWII light bomber; Douglas B-23 *Dragon*—WWII light bomber/transport; Fairchild PT-19 *Cornell*—WWII basic trainer; Fairchild PT-23 *Cornell*—WWII basic trainer; Fairchild PT-26 *Cornell*—WWII basic trainer; Fairchild C-119C *Flying Boxcar*—post-WWII transport; Fleet Model 16B *Finch*—WWII primary trainer; Focke Wulf FW 44J *Stieglitz*—WWII liaison/observation; Grumman F4F *Wildcat*—WWII pursuit; Grumman F6F *Hellcat*—WWII pursuit; Grumman F8F *Bearcat*—WWII pursuit; Grumman TBM-3E *Avenger*—WWII torpedo bomber; Hawker Mk.20 *Sea Fury*—post-WWII fighter-bomber; Heinkel He 111 (CASA C.2111)—WWII medium bomber; Hughes TH-55A *Osage*—post-WWII training helicopter; Junkers Ju 52 (CASA 352)—WWII transport; Lockheed L-18 *Lodestar/Hudson*—WWII transport/bomber; Lockheed P-38L *Lightning*—WWII pursuit; Martin B-26C *Marauder*—WWII medium bomber; Martin AM-1 *Mauler*—post-WWII torpedo bomber; Messerschmitt (Nord) BF-108—WWII light transport; Messerschmitt BF-109G (Hispano HA 1112)—WWII pursuit; Naval Aircraft Factory N3N *Yellow Peril*—WWII primary trainer; North American T-6A/D/G *Texan*—WWII basic trainer; North American P-51D/K *Mustang*—WWII pursuit; North American P-82B *Twin Mustang*—WWII pursuit; North American B-25J/N *Mitchell*—WWII light bomber; North American T-28 *Trojan*—post-WWII basic trainer; North American F-86L *Sabrejet*—post-WWII fighter; Piper L-21B *Super Cub*—post-WWII liaison/observation; Republic P-47N *Thunderbolt*—WWII pursuit; Ryan PT-22 (ST3KR) *Recruit*—WWII primary trainer; Schweitzer TG-3A—WWII training glider; Sikorsky R-4B *Hoverfly*—WWII rescue helicopter; Stinson L-5 *Sentinel*—WWII liaison/observation; Stinson S-10-A *Voyager*—WWII private aircraft; Supermarine Mk. IX *Spitfire*—WWII pursuit; Vought F4U (FG-1D) *Corsair*—WWII pursuit; Vultee BT-13 *Valiant*—WWII basic trainer; Waco CG-4A *Hadrian*—WWII cargo glider.

HISTORY AND TRADITIONS MUSEUM, LGHM, Lackland AFB, 78236; curator, Gloria Livingston. Essentially a branch of the world-renowned U.S. Air Force Museum at Wright-Patterson AFB, Ohio, the Lackland Museum consists of aircraft, engines, instruments, and air weapons spanning the years of aviation development from its origins to the aerospace age. A small museum building houses a large number of interesting exhibits and artifacts, including several large bombs, a World War II–vintage gun turret, several engines, several rare wind tunnel models, and many framed photographs. Most of the actual full-scale aircraft are scattered around the base at various strategic locations, though ten or so surround the actual museum building. Aircraft considered part of the History and Traditions Museum include Beechcraft UC-45J *Expeditor*—WWII cargo and VIP transport; Beechcraft T-34A *Mentor*—1950s-vintage primary trainer; Bell RP-63G *Pinball*—WWII manned fighter target; Bell UH-1B *Huie*—1960s-vintage army helicopter; Boeing (Douglas-built) TB-17G *Flying Fortress*—WWII training medium bomber; Boeing B-52D *Stratofortress*—1950s-vintage heavy bomber; Boeing CIM-10A (IM-99) *Bomarc*—1950s surface-to-air antiaircraft missile; Cessna XT-37—1950s prototype (one of three) jet trainer; Cessna O-2A *Skymaster*—1960s-vintage observation/forward air control; Convair (Ford-built) EB-24M *Liberator*—WWII medium bomber modified for research; Convair VT-29B *Flying Classroom*—1950s-vintage navigator trainer (modified for VIP transport and painted as C-131); Convair F-102A *Delta Dagger*—1960s-vintage fighter; Convair TF-102A *Delta Dagger*—trainer version of F-102A; Douglas B-26C *Intruder*—WWII-vintage light bomber; Douglas XPGM-17A *Thor*—1950s-vintage intermediate-range ballistic missile; Douglas WB-66D *Destroyer*—1950s-vintage light bomber and electronic intelligence system transport; Douglas C-47D *Skytrain*—WWII-vintage transport; Douglas C-118A *Liftmaster*—post-WWII transport; Douglas/MIT VB-10 *Roc*—WWII-vintage guided bomb; Fairchild C-119D *Flying Boxcar*—post-WWII transport; Fairchild C-123K *Provider*—post-WWII transport; Grumman HU-16B *Albatross*—post-WWII amphibious

273

transport and patrol; Hughes XGAR-1 *Falcon*—air-to-air antiaircraft missile; Lockheed T-33A *Shooting Star*—post-WWII trainer; Lockheed EC-121S *Constellation*—post-WWII cargo and electronic intelligence system transport; Lockheed F-80A *Shooting Star*—post-WWII fighter; Lockheed YF-94A *Starfire*—post-WWII radar-equipped fighter; Lockheed F-104C *Star Fighter*—1950s-vintage supersonic fighter; Martin RB-57A *Canberra*—1950s-vintage light bomber/sensor system platform; Martin MGM-1A *Matador*—1950s-vintage intermediate range missile; Martin MGM-13A *Mace*—1950s-vintage intermediate range missile; McDonnell ADM-20A *Quail*—1960s-vintage electronic countermeasures-equipped decoy missile; McDonnell F-101F *Voodoo*—1950s-vintage supersonic interceptor; McDonnell F-4B *Phantom II*—1960s-vintage supersonic fighter; North American T-6 *Texan*—WWII-vintage advanced trainer; North American T-28A *Trojan*—1950s-vintage basic trainer; North American P-51H *Mustang*—WWII-vintage pursuit; North American P-82E *Twin Mustang*—WWII-vintage long-range pursuit; North American B-25H *Mitchell*—WWII-vintage light bomber; North American F-86A *Sabrejet*—Korean War–vintage fighter; North American F-100A *Super Sabre*—1950s-vintage supersonic fighter; North American F-100C *Super Sabre*—1950s-vintage supersonic fighter; Northrop F-89A *Scorpion*—1950s-vintage radar-equipped fighter; Northrop T-38A *Talon*—1960s-vintage supersonic trainer; Northrop F-5A *Freedom Fighter*—1960s-vintage fighter; Republic (Willys) JB-2 *Loon*—1940s-vintage ramjet test vehicle; Republic P-47N *Thunderbolt*—WWII-vintage pursuit; Republic F-84C *Thunderjet*—1950s-vintage fighter; Republic F-84F *Thunderstreak*—1950s-vintage fighter; Republic F-105B *Thunderchief*—1950s-vintage fighter-bomber; Republic F-105D *Thunderchief*—1960s-vintage fighter-bomber.

HISTORY OF AVIATION COLLECTION, University of Texas at Dallas, Dallas, 75221; curator, Mike Quinn. Though in possession of only one full-scale aircraft, the late Alvin Parker's (Odessa, Texas) beautiful Glasflugel BS-1 ultra-high-performance sailplane, this collection contains the best aerospace reference library in the southern United States. It is simply stunning in terms of content and quality. There are over 50,000 volumes on aeronautics, nearly a quarter of a million periodicals, and hundreds of thousands of miscellaneous references in the form of original letters, photographs, transparencies, films, and other materials. Additionally, the memorabilia collection is one of the very best extant. Hundreds of models, many full-scale powerplants, flying clothing, and miscellanea are displayed for public viewing. The collections include the Admiral Rosendahl lighter-than-air library, the Gen. James Doolittle Military Aviation Library, an extensive business and commercial aviation research center, and a comprehensive airline industry library. All are particularly noteworthy, and serve as excellent source collections for scholars and researchers.

JOHNSON SPACE CENTER, Public Services Branch, AP4, NASA Johnson Space Center, Houston, 77058; director, Chuck Biggs. This is a unique, somewhat concentrated collection with a heavy emphasis on education. There are hundreds of exhibit items, including full-scale missiles and spacecraft and numerous audiovisual displays. There are several full-scale space vehicles on view inside the main display building, including a Lunar Module test article and a Boeing-built Lunar Rover trainer. There are too many items in the collection to list here, but among the more important are the following: *Mercury* capsule seat; Rockwell International Command Module A-17—*Apollo 17* capsule from the last *Apollo* mission; *Saturn V* lunar rocket, to date, the largest and heaviest vehicle ever to rise from the earth; Docking Module 1-G trainer; various *Space Shuttle* wind tunnel models; *Mercury* space capsule MA-9; *Gemini V* space capsule; Rocketdyne F-1 rocket engine from a *Saturn V*; space suits from various space programs; the *Skylab* Trainer Complex; a *Mercury-Redstone* rocket; a Pratt & Whitney RL10-A3 rocket engine; a *Gemini* training suit; an *Explorer I* satellite replica; a full-scale Lunar Orbiter mockup; a *Gemini* heat shield sample; and a *Little Joe* Vehicle 3—a launch vehicle for testing emergency recovery systems.

PATE MUSEUM OF TRANSPORTATION, Box 711, Fort Worth, 76101; curator, Jim Peel. A small and relatively unheralded collection arranged through the political connections of Fort Worth oil millionaire "Aggie" Pate. The collection consists of numerous items other than aircraft, including a sizable number of antique automobiles, and bits and pieces of memorabilia too numerous to mention. Several aircraft powerplants are displayed, along with items such as propellers, wheels and tires, and models. The full-scale aircraft collection, which is displayed statically outdoors, consists of the following: Douglas C-117C (DC-3) *Skytrain*—1940s-vintage transport; Fairchild C-119G *Flying Boxcar*—1950s-vintage transport; Grumman F9F-6P *Cougar*—1950s-vintage fighter; Lockheed T-33A *Shooting Star*—1950s-vintage trainer; McDonnell F-101B *Voodoo*—1950s-vintage interceptor; North American F-86H *Sabrejet*—1950s-vintage fighter; Republic RF-84F *Thunderflash*—1950s-vintage photo-reconnaissance fighter; Vertol CH-21B *Shawnee*—1950s-vintage transport helicopter; Vought F8U-1 (F-8A) *Crusader*—1950s-vintage supersonic fighter.

SILENT WINGS MUSEUM, Terrell (Municipal Airport); no acting curator at present. A small and relatively new aviation museum dedicated to preserving the memory of military glider activity in World War II. The museum has numerous vintage memorabilia and a rare vintage Waco CG-4 combat glider. Other full-scale aircraft include a Ryan PT-22 *Recruit*, a Piper L-4 *Grasshopper*, and a Culver *Cadet*.

SOUTHWEST AEROSPACE MUSEUM, Fort Worth (outside the main entrance to the General Dynamics Corporation plant); curator, David Ciocchi. A rapidly growing and relatively new aviation museum dedicated to the preservation of aircraft associated with the Southwest. Though underfunded and lacking strong support from any major backers, this collection continues to grow and modestly prosper due almost totally to the dedication of its volunteer work force. A trailer houses an interesting selection of models, including some rare original General

Dynamics F-111 wind tunnel studies. Other memorabilia scattered about include engines and miscellaneous aircraft parts. At present, the aircraft collection consists of the following: Boeing B-52 *Stratofortress*—strategic bomber; Boeing KC-97L *Stratofreighter*—in-flight refueling tanker; Consolidated Vultee SNV-1 (BT-13) *Valiant*—WWII basic trainer; Convair B-36J *Peacemaker*—post-WWII heavy strategic bomber; Convair TB-58A *Hustler*—supersonic bomber trainer; E-Systems L-450F—experimental turboprop sensor platform; Fairchild AT-21 *Gunner*—WWII advanced trainer; Ford AIM-9 *Sidewinder*—air-to-air missile; Hughes AIM-4G *Super Falcon*—nuclear-tipped air-to-air missile; Lockheed T-33A *Shooting Star*—post-WWII jet trainer; LTV *cruise missile*—nuclear-tipped air-launched missile; McDonnell ADM-20 *Quail*—1960s-vintage decoy drone; North American F-86L *Sabrejet*—1950s-vintage jet fighter; North American F-100D *Super Sabre*—1950s-vintage supersonic fighter; Northrop F-89J (originally F-89D) *Scorpion*—1950s-vintage all-weather fighter; Republic F-105F *Thunderchief*—1950s-vintage fighter trainer.

Appendix 7. Military Airfields and Bases in Texas No Longer Active

AMARILLO AFB, fifteen miles east of Amarillo. Inactivated on December 31, 1968. Now utilized as Amarillo Municipal Airport.

AVENGER FIELD, near Sweetwater; used for WASP training during World War II. City airport.

BIGGS AFB, eight miles northeast of El Paso, named after Lt. James B. Biggs, a World War I fighter pilot. Inactivated in June, 1966. Currently used as Biggs Army Air Field for Fort Bliss support work.

BRYAN AB, six miles west of Bryan. Inactivated in 1959. Now used by Texas A&M University.

CORSICANA AIRFIELD, a contract training school during World War II.

CUERO AIRFIELD, a contract training school during World War II.

DUNCAN FIELD, a division of what is now Kelly AFB in San Antonio. This field came into existence at the end of World War I and was named for Maj. Thomas Duncan of the Air Corps, who was killed in a Washington, D.C., aircraft accident in 1923. Duncan Field covered approximately 800 acres and served primarily as an aircraft repair depot. In 1942, it was merged with Kelly Field.

FOSTER AB, eight miles northeast of Victoria; named for Lt. Arthur L. Foster of Georgetown. Activated in 1954 and inactivated in 1958. Now in use by the City of Victoria as Victoria-Foster Airport.

GARY AB, six miles east of San Marcos; named for 2nd Lt. Edward Gary, a San Marcos native. Following activation as San Marcos Army Air Field, it was utilized as a training facility; it was inactivated in 1945; reactivated as Gary AFB in 1953. It was again inactivated in December, 1956. Now utilized as a civil airport by the City of San Marcos.

GRAY AB, ten miles west of Killeen; named for Capt. Robert M. Gray, a Doolittle Raid pilot. Activated as Camp Hood Army Air Field; inactivated in 1963. Now utilized in support of Fort Hood activities.

HARLINGEN AB, five miles northeast of Harlingen. Inactivated in 1961. Now utilized as a civil airport for the City of Harlingen. Also serves as home field for the Confederate Air Force.

HARTLEE FIELD, near Denton; military training facility during World War II. Currently a private airport.

HONDO AB, one mile northwest of Hondo. Activated as a primary training facility under private contract in 1953; inactivated in 1958.

JAMES CONNALLY AFB, seven miles northeast of Waco; named after Col. James T. Connally, a B-29 pilot and Waco native. Activated as Waco AFB; inactivated in 1950; later reactivated. It was again inactivated in June, 1968. Now utilized as a civil airport (Waco Municipal) and home for one of several branches of Texas State Technical Institute.

LAREDO AFB, northeast of Laredo. Activated in May, 1942, as Laredo Army Air Field; inactivated in 1945 and reactivated in April, 1952. Used as a jet training facility from 1952 until inactivation in 1976. Now used as a civil airport (Laredo International).

LUBBOCK AFB, six miles west of Lubbock. Activated in 1942 as Lubbock Army Air Base and renamed Reese AFB in November, 1954.

MOORE AB, fourteen miles northwest of Mission. Activated in 1954 and named for 2nd Lt. Frank M. Moore, a World War I pilot who was killed in September, 1918; inactivated in 1961. Utilized for primary training under civil contract.

PERRIN AFB, five miles northeast of Sherman. Activated in August, 1941, and named for Lt. Col. Elmer D. Perrin, a native of Boerne; inactivated in 1972. Used as an Air Training Command facility from 1947 through 1964 and later as a training facility for interceptor pilots.

PYOTE AFB, eighteen miles southwest of Monahans. Named for the small town of Pyote; inactivated in 1954. Used as a training facility initially and, following World War II, as a storage facility for aircraft under the auspices of the Air Materiel Command.

WEBB AFB, four miles southwest of Big Spring. Named after 1st Lt. James L. Webb, a World War II fighter pilot and native of Big Spring. Activated as Big Spring AB in September, 1942, and utilized initially as a bombardier school; inactivated in 1977.

WOLTERS AFB, three miles east of Mineral Wells. Activated as Camp Wolters, named for Brig. Gen. Jacob F. Wolters; inactivated in 1956.

Appendix 8. Active Texas-Based Units

12TH AIR FORCE (TACTICAL AIR COMMAND); with headquarters at BERGSTROM AFB—under the jurisdiction of the 12th Air Force are four air divisions, seven tactical fighter wings, four tactical training wings, one tactical reconnaissance wing, and one tactical air control wing. All but one, the 67th TRW, are located at bases outside Texas.

67TH TACTICAL RECONNAISSANCE WING (TACTICAL AIR COMMAND); with headquarters at BERGSTROM AFB—the single 12th AF unit based in Texas is the 67th TRW. Falling under the jurisdiction of the 67th TRW are the 12th Tactical Reconnaissance Squadron, the 45th Tactical Reconnaissance Training Squadron, the 62nd Tactical Reconnaissance Training Squadron, and the 91st Tactical Reconnaissance Squadron. All four squadrons currently operate McDonnell RF-4C tactical reconnaissance aircraft. Planned updates call for the eventual phaseout of the RF-4C and the integration of the General Dynamics F-16C/D as the air force's primary tactical reconnaissance aircraft.

10TH AIR FORCE (TACTICAL AIR COMMAND/AIR FORCE RESERVE); with headquarters at BERGSTROM AFB—the 10th Air Force is one of three major reserve air forces. Six wings fall under its jurisdiction, including the only Texas-based reserve wing, the 301st.

301ST TACTICAL FIGHTER WING/924TH TACTICAL FIGHTER GROUP (TACTICAL AIR COMMAND/AIR FORCE RESERVE); with headquarters at CARSWELL AFB—the 301st TFW is the parent unit to the 924th TFG. Both units currently operate McDonnell F-4D tactical fighter aircraft. The 301st is stationed at Carswell AFB and the 924th is stationed at Bergstrom AFB.

19TH AIR DIVISION/7TH BOMB WING (STRATEGIC AIR COMMAND); with headquarters at CARSWELL AFB—under the jurisdiction of the 19th Air Division are the 340th Air Refueling Group located at Altus AFB, Oklahoma (operating Boeing KC-135s); the 351st Strategic Missile Wing located at Whiteman AFB, Missouri (operating the Boeing *Minuteman III* ICBM); the 381st Strategic Missile Wing located at McConnell AFB, Kansas (operating Martin *Titan II*s); the 384th Air Refueling Wing located at McConnell AFB, Kansas (operating Boeing KC-135s); the 308th Strategic Missile Wing located at Little Rock AFB, Arkansas (operating Martin *Titan II*s); and its only Texas unit, the 7th Bomb Wing, located at Carswell AFB.

7TH BOMB WING (STRATEGIC AIR COMMAND); with headquarters at CARSWELL AFB—under the jurisdiction of the 7th BW are the 9th Bomb Squadron, the 20th Bomb Squadron, and the 7th Air Refueling Squadron. The 9th BS and 20th BS both operate the Boeing B-52H. The 7th ARS operates the Boeing KC-135A. All three units are stationed at Carswell AFB.

12TH AIR DIVISION (STRATEGIC AIR COMMAND); with headquarters at DYESS AFB—the 12th Air Division has under its jurisdiction the 390th Strategic Missile Wing located at Davis-Monthan AFB, Arizona (operating Martin *Titan II* ICBMs); the 22nd Aerial Refueling Wing located at March AFB, California (operating McDonnell Douglas KC-10s and Boeing KC-135s), the 55th Strategic Reconnaissance Wing located at Offutt AFB, Nebraska (operating Boeing RC/KC-135s); and its only Texas-based unit, the 96th BW, located at Dyess AFB.

96TH BOMB WING (STRATEGIC AIR COMMAND); with headquarters at DYESS AFB—under the jurisdiction of the 96th BW are the 337th Bomb Squadron and the 917th Air Refueling Squadron. The 337th BS is currently inactive until the arrival of the Rockwell International B-1B in mid-1986. An interim unit, the 4018th Combat Crew Training Squadron, is due to form during 1985 and will serve as a B-1B training unit next to the 337th BS at the latter unit's home base, Dyess AFB. The 917th ARS, also based at Dyess AFB, operates the Boeing KC-135A.

463RD TACTICAL AIRLIFT WING (MILITARY AIRLIFT COMMAND)—under the jurisdiction of the 463rd TAW at DYESS AFB are the 772nd Tactical Airlift Squadron, the 773rd Tactical Airlift Squadron, and the 774th Tactical Airlift Squadron. All three squadrons operate the Lockheed C-130H.

433RD TACTICAL AIRLIFT WING (MILITARY AIRLIFT COMMAND/AIR FORCE RESERVE)—assigned to the Air Force Reserve's 4th Air Force (headquartered at McClellan AFB, California), the 433rd Tactical Airlift Wing has under its jurisdiction the 68th Tactical Airlift Squadron. The 68th TAS is currently flying Lockheed C-130Bs. However, in 1985 it began converting to a Military Airlift Wing (MAW) and as such will operate the

Lockheed C-5A. the squadron is based at KELLY AFB.

136TH TACTICAL AIRLIFT WING (AIR NATIONAL GUARD)—under the jurisdiction of the 136th Tactical Airlift Wing is the 181st Tactical Airlift Squadron. The 181st TAS operates the Lockheed C-130B and is based at HENSLEY FIELD.

147TH FIGHTER INTERCEPTOR GROUP (AIR NATIONAL GUARD)—under the jurisdiction of the 147th FIG is the 111th Tactical Fighter Squadron, which operates the McDonnell F-4C and is based at ELLINGTON AFB (considered an inactive air force facility).

149TH FIGHTER INTERCEPTOR GROUP (AIR NATIONAL GUARD)—under the jurisdiction of the 149th FIG is the 182nd Tactical Fighter Squadron, which operates the McDonnell F-4C and is based at KELLY AFB. The 182nd TFS is expected to make a transition to the General Dynamics F-16A between July and December, 1985.

47TH FIGHTER TRAINING WING (AIR TRAINING COMMAND)—under the jurisdiction of the 47th FTW are the 85th Fighter Training Squadron and the 86th Fighter Training Squadron. The 8th FTS operates the Cessna T-37B and the 86th operates the Northrop T-38A. Both squadrons are based at LAUGHLIN AFB.

12TH FIGHTER TRAINING WING (AIR TRAINING COMMAND)—under the jurisdiction of the 12th FTW are the 559th Fighter Training Squadron and the 560th Fighter Training Squadron. The 559th FTS operates the Cessna T-37B and the 560th operates the Northrop T-38A. Both squadrons are based at RANDOLPH AFB.

64TH FIGHTER TRAINING WING (AIR TRAINING COMMAND)—under the jurisdiction of the 64th FTW are the 35th Fighter Training Squadron and the 54th Fighter Training Squadron. The 35th FTS operates the Cessna T-37B and the 54th FTS operates the Northrop T-38A. Both squadrons are based at REESE AFB.

80TH FIGHTER TRAINING WING (AIR TRAINING COMMAND)—under the jurisdiction of the 80th FTW are the 89th Fighter Training Squadron and the 90th Fighter Training Squadron. The 89th FTS operates the Cessna T-37B and the 90th FTS operates the Northrop T-38A. Both squadrons are based at SHEPPARD AFB.

CARRIER AIR WING 20 (CVWR-20, NAVY)—under the jurisdiction of Carrier Air Wing 20 are Navy Fighter Squadron 201 (VF-201) and Navy Fighter Squadron 202 (VF-202). Both operate the McDonnell F-4s and are based at DALLAS NAVAL AIR STATION.

MILITARY AIRLIFT GROUP 41 (MAG-41, MARINES)—under the jurisdiction of 4th Marine Air Wing located at NSA New Orleans. Under the jurisdiction of MAG-41 are Marine Attack Squadron 112 (VMFA-112), Heavy Marine Helicopter Squadron 777 (HMH-777), and several support units (HMS-41, HMS-49, and MABS-41). VMFA-112 operates the McDonnell F-4N/S and HMH-777 operates the Sikorsky CH-53A. Both squadrons are based at NAS DALLAS.

TRAINING WING 2 (TRAWING-2, NAVY)—under the jurisdiction of TRAWING-2 are Navy Training Squadron 21 (VT-21), Navy Training Squadron 22 (VT-22), and Navy Training Squadron 23 (VT-23). VT-21 and VT-22 both operate the Douglas TA-4J, and VT-23 operates the Rockwell International (ex–North American) T-2B. All three are based at CHASE FIELD.

TRAINING WING 3 (TRAWING-3, NAVY)—under the jurisdiction of TRAWING-3 are Navy Training Squadron 24 (VT-24), Navy Training Squadron 25 (VT-25), and Navy Training Squadron 26 (VT-26). VT-24 and VT-25 both operate the Douglas TA-4J, and VT-26 operates the Rockwell International (ex–North American) T-2B. All three are based at KINGSVILLE FIELD.

TRAINING WING 4 (TRAWING-4, NAVY)—under the jurisdiction of TRAWING-4 are Navy Training Squadron 27 (VT-27), Navy Training Squadron 28 (VT-28), and Navy Training Squadron 31 (VT-31). VT-27 operates the Beechcraft T-34C, and VT-28 and VT-31 both operate the Beechcraft T-44A. All three are based at CORPUS CHRISTI NAVAL AIR STATION.

The following units are stationed at HOOD ARMY AIR FIELD at Fort Hood: 2nd Squadron/1st Cavalry/2nd Armored Division (assigned Bell AH-1S attack helicopters); Combat Aviation Brigade (assigned OH-58 observation helicopters and AH-1 attack helicopters); 1st Squadron/9th Cavalry/1st Cavalry Division (assigned Bell AH-1S attack helicopters and Bell OH-58C observation helicopters); 4th Squadron/9th Cavalry/6th Cavalry Brigade (Air Combat—assigned Bell AH-1S attack helicopters); 7th Squadron/17th Cavalry/6th Cavalry Brigade (Air Combat—assigned Bell AH-1 attack helicopters, Bell OH-58 observation helicopters, and Bell UH-1 utility helicopters); 34th Support Squadron/6th Cavalry Brigade (Air Combat—assigned Boeing Vertol CH-47 heavy transport helicopters); 163rd Military Intelligence Battalion/504th Military Intelligence Group (assigned Grumman OV-1D observation aircraft); 227th Aviation Battalion/1st Cavalry Division (assigned Bell AH-1S attack helicopters); 228th Aviation Battalion/1st Cavalry Division (assigned Bell AH-1 attack helicopters and bell OH-58 observation helicopters); 502nd Aviation Battalion/2nd Armored Division (assigned Bell UH-1 utility helicopters and Bell OH-58 observation helicopters); 507th Medical Company/3rd Flight Platoon/13th Support Command (DUSTOFF—assigned Bell UH-1 utility helicopters); 200th Aviation Company/1st Platoon (assigned Beechcraft C-12 general transport aircraft, Beechcraft U-21 general utility aircraft, Bell UH-1 utility helicopters, and Bell OH-58 observation helicopters).

The following units are assigned to the Texas Army National Guard:

AUSTIN: HHC 149th Combat Aviation Battalion/Detachment 1 of Company A (assigned Bell OH-58 observation helicopters and Bell UH-1 utility helicopters); Detachment E (-) (assigned Bell UH-1 utility helicopters); Troop D, 1st Battalion, 24th Aviation (assigned Bell OH-58 observation helicopters, Bell UH-1 utility helicopters, and Bell

AH-1 attack helicopters). Additionally, the state Area Command Aviation Section is assigned a Beechcraft C-12 general transport and a Cessna U-3A general transport.

DALLAS: 136th Transportation Company (-) (assigned Boeing Vertol CH-47 heavy transport helicopters); Detachment 2, Company A (assigned Bell OH-58 observation helicopters and Bell UH-1 utility helicopters); Detachment 2, 163rd Air Cavalry Regiment (assigned Bell OH-58 observation helicopters and Bell UH-1 utility helicopters).

HOUSTON: Detachment 1, 136th Transportation Company (assigned Boeing Vertol CH-47 heavy transport helicopters).

SAN ANTONIO: Company A (-) 149th Aviation (assigned Bell OH-58 observation helicopters and Bell UH-1 utility helicopters).

Appendix 9. Subcontractors in Texas Involved in the Production of Parts or Materials Used by the Aerospace Industry by City

ADDISON: Airborne, Inc.; Avicon Corp.; Foster-Edwards Aircraft Co, Inc.

ARLINGTON: Doskocil Mfg. Co., Inc.; Hutson Aerospace, Inc./Teleflex, Inc.; The Hutson Corp.; Jet Research, Inc.; LFC Industries, Inc.; Redifon Simulation, Inc.; T. J. Electronics.

AUSTIN: The Electro-Mechanics Co.; Elkem-Holloway Co.; Tracor Aerospace.

BEAUMONT: Southern Avionics Co.

CARROLLTON: Booth, Inc.

CROCKETT: ASE Texas, Inc./Aero Systems Engineering, Inc.

CROWLEY: Stearns Airport Equipment Co., Inc.

DALLAS: Action Communications Systems, Inc./Plantronics, Inc.; Aero Logistics International; Aircraft Ducting Associates, Inc.; Airmotive Engineering Corp.; Airport Equipment, Inc.; Bailey Hose, Inc.; B.K.M. Company; Cargo Systems Cc.; Continental Electronics Manufacturing Co.; Aerosonic Corp.; Datotek, Inc.; Delta Electronic Mfg. Co.; Foxtronics, Inc.; Geotronics Laboratories, Inc.; Optic-Electronic Corp.; Otis Engineering Corp., Special Products Div.; Surcon Abrado Blast Corp.; The Texacone Co.; Texas Electronics, Inc.; Hamilton Avent Electronics; Ducommon Metals; Earle M. Jorgenson Co.; Carpenter Technology.

DECATUR: Poco Graphite, Inc.

EL PASO: Continental Water Systems Corp.; Electronic Memories & Magnetics.

EULESS: Del Norte Technology, Inc.; Instrument Specialties Co., Inc.; Menasco, Inc.

FORT WORTH: Aerospace Optics, Inc.; The Almasol Corp.; Graphic Datakits International; Howell Instruments, Inc.; Menasco, Inc./Colt Industries; Mosites Rubber Co., Inc.; Williams Instruments, Inc.

GARLAND: Bergman Manufacturing Co., Inc./International Controls Corp.; Cosar Corp.; General Electrodynamics Corp.; Intercontinental Mfg. Co., Inc./International Controls Corp.; Marlow Industries, Inc.; Micropac Industries, Inc.; Precision Cable Mfg. Co., Inc.; Unitron, Inc.; Varo, Inc.

GRAND PRAIRIE: Airline Containers, Inc.; Classical Chemical; Inverted-A, Inc.; Sfena Corp.; STMCO, Inc.; Texstar Plastics.

HOUSTON: All Woods/Schroeder, Inc./Trak Microwave Corp.; A&S Building Systems, Inc.; ATEC, Inc.; Automation Products, Inc.; Aviation Instrument Mfg. Corp.; Griffolyn Co.; Jet-Lube, Inc.; Life Sciences Division/Technology, Inc.; Marathon Metallic Bldg. Corp.; National Steel Products Co.; Precision Aviation, Inc.; Prist Div., PPG Chemicals; The Randolph Co.; Ruska Instrument Corp.; Stewart & Stevenson Services, Inc.; Tech-Sym Corp./Trak Microwave Corp.; Tritan Corp.

HURST: Anchor Metals, Inc.; International Controls Corp.

IRVING: Organic Products Co.

KERRVILLE: Reed Switch Developments Co., Inc.

MANSFIELD: Rhimco Industries, Inc.

MINERAL WELLS: Antenna Products Co.

PLANO: Luninator.

RICHARDSON: Electrospace Systems, Inc.; Vac-Cyclonic, Inc.

SAN ANGELO: Pattco Div./K.J. Law Engineers, Inc.

SAN ANTONIO: Alcor, Inc.; Dee Howard Co.; Eldorado Chemical Co., Inc.; Engine Components, Inc.; Jet Crafters, Inc.; Page Gulfstream, Inc.; Ray Electronics Co.; Texas Trunk Co.

SAN MARCOS: Mensor Corp.; Wide-Lite Corp.

WACO: Marathon Battery Co.; Surry Seal, Inc.; Tymco, Inc.

Appendix 10. Military Aircraft and Missiles Produced by Texas Aerospace Companies (Quantities of Each Type in Parentheses)

BELL HELICOPTER TEXTRON (note: not all H-13/HTL-series helicopters were built at the Hurst facility; some were produced at Bell's Niagara Falls, New York, facility prior to the move to Texas): YR-13 (18); YR-13A (2 from YR-13); H-13B (65); H-13C (16 from H-13B); H-13D (87); H/OH-13E (490): XH-13F (1 from H-13E); H/OH-13G (265); H/OH/UH-13H (468); H/UH-13J (2); H/OH-13K (2 from H-13H); HTL-1 (10); HTL-2 (12); HTL-3 (12); HTL-4/TH-13L (46); HTL-5/TH-13L (36); HTL-6/TH-13M (48); HTL-7/TH-13N (18); HUL-1/UH-13P (28); HUL-1G/UH-13P (2); HUL-1M/UH-13P (2 converted from HUL-1); HH-13Q (2 HUL-1Gs transferred to Coast Guard); UH-13R (2 from HUL-1M); OH 13S (?); TH-13T (?); HTL-3 (12); XHSL-1 (3); HSL-1 (50); XH-33/XV-3 (2); XH-40 (3); YH-40 (6); HU-1 (9); HU-1A (182); HU-1B (1,014); TH-1A (14); YHU-1B (2 from HU-1B); NUH-1B (1 from HU-1B); UH-1C (767); YUH-1D (7); UH-1D/CUH-1D (2,008); TH/UH-1E (270); UH-1F (120); TH-1F (26); TH-1G (?); UH-1H (5,435); CUH-1H (?); HH-1H (30); EH-1H (10 +); HH-1K (27); TH-1L (90); UH-1L (8); UH-1M (?); UH-1N (284); VH-1N (6); CUH-1N (50 +); UH-1P (from UH-1F); UH-1V (220 from UH-1H); Model 533 (1); OH-4A (5); OH-58A (2,212); COH-58A (74); OH-58B (12); OH-58C (278 from OH-58A); OH-58D (578 + from OH-58A); Model 207 (1); Model 209 (1); Model 406CS (1 +); Model 206L *Texas Ranger* (1 +); TH-57A (47); AH-1G (1,078); TH-57B (21); TH-57C (76); TH/AH-1J (271); JAH-1G (1 from AH-1G); AH-1Q (92); YAH-1R (1 from AH-1G); AH-1S (700 + incl. 407 from AH-1G/Q); YAH-1S (1 from AH-1S); AH-1T (57 +); YAH-63 (2); AH-1T + (45); XV-15 (2); Model 412 (6); Model 214ST (10); D292 (1 + 2 for static test).

CONSOLIDATED VULTEE/CONVAIR: B-24D (303); B-24E (144); B-24H (738); B-24J (1,558); C-87 (285? from B-24Ds); C-87A (6); RY-3 (46); AT-22 (5); XB-32 (3); TB/B-32A (114); XB-36 (1); YB-36 (1); B-36A (22); B-36B (73); RB/B-36D (39); RB/B-36D (39); RB/B-36F (58); RB-B-36H (156); B-36J (33); NB-36H (1 from B-36H); YB-60 (2); B/TB-58A (116).

E-SYSTEMS: XQM-93/L-450F (6); EC/RC-135 modifications (over 400); miscellaneous other aircraft modifications (?); E-45 (12); E-55 (?); E-55S (3 from E-55); Axillary (5); E-75 (?); E-90 (?); E-100X (?); E-130 (3); E-150 (?); E-175 (?); E-200 (?); E-260 (?).

GENERAL DYNAMICS: RB-57F (21); F-4E(S) (3); miscellaneous other aircraft modifications (several hundred); YF/RF/F-111A (159); F-111C (24); F-111D (96); F-111E (94); F-111F (106); FB-111A (76); YF-16 (2); F-16/A/B/C/D (over 1,300); F-16XL (2); F-16/79 (1 from F-16A); F-16/101 (1 from F-16A); AFTI/F-16 (1 from F-16A).

GLOBE: MQM-40 (?).

LOCKHEED: XMQM-105 (23); YMQM-105 (28); MQM-105 (548).

LTB: BGM-110 (?).

LTV: VTS-6/YAQM-127A (?).

MOONEY: TX-1 (1).

NORTH AMERICAN: B-24G (430); B-24J (536); C-82 (1); AT-6A (1,210 including 298 as SNJs for navy); AT-6B (?); AT-6C (2,970); AT-6D (4,388 including 675 as SNJs for navy); XAT-6E (1); AT-6F (956 including 931 as SNJs for navy); SNJ-4 (2,400); SNJ-5 (1,573); SNJ-6 (411); P-51C/K (4,790).

TEMCO: YT/T-35/TE-1A (25); TP-51D (?); TT-1 (15); *Plebe* (2); XKDT-1 *Teal* (?); XASM-1 *Corvus* (?); GDD-1 (?).

TEXAS INSTRUMENTS: AGM-45 (several thousand); AGM-83 (several thousand); AGM-88 (several thousand).

TRACOR: ADR-9 (?).

VOUGHT: AU-1 (111); F4U-7 (94); *Regulus I* (514); *Regulus II* (59); XF6U-1 (3); F6U-1 (30); XF7U-1 (3); F7U-1 (14); F7U-3 (180); F7U-3M (98); F7U-3P (12); XF8U-1 (2); TF/DF/QF/F-8A (318); F-8B/F-8L (130); RF-8A/RF-8G (144); NTF-8A (1 from F-8A); F-8C/F-8K (187); F-8D/F-8H (152); F-8E/F-8J (286); F-8E(FN) (42); F8U-3 (5); MGM-52 (?); XC-142A (5); A-7A (199); A-7B/TA-7C (196); A-7C/TA-7C (67); A-7E/TA-7C (692); A-7D (459 +); YA-7H (1); A-7H (60); TA-7H (5); A-7K (31); A-7P (44 from A-7A); TA-7P (6).

WICHITA ENGINEERING: TG-10 (1?).

WINDECKER: YE-5A (1).

Selected References

Hugh Allen. The *Story of the Airship (Non-Rigid)*. Akron, Ohio: Goodyear, 1943.

Frank W. Anderson. *Orders of Magnitude: A History of NACA and NASA, 1915-1980*. Washington, D.C.: Government Printing Office, 1981.

David Anderton. *The History of the United States Air Force*. New York: Crescent Books, 1981.

E. C. Barksdale. *The Genesis of the Aviation Industry in North Texas*. Austin: Bureau of Business Research, University of Texas, 1958.

Roger E. Bilstein. *Flight in America, 1900-1983*. Baltimore and London: Johns Hopkins University Press, 1984.

Peter Bowers and Gordon Swanborough. *United States Military Aircraft since 1908*. London: Putnam & Company Limited, 1971.

Kathleen Brooks-Pazmany. *United States Women in Aviation, 1919-1929*. Washington, D.C.: Smithsonian Institution Press, 1983.

Don Clark. *Wild Blue Yonder, An Air Epic*. Seattle: Superior Publishing Company, 1972.

Douglas Corrigan. *That's My Story*. New York: E. P. Dutton, 1938.

Robert Coulam. *Illusions of Choice, The F-111 and the Problem of Weapons Acquisition Control*. Princeton: Princeton University Press, 1977.

Wesley Craven and James Cate. *The Army Air Forces in World War II*. Chicago: University of Chicago Press, 1948, 7 vols.

Tom D. Crouch. *The Eagle Aloft: Two Centuries of the Balloon in America*. Washington, D.C.: Smithsonian Institution Press, 1983.

R. E. G. Davies. *Airlines of the United States Since 1914*. Washington, D.C.: Smithsonian Institution Press, 1982.

Eaton Manufacturing Co. et al. *A Chronicle of the Aviation Industry in America 1903-1947* (plus supplements for 1948, 1949, 1950, and 1951). Cleveland: Eaton Manufacturing Co., 1948.

Alfred Goldberg. *A History of the United States Air Force*. New York: D. Van Nostrand Company, Inc., 1957.

Joseph P. Juptner. *U.S. Civil Aircraft*. Fallbrook, Cal.: Aero, 1962-82, 9 vols.

Cline Knowles, Jr. "The United States Navy in South Texas, 1945-1955." Unpublished manuscript, 1969.

Manufacturers Aircraft Association. *Aircraft Year Book*, all editions from 1919 to 1971. Various publishers.

Maurer Maurer, ed. *The U.S. Air Service in World War I*. Washington, D.C.: Office of Air Force History, 1978, 4 vols.

Jay Miller. *General Dynamics F-16*. Arlington, Tx.: Aerofax, Inc., 1982.

.*Lockheed U-2*. Arlington, Tx.: Aerofax, Inc., 1983.

Gerard Moran. *Aeroplanes Vought 1917-1977, Historical Aviation Album*. Temple City, Cal.: n.p., 1977.

Claudia Oakes. *United States Women in Aviation through World War I*. Washington, D.C.: Smithsonian Institution Press, 1978.

Stephen B. Oates. "NASA's Manned Space Center at Houston." *Southwestern Historical Quarterly*, vol. 67 (1963-64).

Office of History, San Antonio Air Logistics Center, Kelly AFB, Texas. *A Pictorial History of Kelly Air Force Base*. San Antonio: Air Force Logistics Command, 1984.

Mary Beth Pliska. *A Blacksmith's Aeroplane*. (Copyright by Mary Beth Pliska, 1965.)

Nick Pocock. *Did W. D. Custead Fly First?* China Spring, Tex.: Special Aviation Publications, 1974.

Norman Polmar and Floyd Kennedy, Jr. *Military Helicopters of the World*. Annapolis, Md.: Naval Institute Press, 1981.

Wiley Post and Harold Gatty. *Around the World in Eight Days: The Flight of the Winnie Mae*. New York: Garden City, 1931.

Kenneth B. Ragsdale. *Wings over the Mexican Border: Pioneer Aviation in the Big Bend*. Austin: Texas Press, 1984.

Art Ronnie. *Locklear: The Man Who Walked on Wings*. New York: A. S. Barnes, 1973.

C. R. Roseberry. *The Challenging Skies: The Colorful Study of Aviation's Most Exciting Years, 1919–1939*. Garden City, N.Y.: Doubleday, 1966.

John Shiner. *Foulois and the U.S. Army Air Corps 1931–1935*. Washington, D.C.: Office of Air Force History, 1983.

Hart Stilwell and Slats Rogers. *Old Soggy No. 1: The Uninhibited Story of Slats Rogers*. New York: Julian Messner, 1954.

Texas Aeronautics Commission. *Texas Aeronautical Facilities Plan:* Summary. Austin: Texas Aeronautics Commission, 1984.

L. L. Walker, Jr. "1910: The Year the Air Age Came to Houston." *Houston Review*, vol. 6, no. 1 (1984).

Walter P. Webb, ed. *The Handbook of Texas*. Austin: Texas State Historical Association, 1976, vols. 1, 2, and 3.

Sydney Wise. *Canadian Airmen and the First World War, Vol. 1*. Toronto: University of Toronto Press, 1980.

Bill Yenne. *The History of the United States Air Force*. New York: Exeter Books, 1984.

Magazines

Aero Digest
Aerophile
Southern Flight
Southwestern Aviation

Newspapers

Brownsville Herald
Dallas Morning News
Houston Chronicle
Houston Post
San Antonio Light
Temple Daily Telegram

Archival Holdings

Aviation Collection, University of Texas, Dallas
Barker Texas History Center, University of Texas, Austin
Institute of Texan Cultures, University of Texas, San Antonio
Metropolitan Research Center, Houston Public Library
National Air and Space Museum, Washington, D.C.

Though not a museum item, this rare original WWI-vintage Nieuport 28, owned by Jim Hall of Midland, is worthy of mention. It is still airworthy after three-quarters of a century.

The Confederate Air Force's Boeing B-29 is now the only flyable example extant. The B-29 had the ignominious honor of dropping atomic bombs on Hiroshima and Nagasaki.

Confederate Air Force maintenance personnel doctor a Spanish-built version of the WWII-vintage German Heinkel He-111.

One of the first aircraft acquired by the Confederate Air Force was this North American P-51D. In terms of both aesthetics and performance it remains the archetypical WWII fighter.

The Edward H. White Memorial Museum at Brooks AFB is housed in the historically significant Hangar 9—which is the only remaining WWI hangar still standing on U.S. soil.

The Edward H. White Memorial Museum houses an extensive collection of memorabilia, including numerous photographs and large pieces of full-scale hardware.

The Lackland AFB History and Traditions Museum contains a large collection of air force memorabilia.

Among the larger items in the Lackland AFB collection is this Ford "Loon" pulse-jet powered drone.

The Lackland AFB History and Traditions Museum collection of weapons and models is extensive.

The Lackland AFB History and Traditions Museum outdoor display includes this Douglas "Thor" missile.

A rare North American P-51H "Mustang," considered by some authorities to be the fastest production aircraft of WWII, is among the many types displayed outdoors at Lackland AFB.

The Southwest Aerospace Museum, near the entrance to General Dynamics in Fort Worth, maintains the only example of Convair's B-36 bomber on display in Texas.

Only eight B-58s survive, and one is presently on display at the Southwest Aerospace Museum. This particular example is a TB-58A, one of the few trainer variants of the "Hustler" built.

Index